Annual Education Quote Contest Winner

"Educators Need to Reach Out to Troubled Students!"

Principal Dawn Hochsprung
Sandy Hook Elementary School, Newtown, Connecticut
(June 28, 1965 - December 14, 2012)

What All Parents Need to Know About Their Child's Education

Date:

To:

From:

Message:

SMARTGRADES BRAIN POWER REVOLUTION

"This book has the power to save the lives of millions of American children, solve the problem of education here and abroad, and save the world by planting the seeds of world peace in every corner of the globe."

Sharon Rose Sugar
Paladin of Education for the 21st Century
www.smartgrades.com

What All Parents Need to Know
About Their Child's Education

THE SILENT CRISIS DESTROYING AMERICA'S BRIGHTEST MINDS

BOOK OF THE MONTH
Alma Public Library, Wisconsin

If Children Grew Up According to Early Indications, We Should Have Nothing But Geniuses.
Johann Wolfgang von Goethe

Also By The Author

Student Empowerment For Academic Success

- SMARTGRADES SCHOOL NOTEBOOKS
- EVERY DAY AN EASY A: 3 Editions, ELE, HS, College
- TOTAL RECALL: ACE EVERY TEST EVERY TIME
- YOUR STUDY ROOM IS UNDER NEW MANAGEMENT

Parent Empowerment for Academic Success

- The Silent Crisis Destroying America's Brightest Minds
  BOOK OF THE MONTH, Alma Public Library, Wisconsin
- How to Parent for Academic Success
- Broken Wings Blocked Blessings

Teacher Empowerment for Academic Success

- The Silent Crisis Destroying America's Brightest Minds
  BOOK OF THE MONTH, Alma Public Library, Wisconsin
- The Universal Gold Standard of Education
- How Does Learning Take Place?
- Intrapersonal Integration Therapy Modality

Children's Books

The Smartest Children's Book in the Whole World
(Color-Coded Vocabulary Words)
SCHMALTZY
IN AMERICA EVEN A CAT CAN HAVE A DREAM
Ages: 8-12
www.schmaltzy.com

Why Isn't Sharon Sleeping?
This Book Helps Kids and Adults Fall Asleep Fast

THE SILENT CRISIS DESTROYING AMERICA'S BRIGHTEST MINDS

SHARON ROSE SUGAR

BOOK OF THE MONTH
Alma Public Library, Wisconsin

SMARTGRADES
BRAIN POWER REVOLUTION

Education/Teacher Education/Parenting/World Peace

The Silent Crisis Destroying America's Brightest Minds

© 2023 @ 2009 by Sharon Rose Sugar. All Rights Reserved. No part of this book may be used or reproduced in any manner whatsoever without written permission except in the case of brief quotations embodied in critical articles and reviews.

SMARTGRADES books may be purchased for education, business, or sales promotional use.

SMARTGRADES BRAIN POWER REVOLUTION

Smartgrades.com
EveryDayAnEasyA.com
PhotonSuperhero.com
BooksNotBombs.com
Schmaltzy.com

Library of Congress Catalog Card Number: 2007902018
ISBN Hardcover: 978-1-885872-52-5
ISBN Paperback: 978-1-885872-54-8
ISBN E-Book: 978-1-885872-53-1
UPC: 672180000011

Book design and interior: Sharon Esther Lampert

Pen Name: Sharon Rose Sugar is the Pen Name of Prodigy Sharon Esther Lampert

Illustrations:
By Mark A. Hicks, illustrator. Used with permission.
Artwork pages: Intro, 1, 2, 4, 6, 48, 71, 74, 100, 118, 131, 134, 144, 162, 170, 182, 204, 230, 232, 242, 244, 256, 264, 266, 290, 316, 346, 349, 365, 368, 372, 388, 390, 398, 412, 419, 429, 478, 484, 488, 512, 520, 555. For more information, please visit websites:
www.MARKIX.net and www.markix.net/4teachers.html

For Bulk Orders:
Ingram, 1 Ingram Blvd., La Vergne, TN 37086-3629
Phone: 615-793-5000
Fax orders: 615-287-6990

First Edition

Manufactured in the United States of America

Testimonial

This book is a gold mine of interesting stories and great ideas. Every person will be touched and transformed by its message. Every educator who reads this book will find the will and the way, at a grass roots level, to transform the fifteen stumbling blocks of academic failure into the fifteen stepping stones for academic success. In due time, America will have one of the greatest education systems in the world.

Headmaster John Humphreys
Ardent Fan and Admirer

If We Don't Stand Up for Children,
Then We Don't Stand for Much.
Marian Wright Edelman

Highlights and Hidden Gems: A Quick Study Guide

- Summary of National Crisis in American Education, p. 115
  (this 500-page book is condensed into a page)

- Poetic Summary of National Crisis in American Education, pp. 72-73
  (this 500-page book condensed into a poem)

- Cartoon Summary of National Crisis in American Education, p. 2
  (this 500-page book condensed into a cartoon)

- 8 Goalposts of Education, p. 52

- The Misdiagnosis of A. D. H. D., pp. 57-58

- 13 Steps to Self-Actualization, p. 92

- **SMARTGRADES SUCCESS STRATEGY STUDY SKILLS**, pp. 90-91, p.140

- Two Education Paradigms Side By Side, p. 323, pp. 426-427

- America's Brightest Minds: "I am not as smart as I thought I was!" p. 278

- Quote: Solve the Problem of Education and Save the World, p. 420

- Ms. Sugar's Contributions to Education & World Peace, p. 526

- World Peace Initiative: Democratic Libraries, p. 463

- Cognitive Healing for Depression, p. 455

- The Greatest Lie Ever Told in the Name of God, p. 457

- All You Will Ever Need to Know About God, p. 459

- See the World Through The Eyes of a Creative Genius, p. 567

- Poem: **"BE BORN,"** p. 548

- **First Book Review by a Parent, EDNEWS.org, 2009, p. 502**

Contents

The Five Intentions of the Book
1

Part One
Save America's Children of Privilege
3

If the Truth Be Told
7

There Is Something for Everyone
53

Acknowledgments
63

Notes to the Reader
68

World Famous Poem
EDUCATE NOT
72

Sweet Darling Isabel
79

Every Student Has a Horror Story
103

Summary of the National Crisis of Education in America
115

Part Two
The Malfunctioning American Education System
THE FIFTEEN STUMBLING BLOCKS OF ACADEMIC FAILURE
117

Stumbling Block 1
The Quantity Over Quality Curriculum-Driven American Education System
121

Stumbling Block 2
Poor Learning Tools to Process Voluminous Academic Facts
137

Stumbling Block 3
The Fast Food Restaurant: Cursory Comprehension
147

Contents

Stumbling Block 4
In One Ear and Out the Other Ear: Short-Term Retention
165

Stumbling Block 5
The Academic Pressure Cooker: Hotdog Tests
Read, Cram, Regurgitate, and Test
173

Stumbling Block 6
The Darwinian Grind of Cutthroat Competition
185

Stumbling Block 7
Student Survival Strategies: Cutting Corners and Cheating
195

Stumbling Block 8
Escapism: Seeking Refuge from the "Pain of Inadequacy"
209

World Famous Poem
The Prescription-Drug Pushers
235

Stumbling Block 9
The Downward Spiral of Academic Failure
235

Stumbling Block 10
The War Zone: Few Heroes, Heavy Casualties,
and Senseless Fatalities
247

Stumbling Block 11
The Desert: Wander Aimlessly with No Direction
259

Stumbling Block 12
The Wasteland: One Size Does Not Fit All or Any
269

Stumbling Block 13
American Dreams Deferred, Denied, and Destroyed
279

Stumbling Block 14
Get a Clue: How Does Learning Take Place?
2

Stumbling Block 15
Unintentional Institutionalized Child Abuse
291

Part Three
Reinventing the American Education System
**THE FIFTEEN STEPPING STONES
OF ACADEMIC SUCCESS
REENVISION, REINVENT, REBUILD**
307

Stepping Stone 1
BRAIN POWER
The Human Brain Is the Most Powerful
Biological Machine in the World
311

Contents

Stepping Stone 2
New Education Paradigm
Shift Paradigm from Curriculum-Driven to
a Learning-Processing Education System
321

Stepping Stone 3
In-Depth Comprehension
SMARTGRADES Critical Thinking Tools
329

Stepping Stone 4
NEW LEARNING STRATEGY
SMARTGRADES Processing Tools
335

Stepping Stone 5
New Grading System
Grade A or REDO
341

Stepping Stone 6
Get a Clue: How Learning Takes Place
351

Stepping Stone 7
The Universal Gold Standard of Education
359

Stepping Stone 8
Children have Unique Minds that Require Early Intervention
371

Stepping Stone 9
Educate the Whole Student: Mind, Body, and Spirit
377

Stepping Stone 10
Prepare Students to Meet the Challenges of the Real World
387

Stepping Stone 11
Prepare Students to Further the Progress of Civilization
393

Stepping Stone 12
Remove Stress, Anxiety, Depression, and Suicidal Thoughts from the Learning Environment
401

Stepping Stone 13
Stop the Education Blame Game: There Are No Beneficiaries
417

Stepping Stone 14
Take Responsibility for the Failure to Educate Students
423

World Famous Poem

Sandstorm in Baghdad
433

Stepping Stone 15
Education Is the Only Path to a Peaceful World
437

World Famous Poem

There Is No Flower in Darfur
440

Contents

World Famous Poem
TSUNAMI
444

World Famous Poem
Everyone Is On the Same Page
449

World Famous Poem
Simon Wiesenthal: A Survivor's Burden
465

World Famous Poem
The Militant Palestinian Toddler Terrorist
467

Final Note to the Reader
469

World Famous Poem
The World Trade Center Tragedy
Spiraling Downward, Upward We Stand United
471

Three World Famous Quotes
The Eternal Paradox of the Penis & Two Kinds of Men,
There Are No Believers, 479

World Famous Poem
DEADICATION
481

Take a "Hotdog" Exam on this Book
484

Education Update
Secretary Arne Duncan's "Race to the Bottom"
489

Appendix
493

Appendix A
Definitions: The Fifteen Stumbling Blocks of Academic Failure
495

Appendix B
Definitions: The Fifteen Stepping Stones for Academic Success
503

Appendix C
The Silent Crisis Destroying America's Brightest Minds
513

Appendix D
The Downward Spiral of Academic Failure
517

Appendix E
Academic Insanity
521

Appendix F
Thinkers in Education
Sharon Rose Sugar
Paladin of Education for the 21st Century
525

Appendix G
School Smart Books for Academic Success
56

Contents

About the Alien

PHOTON
SUPERHERO OF EDUCATION
EVERYBODY IS SOMEBODY SPECIAL
www.PHOTONSUPERHERO.com
528

PHOTON SUPERHERO
Spiritual Affirmations
Feed the Whole Child: Mind, Body, and Spirit

- Self-Esteem Affirmation
- Empowerment Affirmation
- Circle of Responsibility Affirmation
- World Peace Equation
- 5 Superpowers of Making Dreams Come True
- 7 Superpowers of Stress-Relief
- Special Gifts
- **SMARTGRADES** Processing Tools for Academic Success
- 22 Spiritual Illuminations
- Moon Quote for Life on Planet Earth

#1 Poetry Website for Student Projects
How to Read a Poem By Sharon Esther Lampert

- BE ART
- TRUE LOVE
- BE BORN
- The 22 Commandments
- The Restless Sunrise
- Finite
- Impossible
- Poetree
- Minus Zero Woman
- Be Hard
- Warm Nobody
- What Other People Think

Contents

About the Creative Genius
SHARON ESTHER LAMPERT

- SharonEstherLampert.com
- WorldFamousPoems.com
- PoetryJewels.com
- PhilosopherQueen.com
- FamousPoetsandPoems.com
- GodIsGoDo.com
- Schmaltzy.com
- WinAtThin.com
- TrueLoveBurnsEternal.com
- WomenHaveAllThePower.com
- BooksArePowerful.com
- Smartgrades.com

Sharon Esther Lampert's Critical Contributions:
- Prophecy
- Poetry
- Philosophy
- Theology
- Children's Books
- Literature
- Education
- Feminism
- Language
- World Peace

The [Wo]Man Who Can Make Hard
Things Easy Is the Educator.
Ralph Waldo Emerson

If One is Lucky, a Solitary Fantasy Can Totally Transform One Million Realities.

Maya Angelou
Compatriot: Poet, Philosopher, and Teacher

The Five Intentions of the Book

The first intention: I single-handedly rescued many children. I wrote this book to rescue millions of American children.

The second intention: To place the new learning technology, **SMARTGRADES SUCCESS STRATEGY STUDY SKILLS,** directly into the hands of all students for self-reliant and life-long learners, "Every Student Is a Success Story!"

The third intention: To address, solve, and resolve the problem of, "The Silent Crisis Destroying America's Brightest Minds" and all hot-button issues in education.

The fourth intention: If we shift the education paradigm to a "Quality-Over-Quantity Learning-Processing Education System," America will have the greatest education system in the world.

The fifth intention: If we just solve one problem in the world "The Problem of Education," then we will be able to solve every other problem in the world: famine, illiteracy, poverty, crime, disease, domestic violence, religious strife, and war.

Teachers — not politicians — are the true peacemakers in the world. Education is the only path to a peaceful world. SOLVE THE PROBLEM OF EDUCATION, SAVE THE ENTIRE WORLD!

Sharon Rose Sugar
The Paladin of Education for the 21st Century

"I am not as smart as I thought I was!"

- Disconnected
- Depressed
- Distracted
- Disillusioned
- Disgruntled
- Disobedient
- Drugged

Student does not have

A.D.H.D.

the incurable brain disorder. Drugs are not the answer.

Student does have a powerful brain — and is a talented and gifted child.

Fall Behind, Flounder, Fail, and Fall Through the Cracks of the Malfunctioning American Education System

Part One
Save America's Children of Privilege

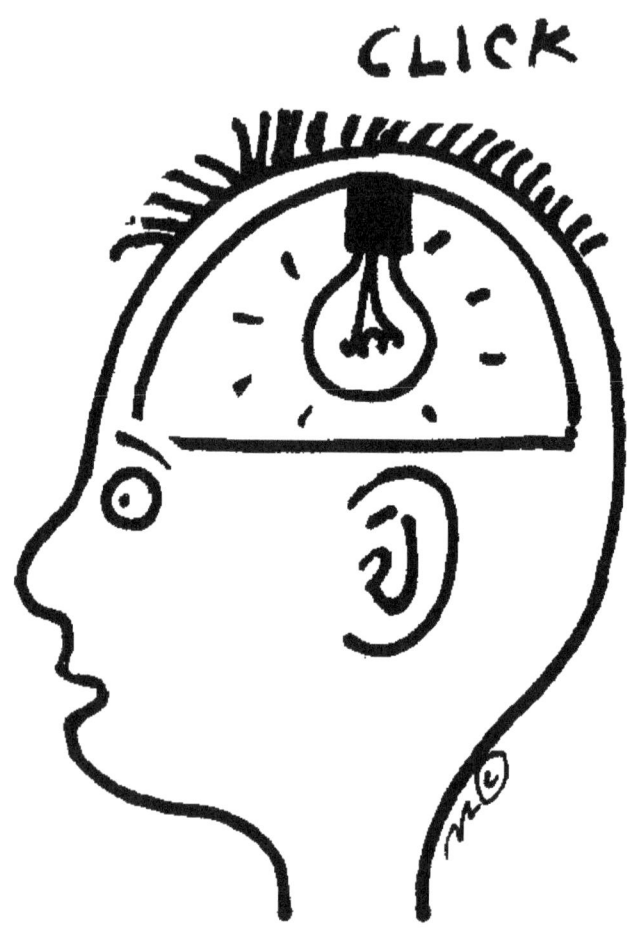

"All Students Want To Do Well,
They Just Don't Know How."

Sharon Rose Sugar
The Paladin of Education for the 21st Century

All of Us Do Not Have Equal Talent,
But All of Us Should Have an
Equal Opportunity to Develop Our Talent.

President John F. Kennedy

The Goal of Education Is the Advancement of Knowledge and the Dissemination of Truth.

President John Fitzgerald Kennedy

If the Truth Be Told

America is the land of democracy, free speech, civil rights, and unlimited personal potential. America is one of the greatest countries in the world. America deserves to have one of the best education systems in the world.

If the truth be told, America's Brightest Minds, are being destroyed. These talented and gifted students are not able to achieve academic success, fulfill their potential, and attain their American dream, because the American education system is malfunctioning. It malfunctions because there are fifteen-stumbling blocks strewn on the path to academic success that cause students to trip, fall, and forfeit their dreams. This is also true for the minority of students who are enrolled in brand name, luxury liner, elite private schools. Private school students are exposed to the same fifteen-stumbling blocks of academic failure as the public school students.

This book exposes the fifteen-stumbling blocks — the jagged-edged pieces of the puzzle of academic failure — and sheds light on the unsolved mystery of why the American education system is malfunctioning. In addition, a critical eye is cast upon the rising A.D.H.D. (Attention-Deficit Hyperactivity Disorder) epidemic.

Most importantly, this book offers four viable solutions to the problem of the national crisis of American education, as follows:

First, we place the new learning technology, **SMARTGRADES SUCCESS STRATEGY STUDY SKILLS,** directly into the hands of all of our students for self-reliant and life-long learners.

Second, we shift the education paradigm to a "Quality Over Quantity Learning-Processing Education System" to ensure in-depth comprehension, long-term retention, and mastery of the academic material. Students will earn a diploma and an education.

Third, we rebuild the American education system from the ground up with the "Fifteen Stepping Stones for Academic Success" to prepare students to meet the challenges of life in the 21st century.

Finally, we adopt the **"40 Universal Gold Standards of Education."**

As a result, America will have the greatest education system in the world. These critical changes will ensure that, "Every Student Is a Success Story." And these monumental changes will bring us closer to a peaceful world.

This book will boldly go where no educator has gone before and courageously attempt to address, solve, and resolve many of the hot-button issues in education that are destroying America's Brightest Minds:

Crisis 1. The Silent Crisis Destroying America's Brightest Minds

Crisis 2. The Rising A. D. H. D. Epidemic

Crisis 3. The Rising Rate of High School Dropouts: DROPOUT NATION

Crisis 4. The Rising Prison Population in America

Crisis 5. The Rising Rate of American Children Living in Poverty

Crisis 6. America's Stop-Loss Soldiers Dying in the Prime of Life

Crisis 7. The Rising Rate of School Shootings and Massacres

Crisis 8. The Rising Rate of School Bomb Scares

Crisis 9. The Rising Rate of College Binge-Drinking and Driving Accidents

Crisis 10. The Rising Rate of College Depression and Suicide

Crisis 11. The Rising Rate of Childhood Obesity and Illness

Crisis 12. The Destruction of Lateral Right-Brain (Creative) Students by Linear Left-Brain Educators

Crisis 13. The Medical System: It can take 5-10 doctors to get the correct diagnosis and more Americans die from medical error than from disease. Rough estimate: 98,000 people die a year from hospital medical errors (Kohn, Corrigan, and Donaldson, *"Building a Safer Health System"* 2000).

Crisis One: The Destruction of America's Brightest Minds

If the truth be told, one of the most devastating consequences of the malfunctioning American education system is that in many elite schools in the country, there are top-notch students who are falling behind, floundering, failing, and dropping out. These students don't really drop out of school. These students fall behind, flounder, fail, and change schools. Properly prepared for greatness by their parents, they have lost their confidence and think **"I am not as smart as I thought I was."** Some of the brightest students in America are losing their way and America is losing her national treasures.

If the truth be told, the vast majority of students who graduate from American schools are walking around with only one shoelace tied. These one-untied shoelace students are struggling to survive. At some point along the way, the untied shoelace is going to trip them up and make them fall flat on their faces. In other words, these students are unprepared to meet the social, economic, science, and technological challenges of life in the 21st century. These students don't know how to get the other shoelace tied, and quite frankly, they don't care, because they have become anxious, stressed, disconnected, depressed, distracted, disgruntled, disillusioned, disobedient, and suicidal. These students are emotionally wounded and suffer from the "Pain of Inadequacy." These deep emotional scars are inflicted by the malfunctioning American education system. Most students who graduate from an American school will suffer from the "Pain of Inadequacy" and bear the "Scars of Incompetence."

Every student enrolled in the American education system has a horror story to tell of an unfair homework assignment, an unfair research report, and an unfair test. There is no one who will listen to the student or stand up for the student. The only advice a student will get is, **"You should study harder!"** When in fact, the student has studied for hours and has had private tutoring sessions, but was sabotaged by tricky test questions on a "Hotdog" exam. The victim, a powerless child, is blamed for the injustices of a malfunctioning education system.

If the truth be told, most students don't learn how to succeed in the American education system; they spend most of their time learning how to survive the American education system.

November 24, 2008, will go on record as one of the saddest days in the history of American education. On this day, the "Officials" of the prestigious Stuyvesant High School in New York City, wanted to install metal detectors to stop their gifted and talented students from cheating on their Regents exams. The malfunctioning American education system had reached its lowest point. This mind-boggling education news bulletin was front page news in every media outlet in the country:

"Officials at Stuyvesant High School told parents that they want to install metal detectors, but not because of concern that students are bringing weapons to school. The prestigious public high school simply wants to catch students who are breaking the Department of Education's ban on cellphones and are using them to text each other test answers" (Billy Parker, "Stuyvesant to Install Metal Detectors--Nerd Alerts Likely, *The Gothamist,* November 24, 2008).

It is a tragedy of colossal proportions that America's Brightest Minds need metal detectors. These gifted and talented students are struggling to survive and have to cut corners and cheat to pass, survive, graduate, and earn a diploma.

Learn to Cheat or Dropout to Earn a Diploma

Paradoxically, educators are completely clueless as to "How Does Learning Take Place." They are fast asleep at the steering wheel. All American students have learned how to cheat to pass, survive, and graduate from a **"Quantity Over Quality, Curriculum-Driven Malfunctioning American Education System"** where teaching and learning are sacrificed to push the curriculum forward at a frenetic pace. Students **"Read, Cram, Regurgitate, and Test"** to earn a diploma. Ironically, it is the dropouts who have not learned how to cheat to survive. The parents have become willing accomplices funding the online purchase of essays and research reports.

The malfunctioning American education system is riddled with "Academic Insanity" that is destroying the emotional, spiritual, and intellectual fabric of America's Brightest Minds. Most American students will earn a diploma, but not an education.

On February 18, 2009, Theodore Graubard, one of America's Brightest Minds, plunged to his death in an apparent suicide, in broad daylight, with other children playing nearby. He was a seventeen-year-old student from one of New York City's finest private schools, The Dalton School. He was an accomplished scholar and athlete. At 11:15 a.m., his suicide was an 11-story plunge from the window of the school's empty dance studio (Yaniv, Lazarowitz, and Lemire, "17-year-old Student Plunges to Death at Manhattan's Elite Dalton School" *Daily News*, February 18, 2009).

It is a tragedy of unimaginable proportions that **AMERICA'S BRIGHTEST MINDS** are committing suicide in every prestigious school in the nation.

The questions that need to be examined are as follows:

Q: Why do the best schools have the highest suicide rates?

Q: Why do gifted and talented students commit suicide?

Q: Why do gifted and talented students cut corners and cheat?

Q: Why humiliate gifted and talented students by asking the entire student body to walk through metal detectors? In America, you are innocent until proven guilty. Why treat gifted and talented students like dishonest thugs?

Q: Why is every day of school a cutthroat competition for academic survival: "Read, Cram, Regurgitate, and Test"?

Q: When will educators understand that test scores have no value if students can't remember the academic facts two weeks after a test?

The human brain is the most powerful biological machine in the world. The only thing that is wrong with a student is that the brain did not come with an instruction manual and a student does not know how to use it. If the truth be told, educators do not know how to nurture and cultivate the awesome power of the human brain. Educators are clueless as to, "How Does Learning Take Place?"

The futile academic games of **"Read, Cram, Regurgitate, Test,"** and **"Hotdog"** exams do not measure education. Moreover, these two games are some of the stressors that contribute to the **"Pain of Inadequacy"** and **"Scars of Incompetence"** of their battle-fatigued students who fight for their American dream on American soil, in American classrooms, across the country.

- Education is not measured by cramming voluminous facts into the mind.

- Education is not measured by regurgitating voluminous facts onto a test.

- Education is not measured by regurgitating voluminous facts under psychological duress onto a test.

- Education is not measured by regurgitating voluminous facts under a stopwatch onto a test.

- Abusive (tricky) "Hotdog" exams do not measure education.

As a result of the **"Academic Pressure Cooker"** the entire student body is suffering from varying degrees of anxiety, stress, and "bouts of depression."

This book will ask and answer the question **"How Does Learning Take Place?"** This is the central question that is at the heart of education (*The Universal Gold Standard of Education* Appendix G, p. 56).

Another critical question that will be addressed in this book is:

Q: Are educators running a school for academic success or an education asylum riddled with academic insanity?

Here is a prototypical example of "Academic Insanity": Teachers don't have time to teach for in-depth comprehension, but they always have time to test you on the significant and trivial details that they don't have time to teach.

The malfunctioning **"Quantity Over Quality, Curriculum-Driven American Education System,"** is a runaway train with a careless conductor manning the controls, randomly bumping into and bruising students or head on decapitating students and putting their powerful brains into virtual wheelchairs. As early as the third grade, the American education system is an insidious form of unintentional child abuse (blind leading the blind) that is destroying the minds, hearts, and spirits of our students, thereby leaving life-long emotional, intellectual, and spiritual wounds. This education system is destroying America's greatest natural resource, America's Brightest Minds.

Some may argue that the Columbine massacre was the lowest point in American education, but I beg to differ, because school shootings and massacres are the direct fault of the broken American psychiatric system that wants to resolve emotional problems with psychotropic drugs, a dangerous crutch with serious side effects. Sometimes negative reactions to these medications can be extreme, such as hallucinations, violent outbursts, volatile temperaments, psychosis, and suicidal behavior.

One of the Columbine gunmen, Eric Harris, was on psychotropic drugs ("Columbine" Wikipedia).

Treating emotional problems, namely depression, with a brain scan to diagnose a brain disorder and psychotropic drugs are failed therapeutic methodologies to mend a wounded soul. You cannot heal a wounded, broken, or shattered spirit (a disintegrated mind) with psychotropic drugs.

There is a new thirteen step therapy modality, "Integration Therapy for Intrapersonal Growth, Development, and Maturity," that heals students who are disconnected, depressed, distracted, disgruntled, disobedient, or misdiagnosed with A.D.H.D., (p. 92). (Intrapersonal *Integration Therapy Modality*, Appendix G, p. 56).

Crisis Two: The Rising A. D. H. D. Epidemic

One of the most devastating consequences of the malfunctioning American education system is the rising A.D.H.D. epidemic. Before the age of puberty, countless American children who were born in perfect health will be misdiagnosed with A.D.H.D., "the incurable brain disorder," because students who fall behind, flounder, fail, and fall through the cracks of the malfunctioning American education system have become disconnected, depressed, distracted, disgruntled, and disobedient. Some students have become blocked. Some students have shutdown. These symptoms resemble the symptoms associated with A.D.H.D., namely inattention, hyperactivity, and impulsivity. Time and again, these students will be misdiagnosed with A.D.H.D., and given Ritalin. These misdiagnosed children will lose much more than their American dream, they will become emotionally handicapped for life. Their self-talk is, "I can't do this and I can't do that, because I have A.D.H.D., an 'incurable brain disorder.'"

According to Dr. Lawrence Diller, "In 1998, nearly five million people in the United States — most of them children — were prescribed Ritalin. Use of this drug has increased by 700 percent since 1990." Moreover, "90 percent of the world's Ritalin is used in America." He concludes that, "This figure — suggests a problem of epidemic proportions" (Dr. Lawrence Diller, "Running on Ritalin," Bantam, 1999).

When I started this book, I wanted to save children from the misdiagnosis of A. D. H. D. I had no idea that the situation had become lethal. A recent news report deftly illustrates how grim the situation has become for America's children and how grave the consequences. It states that the drug Risperdal was not approved to treat A.D.H.D., yet, it is prescribed to treat A.D.H.D., and American children are dying at the hands of clueless psychiatrists (who have a clue).

"Powerful antipsychotic medicines are being used far too cavalierly in children — More than 389,000 children and teenagers were treated last year with Risperdal, one of five popular medicines known as atypical antipsychotics. Of those patients, 240,000 were 12 or younger, according to data presented to the committee. In many cases, the drug was prescribed to treat attention deficit disorders. But Risperdal is not approved for attention deficit problems, and its risks — which include substantial weight gain, metabolic disorders and muscular tics that can be permanent.

From 1993 through the first three months of 2008, 1,207 children given Risperdal suffered serious problems, including 31 who died. Among the deaths was a 9-year-old with attention deficit problems who suffered a fatal stroke 12 days after starting therapy with Risperdal" (Gardiner Harris, "Use of Antipsychotics in Children Is Criticized" *The New York TImes*, November 19, 2008).

Crisis Three: DROPOUT NATION
The Rising Rate of High School Dropouts

Another devastating consequence of the malfunctioning American education system is the rising rate of high school dropouts, because these students fall behind, flounder, fail, and fall through the cracks of a malfunctioning education system. These students have become disconnected, depressed, distracted, disgruntled, and disobedient. Some students have become blocked. Some students have shutdown. Students do not have "time to learn" and learning tools to "learn and process" voluminous academic knowledge: Organization Skills, Time Management Skills, Research Report Skills, and Testing Skills. These students do not know how to play the academic game of "Read, Cram, Regurgitate, and Test," to graduate and earn a diploma. In most cases, students have parents with inadequate parenting tools. In some cases, students have parents with abusive parenting practices and the home is a war zone.

There is a high school dropout epidemic in America. There are almost 2,000 high schools across the country that are called "dropout factories," because they graduate less than 60 percent of their students. "Utah, which has low poverty rates and fewer minorities than most states, is the only state without a dropout factory. Florida and South Carolina have the highest percentages. About half of high schools in those states classify as dropout factories"(Nancy Zuckerbrod, "1 in 10 Schools Are 'Dropout Factories,'" *Associated Press*, November 9, 2007).

"Each year, almost one third of all public high school students – and nearly one half of all Blacks, Hispanics and Native Americans – fail to graduate from public high school with their class (John M. Bridgeland, John J. Dilulio, Jr., and Karen Burke Morison, *"The Silent Epidemic: Perspectives of High School Dropouts,"* Bill and Melinda Gates Foundation, March, 2006).

The Percentage of Students who Graduate from High School
57.8 percent of Hispanics
53.4 percent of African Americans
49.3 percent of American Indians
49.3 percent of Alaska Natives
76.2 percent of Whites
80.2 percent of Asian Americans
(Annie E. Casey Foundation, 2008)

The High School Dropouts by State, 2006
Alabama	Total	24,000
Alaska	Total	3,000
Arizona	Total	31,000
Arkansas	Total	10,000
California	Total	141,000
Colorado	Total	23,000
Connecticut	Total	8,000
Delaware	Total	3,000
District of Columbia	Total	2,000
Florida	Total	74,000
Georgia	Total	52,000
Hawaii	Total	4,000
Idaho	Total	6,000
Illinois	Total	41,000
Indiana	Total	28,000
Iowa	Total	8,000
Kansas	Total	7,000
Kentucky	Total	20,000

Louisiana	Total	31,000
Maine	Total	3,000
Maryland	Total	21,000
Massachusetts	Total	15,000
Michigan	Total	36,000
Minnesota	Total	12,000
Mississippi	Total	19,000
Missouri	Total	20,000
Montana	Total	5,000
Nebraska	Total	6,000
Nevada	Total	13,000
New Hampshire	Total	3,000
New Jersey	Total	22,000
New Mexico	Total	12,000
New York	Total	63,000
North Carolina	Total	36,000
North Dakota	Total	1,000
Ohio	Total	36,000
Oklahoma	Total	16,000
Oregon	Total	14,000
Pennsylvania	Total	42,000
Rhode Island	Total	5,000
South Carolina	Total	20,000
South Dakota	Total	3,000
Tennessee	Total	20,000
Texas	Total	105,000
Utah	Total	10,000
Vermont	Total	2,000

Virginia	Total	23,000
Washington	Total	23,000
West Virginia	Total	8,000
Wisconsin	Total	16,000
Wyoming	Total	2,000

(Annie E. Casey Foundation, 2008)

Crisis Four: The Rising Rate of America's Prison Population
Another devastating consequence of the malfunctioning American education system is the rising rate of America's prison population, because some students who drop out of high school drift aimlessly into trouble. One fantasy is easy work for fast and easy money, e.g., selling drugs. Here are the gross statistics: "As of 2006, it is roughly estimated that at least 9.25 million people are currently imprisoned worldwide. In absolute terms, the United States currently has the largest inmate population in the world, with more than 2.5 million or more than one in a hundred adults in prisons and jails. Although the United States represents less than 5 percent of the world's population, over 25 percent of the people incarcerated around the world are housed in the American prison system" ("Incarceration in the United States" Wikipedia, 2008).

Here are the gross statistics of damages incurred as outlined from a study conducted by the American Youth Policy Forum, "Whatever It Takes: How Twelve Communities Are Reconnecting Out-of-School Youth… The Dropout Problem in Numbers":

• 75 percent of state prison inmates and 59 percent of federal inmates are high school dropouts.

- High school dropouts are 3.5 times more likely than graduates to be incarcerated.

- Dropouts contribute disproportionately to the unemployment rate. In 2001, 55 percent of young adult dropouts were employed, compared to 74 percent of high school graduates and 87 percent of college graduates.

- Dropouts contribute to state and federal tax coffers at about one-half the rate of high school graduates. Over a working lifetime, a dropout will contribute about $60,000 less.

- The 23 million high school dropouts aged 18-67 will contribute roughly $50 billion less annually in state and federal taxes.

- Studies suggest the United States would save $41.8 billion in health care costs if the 600,000 young people who dropped out in 2004 were to complete one additional year of education.

- If 33 percent of dropouts graduated from high school, the federal government would save $10.8 billion each year in food stamps, housing assistance, and temporary assistance for needy families.

- Testifying before Congress, Secretary of Education Margaret Spellings said dropouts cost the United States "more than $260 billion... in lost wages, lost taxes and lost productivity over their lifetimes" (Ben Brudevold-Newman, *"The Cost of Dropping Out"* National Public Radio, March 27, 2006).

Crisis Five: One in Six Children in America Live in Poverty

Another devastating consequence of the malfunctioning American education system is the rising rate of children who live in poverty, because education will be the only lifeline these thirteen million children will have to rise above their unfortunate circumstances and grab hold of a brighter future.

According to a recent report by the Children's Defense Fund, "Child Poverty in America" thirteen million children in America live in poverty (Children's Defense Fund, *"Child Poverty in America"* September, 2007).

According to a recent report by the Center for American Progress, "America is the richest nation in the world, yet 37 million Americans live below the official poverty line and millions more struggle to get by every month. In a nation of 297 million, 12. 6 percent are poor."

Here are some gross statistics on poverty in America:

37 million: Number of Americans who live below the official poverty line — 12.6 percent of the total population.

1 in 8: Proportion of Americans who now live in poverty

1 in 3: Proportion of Americans who are considered low-income

$19,971: A family of four that makes below this income is considered poor – far below what most people believe a family needs to survive

16 million: Number of Americans living in extreme poverty, meaning their incomes are below half the poverty line: less than $9,903 for a family of four or $5,080 for an individual

90 million: Number of Americans who had incomes below 200 percent of federal poverty thresholds; an annual income of $40,000 for a family of four

$500 billion: Persistent childhood poverty's estimated cost to the nation each year because of lost adult productivity and wages, increased crime, and higher health expenditures" (Center for American Progress, "*The Poverty Epidemic in America, by the Numbers,*" April 24, 2007).

"A United Nations (UNICEF) study reports that children in the richest countries are not necessarily the best-off. --UNICEF's Innocenti Research Center in Italy ranked the countries in six categories: material well-being, health, education, relationships, behaviors and risks, and young people's own sense of happiness."

This UNICEF study compared the United States to twenty-one affluent nations, and concluded the following:

- Out of the 21 most affluent nations, the United States has the highest percentage of poor children

- The United States and Britain ranked as the worst places to be a child

(Maggie Farley, "UNICEF Ranks the Well-Being of Youngsters in 21 Developed Countries" *Los Angeles Times*, 2007).

Crisis Six: America's Stop-Loss Soldiers

Another devastating consequence of the malfunctioning American education system is the rising rate of high school students who are voluntarily recruited into the American army. This is because teenagers who are adrift, are drifting into army-recruiting stations. Men in the prime of life will be shipped out to find and capture a handful of "Evil Ones" and along the way, kill others who are guilty by association as well as kill unfortunate innocent bystanders. According to a recent news report, "The percentage of new recruits entering the Army with a high school diploma dropped to a new low in 2007, according to a study released yesterday, and Army officials confirmed that they have lowered their standards to meet high recruiting goals in the middle of two ongoing wars (Josh White, "Army Off Target on Recruits: Percentage of High School Graduates Drops to New Low" *Washington Post,* January 23, 2008). American teenagers will be sacrificed and slaughtered on the altar of democracy.

If our kids were really living in a democracy that practices what it preaches, the barbaric manly ritual of war would have been abolished by the democratic consensus of fellow Americans. The American people don't want their Pit Bull puppies to be turned into "fighting dogs," yet our kids can voluntarily become "fighting soldiers." Last year, "Michael Vick was sentenced to 23 months in prison Monday for running a "cruel and inhumane" dogfighting ring. Dogs that did not perform up to expectations were killed by electrocution, hanging, drowning and other violent means by the dogfighting ring" ("Apologetic Vick gets 23-month sentence on dogfighting charges" ESPN, December 11, 2007).

American teenagers join the army for an all-expenses-paid trip to college and the promise of a good job, and the opportunity to travel to interesting places--not to mediate among the Shia and Sunnis religious factions of Iraq who like "fighting dogs," compete for power, do or die, till death do them part, in the name of Allah, with 40 virgins awaiting them at the pearly gates of heaven.

One American Soldier's Story: Deployed Seven Times

Army Sgt. 1st Class David L. McDowell: Died: April 29, 2008
David had been deployed to Afghanistan and Iraq seven times. He joined the army right after his high school graduation. "He was assigned to the 2nd Battalion, 75th Ranger Regiment, based in Fort Lewis, Wash." Enemy forces attacked using small arms and he died from his wounds. He was 30 years old. "He is survived by his wife, Joleen; son, Joshua, 11; daughter, Erin, 3; his parents; and two sisters." He was a recipient of two Bronze stars and a Purple Heart ("Ramona Army Ranger Killed in Afghanistan," SignonSanDiego.com, May 1, 2008).

The Iraq war began on March 20, 2003 and our kids have been fighting "tit for tat" like "fighting dogs" for more than five years. …And we will still have the problem of worldwide terrorism.

Here are the political conundrums that need analysis:

True, we have not had a terrorist attack on American soil since September 11, 2001, and this has been our primary objective.

Q: Is this because of our billion-dollar bombs and trillion-dollar war effort in Afghanistan and Iraq?

Q: Is this because it takes time for ten to twenty terrorists to fire up their vivid and active imaginations to come up with another game plan, a "low-cost bargain basement special," of martyrdom and murder, that will terrify the American people?

Terrorists tend to travel lightly and at low cost; little more than a dozen young men equipped with cell phones, armed with weapons, who are prepared to commit suicide. The perpetrators all end up dead, so there is no one to bring to justice. If the truth be told, the political problem is really an amalgam of nasty nature and nasty nurture; the earliest education of Islamic fundamentalism, not the lack of a stable governement in need of, democracy, or lack of material goods.

Ironically, "the earliest education" is a top priority among Hamas terrorists who indoctrinate 2-year-old toddlers, their very own beloved children, for martyrdom and murder (Poem, "*The Militant Palestinian Toddler Terrorist*" *Poetry Jewels*, Kadimah Press).

Here is another political conundrum that needs analysis:

On September 11th, 2001, we had 3,000 American fatalities. On September 11th, 2008, we had 7,800 American fatalities and 30,000 American casualties of war. We have doubled our losses and quadrupled our pain, and there is no end in sight, because we have tripled our playmates: Taliban militants, Iraqi insurgents, and Afghani rebels.

Survivors of the Iraq war will transmit war stories for generations to come. As of December 2008, the Iraqi body count hovers around 90,000-98,000 civilian deaths (www.Iraqibodycount.com). The survivors will poison the minds of future generations with stories of horror, humiliation, and hatred. Some will exact revenge. Some will seek justice for the Abu Ghraib torture and prisoner abuse by sadistic American military personnel who boastfully posed to take barbaric photographs. Q: Are our political enemies treated better or worse than Saddam Hussein's political enemies?

And we borrow money from China and have a growing eleven trillion-dollar deficit. And Americans are squeezed financially because of record oil prices. And we have an economy in ruins. As America tries to advance the cause of "Democracy" in Iraq, American banks and businesses are collapsing and are now partially owned by the American government.

And American taxpayers are footing the 45 billion-dollar bill for rebuilding Iraq. Meanwhile, it is estimated that Iraq cleared $100 billion in oil revenues in 2007 and 2008. ("Iraq Oil Revenue Soars, Creating Huge Surplus," *Associated Press*, March 11, 2008)."

Crisis Seven:
The Rising Rate of School Shootings or Massacres in America

Another devastating consequence of the malfunctioning American education system is the rising rate of school shootings and massacres, because depressed, disconnected, distracted, disgruntled, and disobedient students on psychotropic drugs, a dangerous crutch with serious side effects, constitute a recipe for disaster. Here is a short list of disgruntled students:

1927
- Michigan, Bath School **massacre,** school board member, Andrew Kehoe, 45 dead, 58 injured (May 18, 1927)

1966
- Texas, University of Texas, Austin **massacre**. Charles Joseph Whitman, 13 dead, 32 injured (August 1, 1966)

1990's
- Oregon, 14-year-old Kip Kinkel, 2 dead, 22 injured, (May 21, 1998)
- Idaho, 15-year-old Shawn Cooper (April 16, 1999)
- Colorado, Columbine High School **massacre**, Eric Harris and Dylan Klebold, 13 dead, 21 injured (April 20, 1999)
- Georgia, 15-year-old T.J. Solomon, 6 injured (May 20, 1999)

2000-2007
- Pennsylvania, 14-year-old Elizabeth Bush, 1 injury (March 7, 2000)
- California, 18-year-old Jason Hoffman, 5 injured (March 22, 2001)
- Washington, 16-year-old Cory Baadsgaard (April 10, 2001)
- Minnesota, Red Lake High School **massacre**, 16-year-old Jeffrey Weise, 7 dead, 5 injured (March 21, 2005)
- Virginia Tech **massacre,** Seung-Hui Cho, 32 dead, 23 injured (April 16, 2007)
- Delaware State University shooting (September 21, 2007)
- Success Tech Academy shooting (October 10, 2007)

2008: Record Breaking Five School Shootings in One Week
- Notre Dame Elementary School shooting (Feb 7, 2008)
- Louisiana Technical College shooting (February 8, 2008)
- Mitchell High School shooting (February 11, 2008)
- E. O. Green School shooting (February 12, 2008)
- Northern Illinois University **massacre:** (February 14, 2008)

- Central High School shooting (August 21, 2008)
  ("School Shooting" Wikipedia, 2008)

"Eight out of 13 U.S. school shootings were committed by teens taking psychotropic drugs known to cause violent and suicidal behavior" (Jay Baadsgaard, www.drugawareness.org).

Here are newspaper excerpts of a recently reported college shooting and university massacre in America:

School Shooting: February 8, 2008
"A female student shot two other women and herself Friday inside a classroom on the Baton Rouge campus of Louisiana Technical College, authorities said" (Alison Go, "Three Dead After Shooting at Louisiana Technical College," CNN, February 8, 2008).

School Massacre: February 14, 2008
A week later, a school massacre occurred on the campus of Northern Illinois University in DeKalb, Illinois. The shooter, Steven P. Kazmierczak, was a N. I. U. graduate student in sociology (2007). He killed six students and wounded sixteen others before taking his own life ("University Shooter Interested in 'Peace and Social Justice,'" CNN, February 16, 2008).

Ironically, "Mr. Kazmierczak was a former vice president of the Academic Criminal Justice Association at Northern Illinois. The university honored him two years ago with a dean's award for his scholarship in sociology" ("Northern Illinois U. Shooter Was Graduate Student at U. of Illinois at Urbana-Champaign" *Chronicle of Higher Education,* February 15, 2008).

In this case, it was noted that, "The gunman who killed five students and then himself at Northern Illinois University took an anti-anxiety drug and a sleeping aid in addition to the antidepressant Prozac, his girlfriend told CNN" (Catrin Einhorn, "Gunman Took Anti-Anxiety Drug," *The New York Times,* February 22, 2008).

Eric Harris, one of the two gunman of the Columbine High School massacre (April 20, 1999), "was taking the drug Luvox (fluvoxamine), an SSRI antidepressant, which he was required to take as part of court-ordered anger-management therapy." The other Columbine gunman, Dylan Klebold, was once a member of CHIPS (Challenging High Intellectual Potential Students), a program for gifted and talented children" ("Columbine" Wikipedia, 2008). In retrospect, it was two of, America's Brightest Minds, who burned bullet holes into their fellow classmates and murdered them in cold blood.

2009: The Most Brutal in American History

The year began with the decapitation of a college student in a campus cafe, followed by a student murdered and stuffed into a laboratory closet, and ended with the stabbing of a college professor in his office. This is just a small sampling of school violence and is incomplete.

January 22, 2009: *College Murder*
Virginia Tech Student Stabbed and Decapitated in Campus Cafe
"A 22-year-old graduate student who had arrived on campus at Virginia Tech University just two weeks ago was decapitated with what university officials said appeared to be a kitchen knife. She was having coffee with a Chinese doctoral student in a campus cafe Wednesday night. Her killer was 25-year-old Haiyang Zhu of Ningbo, China. He was a doctoral student in agricultural and applied economics" (FOX News).

April 11, 2009: *College Shooting and Suicide*
On Good Friday, at Henry Ford Community College, Anthony Powell, shot Asia McGowan, and then turned the gun on himself in a murder-suicide. "The 17,000-student commuter school sent alerts through an e-mail and cell phone system and locked down the campus ("MI: Murder-Suicide..." gunguys.com, April 11, 2009).

508 Chicago School Students Shot: 36 Students Murdered

May 5, 2009, Rising Murder Rate of Chicago's School Students
More than 36 Chicago public schools students have been murdered since the beginning of the current school year. In 16 months, 508 Chicago school students have been shot. Last year, 27 Chicago school students were murdered in cold blood. On May 4, 2009, in a brutal murder, Alex Arellano, a 15-year-old boy was knocked down by bats, chased and hit by a car, shot in the head with a bullet and burned (Commentary, "508 Chicago Kids Shot in Just 16 months" *Chicago Sun Times*, March 9, 2009).

May 7, 2009, College, Wesleyan University, Connecticut
His journal said: "She Must Die," "Beautiful and Smart," and "I think it okay to kill Jews and go on a killing spree." Gorgeous Johanna Justin-Jinich, is murdered by Stephen Morgan, a disgruntled former Roman Catholic classmate from N.Y.U. The course was on human sexuality. ("Bail raised...." *Hartford Courant*, May 24, 2009).

September 8, 2009: Yale University, Connecticut, Murder
"Annie Le's body was found stuffed behind a basement wall in a high-security school lab. Her wedding date was set for the 13th (CNN).

September 26, 2009: Fenger High School, Chicago
"16-year-old Derrion Albert lay on the gravel, his body dented and damaged from the pummeling. The honor roll student known for his love of computers became the third Chicago teenager killed this month. At least seven more have been shot. The beating death was caught on video and broadcast on YouTube (Banchero and Mack, *Chicago Tribune*, September 26, 2009).

October 9, 2009: College, UCLA, California, Chemistry Class
"Blood gushed from a student's neck and formed a puddle on the floor of a UCLA lab as instructors struggled to stanch the wound. The 20-year-old woman was taken across the hall after being slashed in the neck by a classmate. Stunned students watched in horror" (Staff, *Huffington Post*, October 9, 2009).

October 21, 2009: High School Massacre Attempt Foiled
Teen accused of plotting attack at Monroe-Woodbury on Columbine anniversary. Ex-student had stockpile of explosive materials, trench coat (Oliver Mackson, Times Herald-Record November 29, 2009).

October 27, 2009: High School Student Gang Raped
"Investigators say as many as 20 people were involved in or stood and watched the gang rape of a 15-year-old girl outside a California high school homecoming dance Saturday night. The victim was found unconscious under a bench shortly before midnight Saturday (CNN).

December 5, 2009: Professor Murdered in His Office
"A longtime Binghamton University anthropology professor known on campus as "a really nice guy" was stabbed to death in his office Friday by a grad student whose dissertation he was to judge, authorities said. Cops said the as-yet unidentified attacker plunged a 6-inch kitchen blade into 77-year-old Prof. Emeritus Richard T. Antoun four times, puncturing his lung" (Standora, Daily News December 5, 2009).

December 9, 2009: College Shooting/Massacre Averted
"Mr. Hamilton entered the classroom with a high-powered rifle and when he cocked his weapon the teacher yelled to students to take cover, the police said. A community college student who opened fire on his math professor in a crowded classroom Tuesday was arraigned Wednesday on charges of attempted murder and discharging a firearm in a school zone" Ian Urbina, New York Times, December 9, 2009).

December 12, 2009: High School Massacre Attempt Foiled
Columbine Style Attack Foiled. Monday December 14, 2009 was judgment day at Bridgewater-Raritan High School and Immaculata High School in New Jersey (ABC).

Crisis Eight: The Rising Rate of School Bomb Scares (TIC-TOCK)
Another devastating consequence of the malfunctioning American education system is the rising rate of school bomb scares by disconnected, depressed, distracted, disgruntled and disobedient students. Bogus school bomb scares are a prevalent problem facing every elementary school, high school, and college in America.

Hundreds of times yearly, a bomb threat is made against a school, usually by a disgruntled student. During the 1997-98 school year, one Maryland school district experienced more than 150 bomb threats In these cases, the entire student body is asked to evacuate the premises. Authorities have to empty out every trash can in every classroom. Police dogs have to be brought in to sniff out the real or bogus bomb (www.schoolsecurity.org).

After the Columbine High School tragedy, the Colorado Sheriff's Department of Jefferson County, reported that there were 30 exploded devices and 46 unexploded devices in the school. In addition, 23 other explosive devices were found in the shooters' cars and homes (www.schoolsecurity.org).

Even if more than 90% of bomb threats turn out to be pranks, school districts have to take each threat seriously because of the possibility of death and injury.

Here is an incomplete sample of school bomb scares occurring from March 27- April 25, 2009 (about one month):

March 27, 2009
Bomb Scare Puts School On Lock Down
"Sheriff's deputies and school staff scoured the school for about an hour, searching everywhere from classrooms to trash cans." (Bakersfield News, www.turnto23.com).

March 31, 2009
Bomb Scare Disrupts Methuen High School
"Someone wrote a message on the wall in a men's bathroom at Methuen High School, stating, "There is a bomb in a locker tic toc," police said" (J.J. Huggins, Eagle Tribune).

April 16, 2009
Third Bomb Scare at Fresno High School this Year
"Fresno High Principal Bob Reyes, "It was a lunch nylon bag, but on the bag itself was a note saying this is a bomb" (abclocal.go.com).

In one day, two schools had to be evacuated for bomb scares:

April 24, 2009
Bomb Scare Closes Lake Placid Schools
"Someone left the threat at 7:26 this morning on the middle-high school assistant principal's voice mail" (Peter Crowley, Adirondack Daily Enterprise).

April 24, 2009
Students Evacuated in Bomb Scare at Benson Primary School
A teacher found a second grader with a live grenade. "About 400 primary school students were evacuated to an adjacent ball field, and just over 300 students in the middle school were locked down--it was in intense 40 minutes, but every precaution was taken to assure student and staff safety" (Thelma Grimes, Bensonnews-sun).

April 25, 2009
Police Respond To School Bomb Threat Officers Called To River City High School (West Sacramento, California, MSNBC).

Ironically, disgruntled Taliban militants, Iraqi insurgents, and Hamas suicide bombers, would be appalled to hear that bogus-bomb scares by disgruntled students in American schools constitute an abnormal reality of daily life in an American democracy.

Crisis Nine: The Rising Rate of College Drinking and Driving Accidents and Violence Against Women

Another devastating consequence of the malfunctioning American education system is the rising rate of drinking and driving accidents by college students. This is the leading cause of death among college students.

College binge-drinking is the number-one problem on college campuses, because college students find a mind-numbing escape in alcohol from the psychological wounds inflicted, namely, "The Pain of Inadequacy" and the "Scars of Incompetence" by the "Academic Pressure Cooker" of a malfunctioning American education system.

Binge-drinking is defined as drinking alcohol with the intention of becoming intoxicated. The common pattern is to consume five or more drinks in about one to three hours. A night of binge drinking lasts six to ten hours ("Binge-Drinking" Wikipedia, 2008).

According to a study supported by the National Institute on Alcohol Abuse and Alcoholism (NIAAA), "Drinking to excess by college students contributes to 1,400 deaths, 500,000 injuries, and 70,000 cases of sexual assault and date rape each year" (NIAAA, 2008).

A recently reported death from college binge-drinking was the senseless death of Brett Griffin: "A University of Delaware freshman died early Saturday morning from what police suspect was alcohol poisoning at a party, the News Journal reports. Brett Griffin, 18, was unconscious when police arrived just before 3 a.m. and later died at a nearby hospital. The house that had hosted the party was home to several members of the Sigma Alpha Mu fraternity, which authorities say Griffin—a varsity wrestler at South Brunswick High School in New Jersey—was pledging" (Alison Go, "Delaware Freshman Dies After Party," *U.S. News and World Report*, November 10, 2008).

Crisis Ten: The Rising Rate of College Suicides in America

Another devastating consequence of the malfunctioning American education system is the rising suicide rate among college students. Suicide is the second leading cause of death among college students, because parents sugarcoat harsh realities and children are caught unprepared. In addition, educators set unrealistic expectations and cheat students out of an education: No in-depth comprehension, long-term retention, and mastery of the academic material. Inevitably, the disappointments build up and so does the emotional pain, "I can't take it anymore."

Students do not have any lifelines: Competitive isolation, parents with inadequate parenting skills, the malfunctioning American education system, and the broken American psychiatric system. There is no one to catch these students at any step along the way as they fall and descend down the path towards suicide: Stressors, anxiety, disappointments, pain, rage, "bouts of depression," clinical depression, suicidal thinking (the ticking-time bomb), attempted suicide, and suicide. After the funeral, these distinguished students, some of, America's Brightest Minds, will be written up and written off with an "undiagnosed preexisting mental disorder." Because suicide is an unspeakable tragedy, students, parents, educators, and even psychiatrists will not learn anything from the suicide. Here is what an attempted suicide looks like from a college-dorm room:

Brown University

"On a chilly afternoon in the fall of 2005, 'Jane,' a 19-year-old junior at Brown University, sat on her dorm bed and decided to follow through with her plan to kill herself. In despair over a psychology paper she couldn't finish, and unable to shake her choking depression, she swallowed, two by two, the 120 pills she had stashed--the antidepressant Lexapro, Tylenol, and sleep aids. When she failed to pass out, she got nervous and asked a friend to take her to the hospital, where doctors gave her charcoal to soak up the drugs" (Sarah Elizabeth Richards, "The Suicide Test," Salon.com, March 9, 2007).

According to the Jed Foundation, it is roughly estimated that 24,000 suicide attempts and 1,100 suicides occur annually among U.S. college students aged 18 to 24 years (The Jed Foundation, 2008).

According to a recent study by David Drum, a professor of education psychology at the University of Texas at Austin, "More than half of American college students have considered suicide at some point in their lives." The survey on student suicidal behaviors questioned 26,000 undergraduate and graduate students at 70 U.S. institutions" ("Half of College Students Consider Suicide," MSNBC, August 18, 2008").

According to another recent study by the American College Health Association, *"National College Health Assessment,"* "One out of every ten college students has seriously contemplated committing suicide in the past year" ("Gannett Aims to Reduce Suicides," *The Cornell Daily Sun*, January 23, 2008).

According to another recent study by the, *"Annals of Internal Medicine,"* that looked at stress and its consequences for U.S. medical students: "The study included more than 2,000 students at seven medical schools and looked for evidence of burnout and suicidal thinking. About half the medical students reported the feelings that define burnout (emotional exhaustion, a feeling of a loss of personal identity, a sense of poor personal accomplishment). The most disturbing finding was that each year about 10 percent of the observed students had active suicidal thoughts—a symptom we know carries a substantial risk for a future suicide attempt. Even more—about one student out of four—had thoughts about suicide sometime during medical school" (Sydney Spiesel, "Burnout U," *Slate*, October 2, 2008).

"A few weeks ago, the parents of a Harvard student told Dr. Richard Kadison, the chief of the university's mental health service, that they suspected their daughter had a serious drug problem. Since each student has roughly a 50-50 chance of having some symptoms of depression or other problems, I think it has to be part of the consideration in choosing a college. 'There's this illusion that the university is a safe haven in a stable setting,' said Dr. Dennis Heitzmann, director of psychological services for Penn State. 'But for many students, it's not a carefree environment at all.'" (Mary Duenwald "The Dorms May Be Great, but How's the Counseling?" *New York Times,* October 26, 2004).

According to a report published by the United States Naval Academy:
1. Suicide is preventable.
2. The suicide rate for 15–24 year-olds increased by over 200% in the last 50 years.
3. About 12 young people aged 15-24 will commit suicide today.
4. One person under the age of 25 commits suicide within every 2 hours and 2.5 minutes.
5. One in twelve U.S. college students has made a suicide plan. (United States Naval Academy, "Suicide: Suicide Basics-Just the Facts," www.usna.edu).

The Best Schools in America Have the Highest Suicide Rates
"In a Boston Globe study, the Massachusetts Institute of Technology was cited as having the highest suicide rate out of 12 universities surveyed during the past decade. Harvard University was ranked second after M.I.T. (Sun Kim, "Study Finds M.I.T., Harvard have Highest Rates of Student Suicide" (*The Daily Princetonian,* March 15, 2001).

Massachusetts Institute of Technology: "The Meat Grinder"
A recent suicide is Henning Friedrich, a second year graduate student in the Biology Department (Jan. 5, 2007). The school has been referred to as a "meat grinder" because "over the past 40 years, we've had about 50 suicides" (Editorial, *The Tech,* March 7, 2006).

Harvard University

A recent suicide is, John B. Edwards, 19, December 2007. "Since January 1995, at least 15 Harvard undergraduates have committed suicide" (Reed B. Rayman, "Attempted Suicide Numbers Show No Marked Change," *The Harvard Crimson*, November 9, 2005). "According to survey results released this week by University Health Services, nearly half of Harvard's 6,650 undergraduates report feeling "depressed" at some point over the last year and a disturbing 10 percent admit to having had thoughts of suicide in that time"("Crimson Blues," *The Harvard Crimson*, April 4, 2003).

Yale University

" 'Things just move too fast here.' Brian felt things were going fine during his first year, writing off sporadic anxiety attacks as typical for any freshman. As class work piled up and athletics filled much of his time, his stress level began to climb.

Anxiety plus stress do not mix well, he said. "I was just not functional."

("Facade of Perfection: Depression at Yale Bureaucracy and Social Pressure Prevent Many Students from Seeking Help," *The Yale Herald*, October 31, 2003). Update: On November 4, 2009, Eugerie Andre Narcisse, 19, was found dead in his dorm room. The cause of death is still under investigation. In a poll sent to Yale students, 30% said that they use illicit drugs (Dethy, Yale Daily News, November 19, 2008).

Princeton University: RIP Manzili Davis

A recent suicide is Manzili Davis, 21, of Chicago, April, 2006. In 2003, the school newspaper reported that, "Since September, five or six students have been hospitalized for suicidal tendencies, including one student yesterday morning, said Daniel Silverman, University chief medical officer" ("University Works to Prevent Suicide," *The Daily Princetonian*, October 8, 2003).

Columbia University : RIP Richard Ng
A recent suicide is Richard Ng, who killed himself by jumping off the Brooklyn Bridge on May 7, 2006. Five undergraduate students have killed themselves since Spring 1998. "Almost half of all college students report being depressed at some time, and as many as 10 percent of all college students consider suicide in a given year ("Preventing Suicide Among College Students," Columbia University Medical School, 2008).

Dartmouth University: RIP Katie Cullinan
A recent suicide is Katie Cullinan, August, 2008. "Director of Counseling and Health Services, Mark Reed, estimated that there are two to three suicide attempts by students each term" ("Dartmouth Administrators Hoping to Reach Out to Depressed Students" Mouth of Truth, October 11, 2008).

University of Pennsylvania: RIP Kyle Ambrogi
"According to his family, Kyle Ambrogi, a senior running back at the University of Pennsylvania, had been battling depression and took his own life. Why would a 21-year-old collegiate football player take his own life just two days after his team's 53-7 victory, a game in which both he and his younger brother scored touchdowns that led to the team's success?" (Sam Maniar, NACC, November 7, 2005).

Johns Hopkins University: RIP Austin Rottier
A recent suicide is Austin Rottier, March 29, 2006. According to The Johns Hopkins Newsletter, "Almost half of all college students become so depressed that they are unable to function" ("It's Time to Abandon Stigmas About Mental Illness," *The Johns Hopkins Newsletter,* November 16, 2006).

Cornell University: **"Gorging Out"**
A recent suicide is Ash Thotambilu, May 31, 2006. "Between 1996 and 2006, 21 students at Cornell committed suicide, averaging about two suicides per year, which is close to the national average (Gabriel Arana, "Silent on Suicide," *The Cornell Daily Sun,* April 2, 2008). 15 students identified themselves as being of Asian descent. "Since 1990, at least ten suicides have been attributed to the gorges in the Ithaca area. Stressed-out students sometimes joke about wanting to "gorge out" (Mental Hope News, December 2007). RIP Ash Thotambilu.

Cornell Update: In 2010, 6 Suicides in 6 Months.

Stanford University: RIP Mengyao Zhou and Maurice Morsette
Two recent suicides are Mengyao "May" Zhou (January 2007), and Maurice "Mo" Morsette (April 2007). "The sun is always shining and students are always smiling — this was the likely rationale for the Princeton Review's designation of Stanford as the university with the Happiest Students. Unfortunately, a recent string of student suicides — three between May and August — suggests that all may not be so well under the surface" (Shirin Sharif, "Student Suicides Increase" *Daily Stanford,* October 3, 2005).

"Sarah, a sophomore who also agreed to speak on the condition of anonymity, said she knows this feeling. She suffered from unclassified anxiety in high school, but was never depressed until coming to Stanford. In addition to struggling with feelings of inadequacy in the college environment, Sarah said much of her depression stemmed from what she perceived as everyone around her being happy while she was not. Stanford is characterized by 'a sunny demeanor and an infectious West Coast optimism, an alternative to the gloom that seems to hang over the Ivies.' Yet if recent figures from Stanford's Counseling and Psychological Services Center are any indication, depression is a real problem" (Anne Becker "Unmasking Depression at Stanford" *Daily Stanford,* May 20, 2002).

Brown University: RIP Anthony Abanto and Patrick Tweed

Two recent suicides are Anthony Abanto and Patrick Tweed (2005). "Brown students are supposedly among the happiest in the country, but almost one in five students visits Psychological Services each year. Moreover, that number has risen by 31 percent over the last decade, according to University officials. Though students see Psych Services for test anxiety and psychoses, the most common issue is depression - both short- and long-term. A national college health assessment by the American College Health Association in 2002 reported that 24 percent of all college students are in therapy for depression, and 35 percent of American college students take medication for depression." (Rachel Arndt, "Stressed Out? Visits to Psych Services on the Rise." *Brown Herald*, October 30, 2008).

Wesleyan University; RIP Terence Leary,

A recent suicide is Terence Leary, a 19-year-old sophomore, 2003. "Wesleyan University has settled a lawsuit for an undisclosed amount with a father who alleged that his son's suicide near the Connecticut campus was a result of institutional negligence ("Wesleyan U. Settles Lawsuit With Family of Student Who Committed Suicide" *The Hartford Courant,* May 22, 2009).

Texas A & M University

According to Dr. Maggie Olona, director of Student Counseling Services, "Three Texas A&M students have committed suicide since February 2004, a drastic increase in A&M's historically low suicide rate of one suicide every two years" ("A & M Steps Up Suicide Prevention Efforts," *The Batt,* September 27, 2004).

Michigan State University

Suicide clusters are quite common: "Within three months, six Michigan State University students had taken their own lives. Between January 16 and April 15, 1997, the six students, all of them males, committed suicide. Three of them shot themselves to death; two died by hanging; and the third threw himself in front of a train." ("Suicide on Campus," *Boundless Magazine,* 2000).

New York University: **"The Atrium of Horror"**
The twelve-story atrium of N.Y.U. Bobst Library is called "The Atrium of Horror." The university installed eight-foot-tall Plexiglass walls around the balconies of the library atrium to discourage potential jumpers. In one year, seven N.Y.U. students committed suicide (2003-2004).

"The N.Y.U. community has experienced ten student suicides since 2003. The method of choice for seven out of ten deceased students was death by jumping from buildings" (Green Roofs: Addressing N.Y.U. Student Suicide and Roof Top Security, N.Y.U., March 3, 2008).

"On Sept. 12, 2003 — the day after his 20th birthday — Jeff Skolnik of Evanston, Ill., committed suicide by jumping from the 10th floor of the university's Bobst Library" (Jeane MacIntosh and Andy Geller, "Another N.Y.U. Student Killed in Fall From Building," *New York Post*, March 10, 2004).

"On Oct. 10, 2003 Stephen Bohler, 18, of Irvine, Calif., leaped from the same library floor. His death was ruled accidental because he was under the influence of hallucinogenic drugs" (Ibid., MacIntosh and Geller).

"On Oct. 18, 2003 sophomore Michelle Gluckman jumped from the sixth floor of a Greenwich Village apartment building after smoking a joint and declaring, "I can't take it anymore" (Ibid., MacIntosh and Geller).

"On March 10, 2004, sophomore Diana Chien, 19, jumped from the roof of her boyfriend's 24-story apartment building after quarreling with him" (Ibid., MacIntosh and Geller).

On September 7, 2004, Joanne Michelle Leavy stripped naked and jumped to her death from the roof of a 12-story campus building. She was a second-year graduate student at the Tisch School of the Arts. Leavy was one of five film students honored with prizes in the spring of her senior year. Leavy's grandmother, Jane Campbell, said: "What a tragedy; What on earth could have made her do that?" ("More About the Girl who Jumped off the N.Y.U. Tisch building" *Santa Barbara Beacon*, September 7, 2004).

On September 24, 2007, Allan Oakley Hunter, III, musical genius and art prodigy, who scored a perfect 800 on the verbal portion of his SAT, went to the roof of the 15-story University Hall dorm on East 14th Street and jumped (Scott Martindale, " N.Y. U. Student Eulogized at Memorial Service, *Orange County Register,* September 28, 2007). -- "In a handwritten note addressed to his parents and younger siblings - including a baby sister who had been born just 10 hours earlier - Hunter cited tragic rocker Kurt Cobain's suicide note and offered a simple goodbye and apology. His sudden suicide has shattered his close circle of friends, who were left searching for answers as to why the young man they all called a "genius" would give up on such a promising life" (Larry Celona and Eric Lenkowitz, N.Y. U. Freshman Plunges Eight Floors, *New York Post,* September 24, 2007)."

In November 2007, Pranay Angara, committed suicide, "A New York University sophomore found dead in his Manhattan dorm room suffocated himself with a plastic bag, police said Monday. Pranay Angara's body was discovered Friday night in his Water St. room. It was the second suicide at the university since the start of the fall semester, cops said. Angara, 19, of Dutchess County, had written a farewell note to his family and then pushed a dresser in front of his bedroom door before taking his life, police sources said" (Alison Gendar and Michael White, "N.Y.U. Student Left Note Before Killing Himself" *Daily News,* November 12, 2007).

Update: On November 3, 2009, Andrew Williamson-Noble, 20, managed to leap over the barriers that were put in place to stop him from committing suicide at N.Y.U.'s "Atrium of Horror," and jumped from the 10th floor. He left a suicide note in his dorm. "I have no idea how this happened and why," his shocked mother, Esmeralda Williamson-Noble of Irvington, Westchester County, told the Daily News. "I wish he was here with us and we could hug him" (Daily News Staff Writers, Daily News, November 3, 2009).

"In a 2004 self-study report, N.Y.U. states that 74% of its freshman felt things were hopeless, 97% felt overwhelmed by all they had to do, 41% felt academics suffered as a result of stress, 95% felt exhausted (from other than physical activity), 90% felt very sad, 58% felt so depressed that it was difficult to function, and 16% seriously considered attempting suicide one or more times throughout the 2003-4 school year" ("Green Roofs: Addressing N. Y. U. Student Suicide and Roof Top Security," N.Y. U., March 3, 2008).

Union College
On April 29th, 2002, Jeremy April, eighteen years old, took his own life. "April learned on April 19 that he had been named to the U.S. Aerial Ski Team for the 2002-03 season. On July 4, when he was to turn nineteen, he would have been eligible to perform triple maneuvers" (*Union College Magazine*, 2002). April left a five-page handwritten note, in which he apologized to his parents and his girlfriend and said goodbye to his friends. He gave no explanation for his act, but wrote:

> "Being depressed for as long as I've been, it just gets to a point where even the most precious thing can't save you"

(Adam Lisberg, "Aerial Skier Kills Himself in College Dorm," *The Record*, May 2, 2002).

In mental health clinics on college campuses, students are replacing or supplementing their five cups of caffeine, recreational drugs, and college binge-drinking with psychotropic drugs, a dangerous crutch with serious side effects, to treat their anxiety stress, and depression, as this recent news bulletin stipulates:

"Medication therapy, once a peripheral aspect of college mental health, has moved front and center. Prescriptions rose 39% last year [2003] and have tripled since 1997-1998, most notably for antianxiety medications (up 72%) and antipsychotics (up 173%). UCS [University Counseling Services] medicated approximately 750 students, about one in five who came to the clinic. An increase in prescriptions may require more health professionals trained in psychiatric assessment and psychoparmacotherapy. Securing permanent funding for an additional psychiatric position is a high budgetary priority for UCS (annual report, 2002-2003)" ("Green Roofs: Addressing N.Y. U. Student Suicide and Roof Top Security," N.Y. U., March 3, 2008).

The College Suicide Equation

The first two questions that come to mind and need to be addressed are:

Q: How could this happen?

Q: How can it be prevented?

This book will make a bold attempt to connect the dots ... and explain the complex variables that comprise the college-suicide equation. There is a confluence of internal and external stressors: Family stress, identity stress, academic stress, relationship stress, and financial stress. Disappointments build up and so does the pain. The disappointments, pain, and rage are internalized and "bouts of depression," escalate into clinical depression, suicidal thinking (the ticking time-bomb), attempted suicide, and suicide.

The Truth Will Save the Lives of Millions of American Children

If the truth be told, the American education system needs more than change; the American education system needs a complete academic overhaul: Reenvision, Reinvent, and Rebuild.

Thanks to President Barack Hussein Obama and his inspirational political philosophy of "YES WE CAN!"-- Americans feel empowered to implement the critical changes required to improve their lives. And I agree with this spiritual manifesto of hope: "YES WE CAN!" overhaul the malfunctioning American education system.

SOS: America's Children of Privilege

As of now, you can feel and understand the magnitude of pain and suffering of America's children--and that immediate action must be taken to save the lives of America's privileged children. It is an oxymoron that children of privilege need the world's attention, but they do, because American children are **DYING** at the hands of clueless (no-indepth comprehension of the problem) American parents, educators, psychiatrists, and politicians.

- Save America's Brightest Minds: "I am not as smart as I thought I was"
- Save America's Children Who Live in Poverty
- Save America's Misdiagnosed A. D. H. D. Children
- Save America's High School Dropouts and Prison Inmates
- Save America's Students from Bogus Bomb Scare Threats
- Save America's Binge-Drinking College Students
- Save America's Depressed and Suicidal College Students
- Save America's College Student Drug Pushers from Overdosing

Q: "Why are we all anxious, stressed, depressed, suffering from the 'Pain of Inadequacy' and graduating bearing the 'Scars of Incompetence'?"

- Save America's Children from School Shootings and Massacres

Q: "Why do doctors put disconnected, depressed, and disgruntled students on psychotropic drugs, a crutch with dangerous side effects?

- Save America's Lateral Right-Brain Children Bearing Creative Gifts
Q: "Why was I misdiagnosed with A. D. H. D., an 'incurable brain disorder'?"

- Save America's Overweight Fast Food and Junk-Food Addicted Children from Early Onset of Illness
Q: "Why do I overeat when I eat processed food stripped of fiber?"

- Save America's Stop-Loss Soldiers Dying in the Prime of Life
Q: "Why is there an inexhaustible supply of martyrs dying in the name of Allah and 40 virgins awaiting them at pearly gates?"

SOS: Underprivileged Children in the Developing World

If the truth be told, millions of underprivileged children in the developing world wish that they could be misdiagnosed with A. D. H. D., instead of being diagnosed with A. I. D. S.

If the truth be told, millions of underprivileged children in the developing world wish that they had a malfunctioning American school to go to and suffer the "Pain of Inadequacy" and graduate bearing the "Scars of Incompetence," or drop out and find a job, or commit a crime and go to a warm and well-equipped prison.

If the truth be told, millions of underprivileged children in the developing world wish that they could be anxious, stressed, and depressed college students, on either caffeine, anti-anxiety aids, or anti-depressants, who learn how to cut corners and cheat to pass, survive, and graduate from schools, that ask for astronomical tuition payments, give them a diploma, but also cut corners and cheat them out of an education, and leave them in financial debt for the next twenty-five years bereft of any practical business skills to earn a living, or entrepreneurial skills to start their own businesses.

If the truth be told, millions of underprivileged children in the developing world wish that they could binge on junk food or fatty, fried, and greasy fast foods, and die from the early onset of illness, due to obesity, instead of dying from malnutrition.

If the truth be told, millions of underprivileged children in the developing world wish that they had a box of crayons with five hundred gorgeous colors to draw with, that would then be confiscated, when the linear left-brain educators, slashed the arts-education budget of their lateral right-brain students.

If the truth be told, hundreds of underprivileged children in the developing world, who have been kidnapped from their families, turned into child soldiers, and asked to murder on command with a machete, wish that they could be voluntarily recruited to fight for a cause worth dying for, such as, the American dream of democracy, free speech, civil rights, and unlimited personal potential, and drop million-dollar vacuous bombs on the "Evil Ones" hiding in caves with wireless internet connections who justify killing any infidel who trespasses on holy Islamic turf. In nasty nature, every beast behaves this way. In nasty nurture, religious affiliation compounds the problem of a nasty nature.

A critical question worthy of exploration is the following:
Q: Is America a Democracy or a "Democrisy"?

America is fighting for her soul. America is not a real "democracy." America is really a "democrisy," that is, she is a democracy laden with hypocrisy. The crash of ruthless capitalism is destroying America. President Barack Obama often says that America falls short of meeting her obligations to her fellow Americans. Most people of industrialized nations have the right to a fully government subsidized health care system (ranked 37th) and education system (ranked 18th) vital necessities of a humane civilization.

Education: American educators are clueless as to "How Does Learning Take Place? "Read, Cram, Regurgitate, and Test" is not an education. Most American students will earn a diploma, but not an education.

Healthcare: Forty-seven million Americans do not have adequate healthcare. Americans with healthcare have inadequate coverage. It can take five-twenty doctors to get a correct diagnosis. The first reason the American healthcare system malfunctions is because of the malfunctioning education system. There is no in-depth comprehension, long-term retention, or mastery of academic material. More people die from medical error than from disease (*The Cookbook Doctors,* Read the Fine Print Press).

Home: Many Americans have lost their homes, and for the first time in U.S. history, there are Americans who are living in outdoor tents, such as Sacramento's tent city in California.

Seven years after the fact, America is still justifying the depletion of her economic resources to fight two wars abroad, namely, in Iraq, Afghanistan (and Pakistan) with terrorist organizations who are guilty by association. In an attempt to apprehend a handful of "Evil Ones," who engineered the 9/11 attacks, most of the blood spilled, here and abroad, is of innocent men, women, and children. It appears to be the case that as long as Osama bin Laden is alive and well and a free man, America will have to be at war.

Another critical question that needs to be examined is:

Q: How many people, here and abroad, have to die in trying to find and capture, Osama bin Laden, and a handful of "Evil Ones"?

After 9/11, the American government created the Office of Homeland Security. Americans are told that we are safe. It was reported that violent Mexican drug cartels operate within America's borders, and threaten our national security. On October 23, 2009, 303 La Familia Michoacána drug cartel, were arrested in a raid in 19 states (NDIC, usdoj.gov/ndic).

Nevertheless, these uniquely American social problems have real solutions and these problems will be resolved when the American education system is overhauled to meet the challenges of the 21st century. If the truth be told, reeducation, here and abroad, is the only path to a peaceful world.

He Has the Right to Criticize Who Has the Heart to Help.
President Abraham Lincoln

There Is Nothing Wrong with America That Can't Be Fixed By What's Right with America.

President William Jefferson Clinton

8 Goalposts of Education

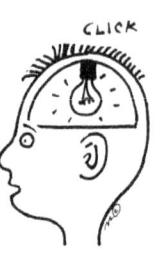

1. EDUCATION: KNOWLEDGE!
2. ENLIGHTENMENT: AHA!
3. EXCELLENCE: MASTERY!
4. EMPOWERMENT: YES I CAN!
5. EMANCIPATION: ALL CAN DO!
6. EGALITARIANISM: EQUAL RIGHTS!
7. EQUALITY: NEW WORLD ORDER!
8. ECONOMIC STABILITY: WORLD PEACE!

Teachers — not —Politicians Are
The True Peacemakers in the World

Education Is the Only Path to a Peaceful World

Sharon Rose Sugar
The Paladin of Education for the 21st Century

SMARTGRADES BRAIN POWER REVOLUTION
www.smartgrades.com

Shop: Classroom Posters

There Is Something for Everyone

In this book, there is something for everyone: Teachers, students, parents, psychiatrists, and even politicians.

Teacher Empowerment
After reading this book, teachers will be able to stand tall and be proud of the work that they do, because teachers--not politicians--are the real peacemakers in the world, and education is the only path to a peaceful world. Teachers will stand strong and united, and refuse to be picked on and bullied as the designated scapegoats for a malfunctioning American education system.

This book will inform and empower teachers and let teachers know that the power to change the "Fifteen Stumbling Blocks of Academic Failure" into the "Fifteen Stepping Stones of Academic Success" is in their hearts and in their hands and within five years, most American schools can become shining beacons of education, enlightenment, empowerment, excellence, and emancipation.

The Myth of Teacher Quality as the Predominant Factor
"There is growing consensus among researchers and educators that the single most important factor in determining a student's performance is the quality of his or her teacher" (Alliance for Excellent Education, all4ed.org, 2008).

If the Truth Be Told: Teacher Quality is Secondary Not Primary
You can't expect two parents to be trailing behind one child everywhere he or she goes and giving directions every step of the way; even more so, it is unreasonable to expect that one teacher can be responsible for the academic performance of five or forty classroom students.

Self-Reliant and Life-Long Learners: SMARTGRADES Processing Tools. The single most important factor in determining a student's academic performance is, SMARTGRADES Processing Tools, to process (absorb) the academic material for long-term retention. Good teaching practices, namely, instilling learning tools into students will result in students who are self-reliant and life-long learners. Good teachers are like coaches who stand on the sidelines of the basketball court and offer instruction, supervision, understanding, and insight. The goalpost of an excellent education is students who are self-reliant and life-long learners.

Student Empowerment
After reading this book, students will know that there is a new learning technology available, SMARTGRADES Processing Tools, to help them achieve academic success in school and secure their American dream. SMARTGRADES Processing Tools give students their power back, because it puts them back in the driver's seat, and gives them control of the steering wheel. As a result, students can drive safely on, "The Superhighway of Academic Success," and achieve their American dream.

New Learning Technology: **SMARTGRADES** Test Preparation Tools
Step 1. Estimation Tool
Step 2. Divide and Conquer Tool
Step 3. Active-Reading Tool
Step 4. Extraction Tool
Step 5. Condensation Tool
Step 6. Association Tool
Step 7. Test-Review Note Tool
Step 8. Conversion Tool
Step 9. Visualization Tool
Step 10. Self-Testing Tool

(**EVERY DAY AN EASY A**, SMARTGRADES, Appendix G).

EVERY DAY AN EASY A

3 Editions:
Elementary: ISBN: 978-1-885872-94-4
High School: ISBN: 978-1-885872-96-8
College: ISBN: 978-1-885872-98-2

3 Formats:
Hardcover, Paperback, and E-Book

Parent Empowerment
After reading this book, parents will become empowered with parenting skills and will be able to take constructive action to get their children back on track for academic success (Broken Wings, Blocked Blessings, SMARTGRADES BOOKS p.56).

Let's Recap: The human brain is the most powerful biological machine in the world and the only thing that is wrong with a student is that the brain does not come with an instruction manual and a student does not know how to use it. Children cannot raise themselves. If a child is failing, it is never the child's fault.

Parent Empowerment Books for Academic Success

Here are self-help books that every parent should have to keep them on their toes, and keep their bright and beautiful children on track for academic success and a lifetime filled with purpose, passion, prosperity, and peace.

The First Steps in Education Last a Lifetime
These Books Are Gifts That Keeps Giving: Elementary School, High School, College, and Graduate School

SMARTGRADES BRAIN POWER REVOLUTION
Global School Supply Company
www.smartgrades.com

1. SMARTGRADES BRAIN POWER SCHOOL NOtEBOOKS
   40+ Success Strategy Study Skills

2. **MY DAY! MY DREAM! MY DESTINY!**
   SMARTGRADES Planner with **SELFCARE** Journal

3. Your Study Room Is Under New Management
   1 Edition
   3 Formats: Hardcover, Paperback, and E-Book

4. EVERY DAY AN EASY A
   3 Editions: Elementary, High School, and College
   3 Formats: Hardcover, Paperback, and E-Book

5. TOTAL RECALL: ACE EVERY TEST EVERY TIME
   3 Editions: Elementary, High School, and College
   3 Formats: Hardcover, Paperback, and E-Book

6. How to Parent for Academic Success
   3 Formats: Hardcover, Paperback, and E-Book

7. Broken Wings Blocked Blessings
   3 Formats: Hardcover, Paperback, and E-Book

The Students with Broken Wings

Children who fall behind, flounder, fail, and fall through the cracks of the malfunctioning education system have become disconnected, depressed, distracted, disgruntled, and disobedient. These students need to rebuild their self-esteem and acquire learning tools; and not get beaten down further by the devastating misdiagnosis of A.D.H.D., the "incurable brain disorder."

More often than not, psychiatrists misdiagnose children with A.D.H.D., "the incurable brain disorder"--and put a child on the road to ... HELL.

The question that needs to be examined is:

> **Q: Do you want to put your child's brain, the most powerful biological machine in the world, into a virtual wheelchair for life?**

Spiritual Healers Not Prescription-Pushing Drug Dealers

After reading this book, parents will be able to find psychiatrists who are therapeutic spiritual healers and do not behave like pill-pushing, prescription-drug dealers.

a. Find a therapist who can heal the wounded spirit of the child.

b. Find a therapist who can build the internal resources of the child: Self-Love, Self-Esteem, and Self-Reliance.

c. Find a therapist who can help integrate the mind, body, and spirit of the child.

d. Find a therapist who can help a child grow, develop, and mature taking into account innate and environmental differences (www.privatetutor.com).

Psychiatrist Empowerment
One of the reasons for writing this book was to inform and empower psychiatrists to heal disconnected, depressed, distracted, disgruntled, and disobedient students instead of misdiagnosing them with A.D.H.D., the "incurable brain disorder."

The symptoms of A.D.H.D., namely, inattention (can't focus), impulsivity (acts out), and hyperactivity (can't sit still), resemble the symptoms that floundering and failing students exhibit, namely, disconnection (can't focus), the "Pain of Inadequacy"(acts out), and escapism (can't sit still):

Q: Are you inattentive (can't focus)?   Bad Grades Hurt
"Pain of Inadequacy"
Depressed, Disconnected

Q: Are you impulsive (acts out)?   Raging and Acting Out
Disgruntled

Q: Are you hyperactive (can't sit still)?   Distraction and Escapism

In most cases, floundering and failing students are blamed and mislabeled as disobedient children. In some cases, failing students are misdiagnosed with A.D.H.D., and their developing brains are put into virtual wheelchairs for life.

Finally, parents, teachers, and psychiatrists must adhere to the following dictum of, "The Second Universal Gold Standard of Education" that will be discussed in part three of this book.

To reiterate ad nauseam, if necessary:

The Second Universal Gold Standard of Education

Children Cannot Raise Themselves
If a Child is Failing, It Is Never the Child's Fault!

Political Empowerment: "The Race to the Top Fund"
Secretary of Education, Arne Duncan, has a 100-billion dollar education budget. He thinks that he is going to be able to use this money properly to reform the malfunctioning American education system.

The first question that must be addressed is:
Q: When will America's Children Become America's First Priority?

The second question that must be addressed is:
Q: How Do You Nurture and Cultivate the Awesome Power of the Human Brain?

The third question that must be addressed is:
Q: How Does Learning Take Place?

Quite frankly, with all due respect, American politicians are clueless as to the gravity of the education problem. Let's Recap: American children are dying at the hands of clueless parents, educators, psychiatrists, and politicians. Get a clue: "The Fifteen Stumbling Blocks of Academic Failure." I am ever hopeful, "President Obama's Audacity of Hope," that after reading this book, politicians will understand that education reform is insufficient, and that a complete academic overhaul is required to meet the social, economic, scientific, and technological challenges of the 21st century.

Unless Someone Like You Cares a Whole Awful Lot,
Nothing Is Going to Get Better. It's Not.
Dr. Seuss

This Study Room Is Under New Management

www.privatetutor.com

Every Student Is a Success Story

SCHMALTZY
THE STUDY BUDDY
www.schmaltzy.com

STUDY TIP:
ALWAYS
LOOK
BEFORE
YOU
LEAP!

NEW: Check Out His Children's Book
with Color-Coded Vocabulary Words

Acknowledgments

First and foremost, I want to extend my deepest appreciation and gratitude to the students who let me post my sign, **"THIS STUDY ROOM IS UNDER NEW MANAGEMENT"** to their bedroom doors.

In a matter of days, they let me reorganize their desks, chairs, computers, bookcases, and book bags.

In a matter of weeks, they let me change their eating habits, sleeping habits, reading habits, writing habits, and testing habits. They let me organize their time to make every day count, and to imbue every hour with purpose, meaning, and value.

In a matter of months, they let me into their hearts and allowed me to heal their "Pain of Inadequacy," mend their "Scars of Incompetence," and rebuild their self-esteem with the new therapy modality, Intrapersonal-Integration Therapy.

They let me into their minds, and I repaired their broken wings with the new learning technology, SMARTGRADES SUCCESS STRATEGY STUDY SKILLS.

In return for all of these monumental renovations of space, mind, and spirit, my students are now able to earn A grades on their homework assignments, research reports, and tests.

Most importantly, they let me rip the deleterious label of A.D.H.D., the "incurable brain disorder," off their foreheads, and take their powerful brains out of the virtual wheelchairs and set them free.

I wish to thank the school administration, namely, the principal, guidance counselors, and teachers for adding this service to their list of educational resources and making it available to parents (www.everydayaneasya.com). As promised, the new learning technology, SMARTGRADES SUCCESS STRATEGY STUDY SKILLS, transforms borderline students into excellent students on the very next test: "Every Student Is a Success Story."

I wish to thank my dear friend and advisor, Karl Bardosh, for supporting my artistic and intellectual endeavors in film, poetry, philosophy, and education. His patience is inexhaustible. His advice is invaluable. His kindness is immeasurable.

I wish to thank my dear friend and advisor, Laurin Raiken, for reading my book in its infancy and making valuable suggestions. He steadfastly has supported my eclectic scholarly works across multiple disciplines: Poetry, philosophy, literature, and education.

I wish to thank my dear friends and devoted editors, Richard Simon, Philip Winters, Irving Ruderman, and Ziv Hellman for their constructive criticisms and invaluable suggestions. Ziv nicknamed me "PHOTON," A.K.A. "SUPERHERO OF EDUCATION."

I wish to thank my best friend, the creative genius, Sharon Esther Lampert, for the world-famous poem, "EDUCATE NOT." She also authored the following gifts of immortal creative genius that help students spiritually grow, develop, and mature. The immortal spiritual gems found within this book are as follows:

- Self-Esteem Affirmation
- Empowerment Affirmation
- Special Gifts Affirmation
- Circle of Responsibility Affirmation
- Five Superpowers for Making Dreams Come True

- Seven Superpowers of Stress-Relief
- 22 Spiritual Illuminations
- World Peace Equation
- Superhero Pledge
- Poem: TRUE LOVE
- Poem: BE BORN
- Poem: FINITE
- Poem: The Restless Sunrise
- Poem: Sandstorm in Baghdad
- Poem: Tsunami
- Poem: Spiraling Downward, Upward We Stand United
- Poem: The Prescription Drug-Pushers
- Poem: The Militant Palestinian Toddler Terrorist

Bonus Materials:
Sharon Esther Lampert has written many of the world's greatest poems. Her poems are used by English teachers in colleges, high schools, and elementary schools throughout the world. Students the world over send Sharon letters written on school stationery, and choose to write about her for their school projects. Her website, www.worldfamouspoems.com, is the **#1 Poetry Website for School Projects**. The poet's personal website is www.SharonEstherLampert.com. In addition, her poetry is published in numerous publications and websites around the world. Sharon Esther Lampert is also a prodigy-prophet-philosopher-poet. Her critical contributions are:

- Unleash The Creator, The God Within: 10 Esoteric Laws of Genius and Creativity
- Who Knew God Was Such a Chatterbox!
- God of What? 11 Esoteric Laws of Inextricability
- The 22 Commandments: All You Will Ever Need to Know About God"

Last but not least, I want to thank my PURRfect kids: Schmaltzy, the "World Famous Piano Virtuoso," and Falafel, the "World Class Soccer Phenomenon." From the start of this book through the final chapter, my cats changed their napping grounds from the luminous windowsill to my desk to keep me company. They have learned how to wrap their bodies around my MAC and not interfere with the computer keyboard. On occasion, when in need of my undivided attention, Schmaltzy, will pounce on the keyboard and type in his opinion.

Animal Fair Magazine featured, Schmaltzy, as a "Feline Prodigy." The New York Post Newspaper picked Schmaltzy for one of "The Most Eligible Pets of 2008" and called him a "Celebrity in His Own Right." This means that, Schmaltzy, doesn't need a Hollywood celebrity to have his adorable face plastered in the newspaper. He is usually the stand-alone star cat in a group of top dogs.

Schmaltzy is also the "American Ambassador Cat" to the Cat Welfare Society in Israel. He uses his celebrity clout to help abandoned cats find loving homes. He was once in a similar predicament. He was once an abandoned kitten in need of a loving home. He was adopted from the, North Shore Animal League, in Port Washington, New York.

If you don't have a furry best friend who makes sure that you are up at the crack of dawn, greets you at the door when you return home after work, is by your side through thick and thin, and loves you unconditionally, then it is time to adopt a "Furry Best Friend" at the North Shore Animal League (516-883-7575). **Tell them that SCHMALTZY sent you.**

Schmaltzy is also a devoted study buddy to my students and curls himself around their schoolbooks while they study for exams. Schmaltzy's study tip is: **"Always Look Before You Leap!"** The story of his extraordinary life can be found in a book entitled, "In America, Even a Cat Can Have a Dream" (Appendix G). To see Schmaltzy play piano, or Falafel play a game of world-class soccer, please visit their website: www.schmaltzy.com.

In America, Even a Cat Can Have a Dream
SCHMALTZY

The World Famous Piano Playing Virtuoso
www.schmaltzy.com

My 6 a.m. Alarm Clock
CEO and Office Manager
American Ambassador Cat to Israel
Best-Dressed Cat in Town
Falafel's Dapper Boyfriend
Study Buddy for Students
World Famous Piano Virtuoso
"Celebrity in His Own Right"
My Best Friend

Schmaltzy was Adopted from
The North Shore Animal League
25 Davis Avenue. Port Washington, N.Y. 11050
Adopt a Furry Best Friend: 516-883-7575
Tell Them SCHMALTZY Sent You

Notes to the Reader

SMARTGRADES SUCCESS STRATEGY STUDY SKILLS
My first noteworthy achievement was to pioneer the new learning technology, **SMARTGRADES PROCESSING TOOLS**, that transform students into self-reliant and life-long learners. Every student earns an A grade on the next test.

Integration Therapy:
13 Steps to True and Everlasting Happiness
My second noteworthy achievement was to pioneer the new therapy modality, Intrapersonal-Integration Therapy, that rebuilds the self-esteem of students who have become anxious, stressed, disconnected, depressed, distracted, and disobedient. Some students rage and act out. Some students have suicidal thoughts. Some students have become blocked. Some students shutdown.

The Silent Crisis Destroying America's Brightest Minds
My third noteworthy achievement was accepting the challenge of helping elementary, high school, and college students from elite private and public schools. Some of the brightest students in America are dropping out of school. They don't really drop out of school; they fall behind, flounder, fail, and change schools. These gifted and talented students are back on track for a bright academic future.

The Rising A.D.H.D. Epidemic in America
My fourth noteworthy achievement was helping students who are misdiagnosed with A.D.H.D., the "incurable brain disorder." Every phone call is an emergency: "The psychiatrist wants to diagnose my child with A.D.H.D., 'the incurable brain disorder' and put my child on Ritalin." Their growing, developing, and maturing brains,

the most powerful biological machines in the world, had been placed into virtual wheelchairs by clueless psychiatrists (who have a clue). Their brains have been taken out of virtual wheelchairs and set free.

Your Study Room Is Under Management
My fifth noteworthy achievement was transforming F students into A students. These students have put their unruly past behind them. As of now, these students are among the top students in the class and compete with the class nerd for the best grades.

Parenting Skills for Academic Success
My sixth noteworthy achievement was empowering parents with the parenting skills for academic success. Every child grows, develops, and matures at a different rate and these innate and environmental differences have to be taken into account by parents, teachers, and psychiatrists.

America's Brightest Minds: America's Buried Treasures
Every student is like a buried treasure who is unearthed to find the precious jewels within: Garnet, Amethyst, Aquamarine, Diamond, Emerald, Alexandrite, Ruby, Peridot, Sapphire, Tourmaline, Imperial Topaz, and Turquoise.

EVERY STUDENT IS A SUCCESS STORY!

Sharon Rose Sugar
The Paladin of Education for the 21st Century

P.S. Please send your compliments and criticisms. Thank you.
 E-Mail: educate@smartgrades.com

VESSEL
very. extra. special. sharon. esther. lampert.

Food Is for the Body
Education Is for the Mind
Poetry Is for the Soul

Sharon Esther Lampert

EDUCATE NOT

No Time to Teach:
In Class, They Give a General Overview.
On Tests, They Want Particular Details.

No Time to Learn:
All By Myself, I Got to Teach Myself a Gazillion Facts:
I Got No Study Skills, I Got No Tutor,
The First Day of School, I Gotta Be Behind.

Students Got a Cheat-Sheet:
I Use Citations From Books
I Got No Time to Read.

Teachers Got a Cheat Sheet:
They Got No Time to Read IT.
They Weigh IT:
Looks Beautiful
They Grade IT A.
Looks Pretty
They Grade IT B.
Looks OK
They Grade IT C.
Looks Ugly
They Grade IT D.
Looks Can Kill
They Grade IT F.

Quantity Over Quality:
Education System is Dumb
And is Gonna Get Dumber,
Wastes My Good Dime,
My Good Mind,
And My Good Time.
I Survive, I Don't Thrive.

Facts Move From Textbook
To Blackboard to Notebook.
Gotta Get the Facts INSIDE OF ME:
No Time to Think,
No Time to Write an Outline,
No Time for Research,
No Time to Write a Rough Draft,
No Time to Reread, Revise, and Rewrite,
No Time to Write a Final Draft,
No TIme to Write My Masterpiece.
When I Get IT Back, My Work-In-Progress,
I Trash IT. I Got No Time for Junk.

Teachers Got No Time to Teach.
I Got No Time to Learn.
No Time to Educate.
EDUCATE NOT.

By Sharon Esther Lampert
Poet, Philosopher, Paladin of Education
Book: **IMMORTALITY IS MINE**

The Greatest Poems Ever Written on Extraordinary World Events
www.worldfamouspoems.com

EVERY DAY AN EASY A

SMARTGRADES
SUCCESS STRATEGY STUDY SKILLS

10 Step Processing Tools to
Ace Every Test Every Time
- In-Depth Comprehension
- Long-Term Retention
- Mastery of the Material

Note to the Reader

These stories are case studies written
from the point of view of a woman scientist.

All of the stories are true.

All of the names are changed.

Every student earned an A grade on the next test
thanks to the new learning technology,
SMARTGRADES SUCCESS STRATEGY STUDY SKILLS

SMART POWER IS BACK IN THE HANDS OF STUDENTS

EVERY STUDENT IS A SUCCESS STORY

Note to Future Editors:
Dr. Phil McGraw always asks his patients to read his
books ten times to absorb the self-help information.
This book has built-in repetition, so one reading will suffice.
After my death, please do not alter this book because the
repetition, ad nauseam, is required for processing for
in-depth-comprehension, long-term retention, and
mastery of the material.

"I Am Not As Smart As I Thought I Was!"

Where did we ever get the crazy idea that in order to make children do better, first we have to make them feel worse? Think of the last time you felt humiliated or treated unfairly. Did you feel like cooperating or doing better?

Jane Nelsen

Note for the Reader

Clueless = No Understanding of the Problem or of the Solution to the Problem

Sweet Darling Isabel

Her name is Isabel. She is black. She is ten years old. She is very pretty. She is shy. She has a crush on a boy named Frank. She is a child with a broken wing. She can't read.

Isabel thinks that she is stupid. The teacher tells her parents to have her tested for learning disabilities. The psychiatrist tells her that she has A.D.H.D., the "incurable brain disorder," and wants to prescribe Ritalin.

Isabel has probably failed a test or two. Failure is painful. She has become disconnected. She has become depressed. She has become distracted. She has become blocked. She has shutdown.

I have yet to meet Isabel, but I know that there is nothing seriously wrong* with her. Why? Because the human brain is the most powerful biological machine in the world, and what is wrong is that her brain did not come with an instruction manual and she does not know how to use it.

*"seriously wrong" as in an "incurable brain disorder"

Isabel does not have "time to learn" or learning tools to "learn and process" voluminous academic material to achieve academic success:
- She does not know how to get organized
- She does not know how to write "Test Review Notes"
- She does not know how to write an English essay
- She does not know how to memorize voluminous facts
- She does not have test preparation skills

It is important at the start to inform parents that they are in good hands. I know that I can make the critical difference and transform a student with a pair of broken wings into an excellent student. I am the only expert in the country (perhaps the world) who can transform an F student into an A student, and put a student back on the grade-A track on the very next test.

I inform the parents that I pioneered the development of the new learning technology, SMARTGRADES Processing Tools and promise them that, "Isabel will earn an A grade on the very next test."

I continue, "There is nothing seriously wrong with your child," I inform the heart-broken and deeply worried parent who called my office asking for emergency help for a child who is in the fifth grade and unable to read English.

As soon as Isabel masters the SMARTGRADES Processing Tools, the new learning technology for academic achievement, she will no longer be a senseless casualty of the malfunctioning "Quantity Over Quality Curriculum-Driven American Education System." She will prevail. She will succeed.

"You have two choices: You can learn to live with the problem or you can solve the problem. What do you want to do?" The parent makes an appointment and keeps the appointment.

"Do you want to be an A student?"

I ask the child when she appears at my door with a ready smile, open arms, and in need of a miracle.

"Yes," she says without hesitation. All students want to do well, they just don't know how. She is a lovely little girl, very sweet, and she listens carefully to everything I say to her.

I ask her to put her hands on her head and tell me what she feels. She replies, "nothing." I then tell Isabel, "That "nothing" that you feel is your brain and your brain is the greatest biological machine in the world. The only thing you are missing is the instruction manual."

I am delighted to tell Isabel the good news: "You are a smart, sweet, and beautiful girl, and don't ever let anybody ever tell you that you are the problem." And I repeat myself: "Your brain is the greatest biological machine in the world, and I am going to teach you how to use it."

I start by asking her three basic questions:

Q1: What do you eat for breakfast?

Q2: What time do you go to sleep?

Q3: Do you have a study room?

As is usually the case, the student doesn't eat breakfast, doesn't have a regular bedtime, and doesn't have her own study room. I have my work cut out for me because I have to get both the parents and the child back on track. The well-intentioned teacher will be delighted to see Isabel return to school as an A-grade student. However, the clueless psychiatrist (who has a clue), who put Isabel on the road to HELL... A. D. H. D., the "incurable brain disorder" is beyond redemption, and for this reason. Inadequate/abusive parenting and a malfunctioning education system has generated a "feeding frenzy" of disconnected, depressed, and distracted students who will be misdiagnosed with A. D. H. D. As far as I am concerned, we are still living in the dark ages of an antiquated school system and a pill-pushing toxic psychiatric system, who add insult to injury. To reiterate, ad nauseam: Parents, educators, and psychiatrists have not yet learned the most basic principle of child rearing:

The Second Universal Gold Standard of Education

Children Cannot Raise Themselves
If a Child Is Failing, It Is Never the Child's Fault

My job is to focus all of my attention on sweet darling Isabel, and rescue this sweet and adorable child from four very scary monsters:

Scary Monster 1. Parents with Inadequate/Abusive Parenting Tools

Scary Monster 2. Clueless Educators "How Does Learning Take Place?"

Scary Monster 3. Psychiatrists Who Add Insult to Injury (Vacuous Pills)

Scary Monster 4. Politicians and their "Education Race to the Bottom"

Back to Sweet Darling Isabel

What did you eat this morning?, I ask. "Nothing," she replies. It takes energy to learn. Energy comes from good nutrition and from sufficient sleep. I hand out a healthy study snack. You can't learn on an empty stomach. I show Isabel my electrical appliances. These machines will not turn on without electricity, I explain. The machines feed on electricity. Your brain will not turn on without food. First you feed your body with food and then you feed your mind with facts. Think of yourself as a car with a gas tank that has to be filled up to be able to take you places. First, you fill your tank and then you drive. First, you eat a nutritious meal and then you go to school to learn. If you don't eat properly, your brain will not have the "full tank of fuel" to be able to read, think, question, write, research, memorize, and test.

Education is food for the brain, I continue. Students spend the entire day eating facts and building their brain. School is a gym to build your brain muscles. If I give you a sandwich to eat, you cannot stuff the entire sandwich into your mouth. You have to take small bites and chew, chew, chew, and digest. Eating facts is like eating a sandwich. You have to take small amounts of information and chew (in-depth comprehension), chew (long-term retention), chew (mastery of academic material), and digest.

I cut a slice of my homemade oatmeal pie, add a dollop of yogurt, a few chopped walnuts, red apple slices and feed mother and child. The pie is completely fat free and full of fiber and energy. There is no sugar or salt. I do sprinkle cinnamon, flax seeds, chia seeds, and almonds, pecans, or walnuts on top of the oatmeal pie before I place it in the refrigerator to gel. I give them the recipe for my signature energy meal, the oatmeal pie (**SMARTGRADES: BRAIN POWER REVOLUTION**, p. 56).

I ask Isabel to read a simple sentence. She reads slowly and stumbles. I break the words down into syllables and cheer her on as if I am watching the final soccer game at The World Cup. I am enthusiastic and my energy propels her forward and onward, and lo and behold, she is reading without my intervention.

Good Grades Deserve Great Rewards
I reward Isabel with a delicious and nutritious study snack. I tell her, "I am very proud of you. You are reading and we are back on track" (*Yummy in My Tummy: Good Grades Deserve Great Rewards and Great Desserts*, Appendix G).

Q: What did I do to make a difference?
To rebuild her confidence, I praised her. I encouraged her. I broke the sentence into smaller "bites" of information that are simple and easy to digest. She is now unblocked. She likes me. She trusts me. We can now move forward and begin reading sentences and paragraphs.

Q: How does this happen to a child?
It happens because she made mistakes and instead of receiving help, namely, the learning tools to correct her errors, she was criticized. Her parents, teacher, and psychiatrist call her all sorts of names: Lazy, unmotivated, and A.D.H.D. All are found guilty of name calling. The child also engages in name calling as she will internalize the harmful labels, agree with the adults, and tell herself, "I am stupid." Every student will make mistakes. The learning curve is steep. Learning takes time. Learning takes practice. Learning takes trial and error. Learning requires infinite patience. Learning requires a support system of encouragement from parents, as well as from the teacher and psychiatrist.

Introduction: Sweet Darling Isabel

As is usually the case, I have my work cut out for me because Isabel needs a complete academic overhaul. Here is the game plan; the five academic interventions that transform Isabel into an A-grade student:

YOUR STUDY ROOM IS UNDER NEW MANAGEMENT
Grade A Students are MADE not Born
Website: www.everydayaneasya.com

Step 1. New School Notebooks
SMARTGRADES School Notebooks contain the new learning technology, SMARTGRADES Processing Tools.

Step 2. New Learning Tools for Self-Reliant and Life-Long Learners
SMARTGRADES Processing Tools: New Learning Technology
Every Student Earns an A Grade on the Very Next Test
(*EVERY DAY AN EASY A*, p. 59)

Step 3. Rebuild Self-Esteem and Repair Broken Wings
Integration Therapy for Intrapersonal Growth, Development, and Maturity (*Integration Therapy*, p.56)

Step 4. Parent Empowerment
Parenting Skills and Strategies for Academic Success (*Your Study Room Is Under New Management*, p. 56)

Step 5. Eat for the Energy to Learn
It takes tremendous energy to read, write, and test. Students need fiber-rich meals with fresh fruits and vegetables for ENERGY!

All Students Want to Do Well, They Just Don't Know How

There Is No Such Thing As Too Much Love

Learning requires love. You have to put love into it. Your heart and your mind have to be working together. I always ask my students:

"Did you put some love into it?"

You don't find love, you create love. Love has to be created. Like my oatmeal pie, you have to make an oatmeal pie for an oatmeal pie to come into existence. On a daily basis, you have to bring love into the world.

I hand out two oversized cue cards to the mother and child. One cue card says," I Love You and You Are the Greatest Mom in the Whole World." The other cue card says," I Love You and I Am Very Proud of You." And we end with the sports cliché, "and now say TEAM." The parent and child practice this two-way communication until they have it memorized and until it becomes a regular daily habit. When they visit, I enforce this routine, and start and end every session with it. On occasion, there is even some physical affection of mushy kisses and bear hugs shared by parent and child.

Parent
"I Love You and I Am Very Proud of You"

Student
"I Love You and You Are the Greatest Mom/Dad in the World"

Introduction: Sweet Darling Isabel

"I Hate You"

I have experienced a child rewriting my cue card and blurting out "I Hate You." On one hand, the rage was a sign that the child felt safe and secure and could release the pent-up pain, frustration, and rage in my presence. On the other hand, this particular child was experiencing the painful stress of a divorce in addition to academic distress.

Many times there is a confluence of stressors that contribute to a child's downfall, namely:
- Divorce
- Parent with a chronic illness
- Sibling rivalry
- Parent with inadequate/abusive parenting tools
- A home that is a war zone

There are children who live on a daily basis with multiple problems and experience all of the aforementioned stressors.

Messy School Notebooks

I take a look at Isabel's school notebooks. They are disorganized. Every teacher gives out three types of loose papers: Homework, handouts, and tests. If you have five classes, then you have three papers per class and that adds up to fifteen loose papers that have to be hole-punched and filed per week.

File, File, File

On a daily basis, students have to spend time filing. Some students spend one hour a week punching holes into their loose papers and filing them into a 3-hole loose-leaf binder. Most students just stuff them into a folder and sort them out the day before a test and then ask themselves, "Where are my science handouts?"

All Students Want to Do Well, They Just Don't Know How

SMARTGRADES Fuss-Free Instant-Organization School Notebooks

I give Isabel a set of five notebooks that I designed that will put an end to her disorganization. The notebooks are color-coded with white labels that specify her subjects:

Math: Red Notebook

History: Blue Notebook

Science: Green Notebook

English: Black Notebook

Language: Orange Notebook

My special school notebooks have four built-in pockets. In less than ten seconds, a student is able to file a loose paper (test, homework, handout) into an SMARTGRADES fuss-free instant-organization school notebook.

Pocket 1. Today's Handouts

The Loose-Leaf Paper

Pocket 2. Homework

Pocket 3. Tests

Pocket 4. Old Handouts

The School Book Bag
I peek inside her book bag. I hesitate. You never know what can be brewing inside a child's book bag. There can be the remains of gooey, sticky, and chewy snacks. I move slowly. And sure enough, there is an empty bag of chips with some crumbs that will really make a mess if and when it capsizes inside a child's book bag. I remove it carefully, evading an avalanche of potato chips and of having to clean out her book bag with soap and water.

The Pencil Case
"Do you have a pencil case?," I ask. It is a minor but critical item. Do you know how many children go to school with only one pen and one pencil? The pencil breaks and the pen's ink runs out. Then these children are stranded and can't write until they interrupt the class and borrow a pen or pencil from a student or teacher. Five pens and five pencils may sound excessive, but I think this is the right number because one pen is left behind on the desk, one pen is lent to a friend, one pen runs out of ink, and now we only have two pens left. Five pens is the right number when you are planning for a worst-case scenario.

The Academic Homework Planner
Isabel learns how to use a homework planner to record and keep track of her homework assignments, research reports, and tests.

The School Textbooks
I take a look at her textbooks. If they are too dense and difficult to read, I will find easier supplementary textbooks.

SMARTGRADES SUCCESS STRATEDY STUDY SKILLS

Isabel learns how to retrieve the facts from her textbook, and return the facts to the teacher on a test. She learns how to "learn and process" academic material for instant recognition and recall to ace her tests:

1. SMARTGRADES Estimation Tools
Isabel learns how to break down the reading assignment into smaller tasks.

2. SMARTGRADES Active-Reading Tools
Isabel learns how to read for main ideas and supporting details.

3. SMARTGRADES Critical Thinking Tools
Isabel learns how to read, think, and question. She learns how to synthesize, analyze, and evaluate what she is reading for meaning, understanding, and value. She learns how to read for the facts, belief systems, and personal opinions of the author.

4. SMARTGRADES Extraction Tools
Isabel learns how to read a sentence and extract the key facts: Who, what, where, when, and why.

5. SMARTGRADES Condensation Tools
Isabel learns how to condense the facts, as if folding them into a suitcase to transport the facts to a test.

6. SMARTGRADES Association Tools
Isabel learns how to link the unknown information to the known information in her brain for instant recognition and instant recall. She has to become a "human toaster" and pop the facts out in mere seconds to ace her tests.

7. SMARTGRADES Test-Review Tools
Isabel learns how to write a, Test-Review Note, of the main ideas, supporting details, and association cues.

8. SMARTGRADES Conversion Tools
Isabel learns how to convert her reading material into test questions.

9. SMARTGRADES Visualization Tools
Isabel learns how to visualize the facts as test questions.

10. SMARTGRADES Self-Test Tools
Isabel learns to self-test checking for her strengths and weaknesses (**EVERY DAY AN EASY A**, Appendix G).

Intrapersonal - Integration Therapy Modality
I pioneered a new therapy modality to develop the inner voice of students — and to help them help themselves.

Developing Isabel's Internal Voice
I ask Isabel to raise both hands in the air. Your right hand is your strength. Your left hand is your weakness. I want your hands to have a conversation about your book bag. I want your strengths to help your weaknesses so that you will no longer forget to bring your book bag home or forget to write down your homework assignments in your new academic planner.

Strengths Over Weaknesses
Paradoxically, her strengths are being overpowered by her weaknesses, and we want to reverse this situation. We want her strengths (fight) to lead the way and her weaknesses (flight) to be under her control.

Spiritual Education: Let the Healing Begin and Make It Last Forever

Integration Therapy is a powerful new therapy modality that builds the child's internal voice, and as a result, Isabel can exercise control over her own behavior. Isabel can police herself. Isabel can teach herself. Isabel begins to hear her own voice and begins the negotiation of flight or fight. Intrapersonal-Integration Therapy is composed of thirteen steps:

1. Self-Talk
2. Self-Love
3. Self-Reliance
4. Self-Esteem
5. Self-Respect
6. Self-Awareness
7. Self-Regulation
8. Self-Reflection
9. Self-Education
10. Self-Parenting
11. Self-Renewal
12. Self-Actualization
13. Self-Definition

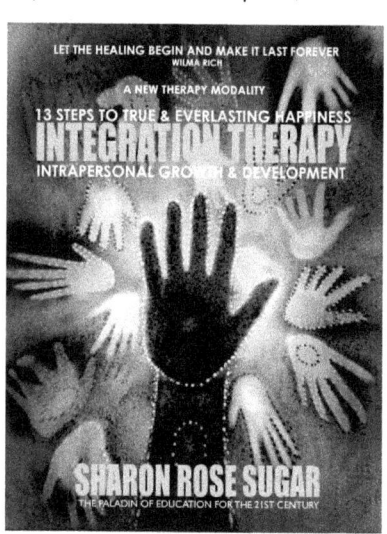

Thirteen Steps to
True and Everlasting Happiness

INTEGRATION THERAPY
Intrapersonal Growth, Development, and Maturity

www.smartgrades.com

(Intrapersonal *Integration Therapy: 13 Steps to Self-Actualization: Let the Healing Begin and Make It Last Forever*, Smartgrades Brain Power Revolution).

Children Cannot Raise Themselves

Self-Talk: Self-Esteem Affirmation

I will teach Isabel "Self-Talk," and rebuild her self-esteem that was damaged by the following three factors:

1. The emotional pain from failing her test.

2. The emotional pain of being blamed for her failure and the pain of abusive name calling: lazy, unmotivated, and A.D.H.D.

3. The internalization of the misdiagnosis of A.D.H.D., into her unconscious, "I can't do this and I can't do that because I have A.D.H.D., an incurable brain disorder"

I want Isabel to have one daily conversation with herself. She will learn to look in the mirror, talk to herself, and recite Photon's Self-Esteem Affirmation*:

"I love you Isabel.
I will do everything in my power to help
you achieve your dream.
My dream is to become a ....
Everything else that I say to myself is just NOISE."

Self-Talk: Self-Reliance Affirmation
Isabel learns Photon's Circle of Responsibility Affirmation*:

"My Problems Have Solutions...
when I take responsibility for my problems have solutions
when I take responsibility for my problems have solutions
when I take responsibility for my problems have solutions
...When I Take Responsibility For My Problems..."

*Photon Is the SuperHero of Education on Planet Earth
Her website is BooksNotBombs.com

All Students Want to Do Well, They Just Don't Know How

Parenting: Bonding Issues

Every parent has a bonding issue. When a child is born, the parent has to do 100%. As a child grows and develops, the parent has to do less and the child has to do more. A good parent is one that is doing 20% while the child is doing 80%. This transition from 100% to 20% is an ongoing process from birth to maturity. A self-reliant child is the goalpost. Self-talk build's self-reliance: Photon's, Self-Responsibility Affirmation, empowers children to take responsibility for healthy eating habits, regular bedtimes, homework assignments, research reports, and test preparation.

Parenting: Control Issues: "I'll Think About It"

Every parent has a control issue with a child. Before I start telling a child what to do and what not to do, I tell the child the following: "You don't have to say yes, and you don't have to say no. Just say 'I'll think about it.' And then, I give the child time to think about it. It is important to give students time to think about it and listen to what they have to say. They need to learn how to evaluate the strengths and weaknesses or the advantages and disadvantages of every decision that they make. They have to learn how to take a stand, make a decision, and take responsibility for the decision.

Sweet Darling Isabel is Back on the A-Grade Track

For a year, the family commuted back and forth to my office from Long Island every Saturday, and the trip took four hours because of heavy weekend traffic, but it was well worth the effort. Isabel made a 360-degree turn-around from a child whose brain was placed into a virtual wheelchair for life because of the misdiagnosis of A.H.D.D., the "incurable brain disorder," to an empowered child who has learning tools and is able to earn A grades on tests. Her mother blessed me for doing God's work. This lovely young lady rebuilt her self-esteem, mastered the SMARTGRADES Processing Tools, and became an excellent student.

Children Cannot Raise Themselves

Introduction: Sweet Darling Isabel

To this day, Isabel's straight-A-grade spelling tests decorate my bulletin board.

Let's Recap: What Really Happened to Sweet Darling Isabel? (Let's play my favorite game of "connect the dots")

1. Brain Power: The human brain is the most powerful biological machine in the world. It does not come with an instruction manual and Isabel does not know how to use it.

2. The Second Universal Gold Standard of Education: Children cannot raise themselves. If a child is failing, it is never the child's fault.

3. Educators are clueless as to "How Does Learning Take Place?" They do not know how to nurture and cultivate the awesome power of the human brain.

4. Isabel is enrolled in a malfunctioning "Quantity Over Quality Curriculum-Driven American Education System."

5. Teaching and learning are sacrificed to push the curriculum forward at a frenetic pace to meet the goals of the "Higher Standards."

6. Parents are asked to fill in the gaps (gigantic potholes) of a malfunctioning education system.

7. In the first week of school, Isabel falls behind and can't catch up.

8. Isabel studies for hours, but does not have "time to learn" or learning tools to "learn and process" voluminous academic material.

9. After the first month of school, Isabel is floundering.

10. Isabel fails a test. A bad grade feels like a punch in the face.

11. Failure is painful. Isabel has become disconnected, depressed, and distracted.

12. Isabel is blamed for her failure. What is wrong with Isabel? Name calling hurts, e.g., "lazy, apathetic, and A.D.H.D." Isabel has become blocked. Isabel has shutdown.

13. Isabel does not have learning deficits, learning disabilities, or A.D.H.D., the "incurable brain disorder."

14. Isabel needs to heal her wounded spirit and rebuild her self-esteem: Intrapersonal-Integration Therapy Modality.

15. Isabel needs to acquire learning tools, **SMARTGRADES** Processing Tools, to become a self-reliant learner and achieve academic success.

16. Isabel needs an Academic Planner to map out her day.

17. Isabel needs a healthy breakfast for the energy to learn.

18. Isabel needs three daily doses of emotional food to feed her soul, "I love you and I am very proud of you." You don't find love, you create love. There is no such thing as too much love.

Children Cannot Raise Themselves

19. Isabel needs a quiet study space to do her schoolwork.

20. Isabel needs color-coded notebooks to stay organized.

21. Isabel needs a daily reward system to stay motivated.

22. Isabel needs a bulletin board to hang up her A grades as a constant reminder that she is an excellent student.

23. Isabel needs a regular bedtime for the energy to learn.

24. Isabel is an A-grade student.

25. Isabel still needs "time to learn."

Reinventing the American Education System

In America, there are countless children facing the same fate as Isabel. They will fall behind, flounder, fail, and fall through the cracks of the "Quantity Over Quality Curriculum-Driven Malfunctioning American Education System." Most of these students will be blamed for their academic failure "What is wrong with that student?" is the constant refrain uttered by parents and teachers. The clueless psychiatrist is the only professional who has a clue, "A.D.H.D., the incurable brain disorder." In some cases, floundering and failing students will be misdiagnosed with, A.D.H.D., "the incurable brain disorder." Their brain will be placed into a virtual wheelchair for life. These growing children will not be able to develop properly because they will internalize the label A.D.H.D. The child's self-talk is, "I can't do this and I can't do that, because I have A.D.H.D., the incurable brain disorder."

Quite frankly, the situation is so out of control that parents have begun labeling their own children with A.D.H.D., for any kind of behavioral infraction. It is not uncommon for me to hear that, "My mom told me that I have A.D.H.D."

To reiterate ad nauseam, if necessary: Parents, educators, and psychiatrists must adhere to the most basic principle of child rearing:

The Second Universal Gold Standard of Education

Children Cannot Raise Themselves
If a Child Is Failing, It Is Never the Child's Fault

If this message is all that you remember (process for long-term retention), after reading this magnum opus on the malfunctioning American education system, then the first goal of this book is accomplished.

It's Better to Build Children Than Repair Men

Grace Mutzabaugh
Co-Founder National Institute of Learning Disabilities

More money is put into prisons than into schools. That, in itself, is the description of a nation bent on suicide. I mean, what is more precious to us than our own children? We are going to build a lot more prisons if we do not deal with the schools and their inequalities.

Jonathan Kozol

Let Us Reform Our Schools, and We Shall Find Little Need of Reform in Our Prisons.

John Ruskin

A little boy had just finished his first week of school.
"I'm just wasting my time," he said to his mother.
"I can't read, I can't write, and they won't let me talk!"

e-mail communication

Every Student Has a Horror Story

The horror stories are all the same. The horror stories are about the bumps and bruises sustained and the injustices suffered by students who are victimized by a malfunctioning American education system.

Abusive (Tricky) "Hotdog" Exams
All students have horror stories about having to "Read, Cram and Regurgitate" voluminous academic facts under psychological duress and a stopwatch onto an abusive (tricky) "Hotdog" test.

Q: How many hotdogs do you have to stuff into your mouth in an hour to win the Coney Island Hotdog Contest in Brooklyn?

Q: How many academic facts do students have to cram into their mind, with meager comprehension, no learning tools, and for short-term retention, to regurgitate onto a stressful time-sensitive abusive (tricky) "Hotdog" test to earn a diploma?

Abusive(Tricky) Testing Practices
Every student has a horror story about studying for hours, and being sabotaged by an unfair tricky test question.

Students have horror stories about having to take three "Hotdog" exams in one day.

Students have horror stories about an unfair exam that three-quarters of the class fails, and then the test is graded on a curve. After the test, most students will feel the "Pain of Inadequacy."

The Academic Pressure Cooker
Students have horror stories about playing the futile academic game of "Read, Cram, Regurgitate, and Test" to earn a diploma.

Escapism: Seek Relief from the Academic Pressure Cooker
Students have horror stories about escaping into mind-numbing activities to find relief from their "Pain of Inadequacy" and "Scars of Incompetence."

Cutting Corners and Cheating to Pass, Survive & Graduate
- Students have horror stories about padding their papers with bibliographic material that they have no time to read.

- Students have horror stories about buying on-line essays and research papers.

- Students have horror stories about the black market of recycled exams.

Stressful School Environment
Students have horror stories about feeling anxious, stressed, overwhelmed, depressed, disconnected, distracted, disgruntled, apathetic, burnt out, and suicidal.

Remedial Courses in College for Poor Writing Skills
After twelve years of school, students have horror stories about having to take remedial English writing courses in college.

Astronomical Tuition Costs/ No Practical Business Skills
Students have horror stories about having to take out hefty school loans, e.g., $125,000, that will take twenty-five years to repay. Students graduate without basic business skills to earn a living or entrepreneurial skills to start their own businesses.

- Students have horror stories about selling drugs to pay for college tuition.

- Students have horror stories about dancing in a strip club to pay for college tuition.

- Students have horror stories about engaging in prostitution and selling their bodies to pay for college tuition.

N.Y.C. Social Promotion, 2004: "Academic Insanity"
Ten thousand New York City students have horror stories about not making the grade and being left back in the third grade for failing a citywide exam. "Social promotion" is a better problem than "Pain 'of Inadequacy." This is proof positive that the American education system is malfunctioning as early as the third grade. For more commentary on this, "Academic Insanity" read chapter fifteen.

Summer School Students: "Academic Insanity"
Students have horror stories about falling behind, floundering, and failing, and going to summer school. The first C grade is a warning sign that students are struggling and need to acquire, SMARTGRADES Processing Tools, to achieve academic success.

The Misdiagnosis of A.D.H.D.
Students have horror stories about falling behind, floundering, failing, and being misdiagnosed with A.D.H.D., the "incurable brain disorder."

DROPOUT NATION
Students have horror stories about falling behind, floundering, failing, falling through the cracks, and dropping out.

American Dreams Denied

Students have horror stories about not being able to realize a dream because of faulty regurgitation of an academic fact on a test. Students spend countless hours studying and spent countless dollars for tutoring services, but they were anxious, drew blanks, and performed poorly. To add insult to injury, two weeks after an exam, the academic facts stored in their short-term memory have disappeared into a black hole in their mind, and vanished into thin air, along with their American Dream.

Every Parent Has a Horror Story

Parents are asked to fill in the gigantic potholes of a "Quantity Over Quality, Curriculum-Driven Malfunctioning American Education System." Before children reach the age of puberty, parents will see children become anxious, stressed, and depressed; dreams that they have for their children will vanish into thin air.

Regular Tutoring Services

Parents are expected to return home after a full day of work to teach their kids schoolwork, because teachers only have time to give a brief overview of a subject, and have no time for in-depth comprehension. Parents pay for tutoring services to help their children learn the academic material that the teachers don't have time to teach. Regular tutoring helps students with the academic problem of the day, but every day there is a new problem. Tutors do help students pass tests, but they do not teach students the learning tools required to become self-reliant and life-long learners.

Private Schools: "Pain of Inadequacy" & "Scars of Incompetence"

Some parents are working more than two jobs to pay for private school tuition because these parents feel that the public school system is failing. Parents later learn that their children do not fare any better in a private school because their children experience the same, "Fifteen Stumbling Blocks of Academic Failure." Private school students will also earn a diploma, but not an education.

Standardized "Hotdog" Exams: The Vacuous Test Scores
Parents pay for expensive preparatory classes to help their children earn good scores on standardized "Hotdog" exams. These "Hotdog" tests require more than two years of expensive after-school private classes.

The Broken American Psychiatric System: The Vacuous Pills
Parents pay psychiatrists to counsel their children for anxiety, stress, and depression. Parents have horror stories about psychiatrists who add insult to injury by prescribing psychotropic drugs, a dangerous crutch with serious side effects.

Senseless School Shootings and School Massacres by Some of America's Brightest Minds
Parents have horror stories about losing their children to school shootings or massacres, or of having their children permanently injured, by a disgruntled student on a psychotropic drug.

Senseless Student Suicides of America's Brightest Minds
Some parents have horror stories about their children committing suicide on school grounds. In these cases, anxiety, stress, and "bouts of depression" escalate into debilitating clinical depression, suicidal thoughts (the ticking-time bomb), attempted suicide, and suicide. Some parents have sued the schools: M.I.T. student, Elizabeth Shin; George Washington student, Jordan Nott; and Allegheny College student, Charles Mahoney ("Suicide" Wikipedia).

Internet Parenting Blogs: Millions of Horror Stories

The Internet parenting blogs are littered with horror stories of parents who are doing whatever they can to help their children pass, survive, and graduate from the malfunctioning American education system.

Here is a letter from a parent blog. A mother is trying to help her twelve-year-old son who was floundering in a math class:

A Parent's Letter

"We have some of the top schools in the country in Arlington County. Is there some point with our children at which we could back off and not continue to push for rising achievement, an official goal of the county schools? Is there a way we can say, good enough is good enough?

My oldest son is in middle school. He is a talented but not gifted math student. Midway through this past school year, it was clear that he was not ready for algebraic thinking, and his seventh-grade math teacher compassionately helped us help him decide to move back to a more appropriate math level. Because I teach human development, I was able to help him understand that this wasn't about being dumb, but a developmental marker he had not yet hit. He moved back to repeat the math class he took last year.

Now I have a boy who is not enthusiastic about math. He doesn't believe he is good at it and doesn't think math is fun, all because we want rising achievement for all students. We don't need him to be doing homework all night. We need him to feel confident and competent. We need him to feel balanced. We want him to do well and we believe in effort, but we want him to not feel lost or deficient.

This need to ensure that we raise achievement for all students is outrageous in a county such as Arlington. We need to ensure that all students are stimulated and excited about learning, but at some point, enough is enough."

Q: What Really Happened to Her Talented, But Not Gifted Child? As this letter explains, her son was told to repeat the same math class he took last year. This child is exhibiting anxiety, stress, and low self-esteem, "He doesn't believe he is good at it." The "talented but not gifted," child is already suffering from the "Pain of Inadequacy," and will eventually graduate bearing the "Scars of Incompetence."

It is true that students grow, develop, and mature at different rates. It is within reason to argue that "gifted" students are stimulated by a fast-paced learning environment, while the "talented but not gifted" students fall behind, flounder, fail, and fall through the cracks of the malfunctioning "Quantity Over Quality Curriculum-Driven American Education System."

If the truth be told, the "talented and gifted" students who forge ahead at top speed have mastered the academic game of "Read, Cram, Regurgitate, and Test." These top-notch students do not process the academic material for long-term retention. Two weeks after the test, the academic material disappears into a black hole in the mind and vanishes into thin air.

I make it perfectly clear to my broken-winged students who master the SMARTGRADES Processing Tools, earn an A grade on the very next test, and begin to feel like "gifted" students, that this was a hard-won victory, but it was only a temporary victory. There is only time to store the academic facts for short-term retention and regurgitate them onto a "Hotdog" test. There is no "time to learn" the academic material for in-depth comprehension, long-term retention, and mastery of the academic material.

Public school students will earn a diploma, but not an education. There is only time to play the futile academic game of "Read, Cram, Regurgitate, Test, Pass, Survive, and Graduate."

This is also the case for students enrolled in elite private schools. Private school students are also asked to play the same academic game of "Read, Cram, Regurgitate, and Test." Private school students will also earn a diploma, but not an education.

The students who fall behind, flounder, fail, and fall through the cracks of a malfunctioning American education system did not learn how to play the academic game of, "Read, Cram, Regurgitate, and Test." In addition, one bad grade can send students into a tailspin, and students will become disconnected, depressed, distracted, disgruntled, and disobedient. Students study for hours by reading and rereading the academic material, but do not have learning tools of, extraction, condensation, association, and conversion, to memorize academic facts for long-term retention to pop out the facts, like a human toaster, onto a test.

According to Tiffany Clay, a top violinist for the Newark High School Sinfonia in Ohio, "I think that kids start out saying that as long as I graduate, I'll be fine. And then it turns into, well, I don't have to graduate and if I don't graduate, I can get a G.E.D., and then it becomes, there is always welfare" (Tiffany Clay, "This Land: Ohio Serenade" Dan Barry, *New York Times*, April 14, 2009).

Our first lady, "Mommy-in-Chief," Mrs. Michelle Obama, has her own childhood horror story of "Academic Insanity," and shared her lingering bad childhood memory in a women's magazine:

"In high school, Michelle once had a typing teacher who started the class by handing out a chart showing students what grades they could expect based on how many words per minute they typed. According to the formula, Michelle earned an A, but when the time came for grades, the teacher said she didn't give A's. Michelle was outraged: How dare she set forth the rules and then not abide by them?" (Holly Yeager, "The Heart and Mind of Michelle Obama" *Oprah Magazine*, April 2009).

A Sense of Entitlement: "Academic Insanity"

Students who fight for a well deserved A grade are referred to by educators as students who have a "sense of entitlement." This is just one more example of "Academic Insanity." Even, America's Brightest Minds, have horror stories of fighting tooth and nail for the correct grade that they earned and deserve.

The definitive horror story is that before the age of puberty, most American students in public and private schools will suffer from the "Pain of Inadequacy," and graduate bearing the "Scars of Incompetence." There is no in-depth comprehension, long-term retention, and mastery of the academic material. This is: The Silent Crisis Destroying America's Brightest Minds.

The Dirty Little Secret of Education in America

"On education, we must summon the moral courage to confront the unjust system that the Democrats desperately cling to and therefore perpetuate. The left has not had an original idea on education since the invention of the chalk board. Our party believes in education reform. We have nurtured a sincere education reform movement. We know the current system is broken for too many kids. We all believe it.

Everyone knows the dirty little secret of education in America -- the idea that all kids, regardless of class, geography, income, or any other factor, the idea that all kids deserve and have a right to equal opportunity in education… that idea is not a reality in America today. And that is a shame.

Now we must have the fortitude to win the political battles it will take to make fundamental changes in our schools, to allow for new ideas, to allow parents to have more choices, to break from the old model and move to a new model which demands equal opportunity in education."

Louisiana Governor Piyush Jindal

(Remarks to Republican National Politics Congressional Committee, March 24, 2009)

> A Problem Well Defined Is a Problem Half Solved.
>
> John Dewey

The U.S Spends more per capita than any other country on education. Yet, by every international measurement, in math and science competence, from kindergarten through the 12th grade, we trail most of the countries in the world. The implications of this are clearly obvious. Some even say it poses a threat to our national security.

Bob Schieffer
The Presidential Debate
October 15, 2008

Summary of the National Crisis of Education in America

Students are enrolled in a "Quantity Over Quality, Curriculum-Driven Malfunctioning American Education System." Teaching and learning are sacrificed to push the curriculum forward at a frenetic pace to meet the goals dictated by the "Higher Standards." Parents are asked to fill in the gaps, the gigantic potholes, of a malfunctioning education system.

In the first week of school, students fall behind and start playing the game of catch up. Students study for hours, but do not have "time to learn" or learning tools to "learn and process" voluminous academic material. Q: "Why don't I have time to read the textbooks, write the papers, and prepare to take tests?" Students suffer the "Pain of Inadequacy. Their self talk is, "I am not as smart as I thought I was."

The Academic Pressure Cooker: Students are asked to "Read, Cram, Regurgitate, and Test." Academic achievement is measured by regurgitating voluminous facts under psychological duress and a stopwatch onto an abusive (tricky) "Hotdog" exam. Hotdog exams are an exercise in futility. Two weeks after a test, facts disappear into a black hole in the mind and vanish into thin air. Students are uneducated. They will not be able to use the academic knowledge to enhance their own lives or to further the progress of civilization. American dreams are destroyed by faulty regurgitation of academic facts or sabotaged by abusive (tricky) test questions. Every student has a horror story of an injustice suffered. American schools resemble a war zone: Few heroes, heavy casualties, and senseless fatalities. Students seek relief from the "Academic Pressure Cooker" and the "Pain of Inadequacy" in mind-numbing escapes: TV; video games; drugs; alcohol; sex, and gambling, to name a few. All students have become anxious and stressed. Some students have become disconnected, depressed, distracted, disillusioned, disgruntled, and disobedient. A few students have been misdiagnosed with A.D.H.D., "the incurable brain disorder." The majority of students are surviving, but not thriving. Students will earn a diploma, but not an education.

Educators are clueless as to "How Does Learning Take Place?" They do not know how to nurture and cultivate the awesome power of the human brain. Q: Are educators running a school for academic success or an education asylum riddled with academic insanity? For example, educators do not have time to teach for in-depth comprehension, but they do have time to test students on the significant and trivial details that they don't have time to teach.

Educators cut corners and cheat students out of an education: There is no time for in-depth comprehension, long-term retention, and mastery of academic material. In return, students also learn how to cut corners and cheat to pass, survive, and graduate. There is no time for continuous feedback of strengths and weaknesses, and students graduate bearing the "Scars of Incompetence."

Failure is instructive.
The person who really thinks,
learns quite as much from his
failures as from his successes.

John Dewey

Part Two
The Malfunctioning American Education System

THE FIFTEEN STUMBLING BLOCKS OF ACADEMIC FAILURE

The Quantity Over Quality
Curriculum-Driven
American Education System

Fall Behind, Flounder, Fail, and Fall Through the Cracks

Here's Your C Grade, Here's Your Diploma!

Students Earn a Diploma! But Not an Education

"Deepa Sannidhi, a second-year medical student at New Jersey Medical School in Newark, struggled her first year. "I came to medical school because of a love of learning, and I felt like I wasn't learning. It was so hard to keep up with the curriculum."

(Kathleen Phalen Tomaselli, *"Medical Student Stress and Burnout Leave Some with Thoughts of Suicide,"* amednews.com, Oct. 20, 2008).

The Malfunctioning American Medical System

The "Quantity Over Quality Curriculum-Driven American Education System" is the first reason that the American medical system malfunctions. It is not uncommon to hear that it took five-twenty doctors to get the correct diagnosis and for this reason: Medical students do not process medical facts with in-depth comprehension, long-term retention, or mastery of the medical facts.

Here are the critical questions that are medical emergencies?
Q: Why does it take 5-10 doctors to get the correct diagnosis?
Q: Why do more people die from medical errors than from disease?
Q: Why do Americans pay for health insurance and still get inadequate coverage?
Q: Why are there more than 46 million Americans without health insurance?
Q: Why is the American healthcare system ranked 37th in the world?

It is Possible to Store the Mind
with a Million Facts and Still
Be Entirely Uneducated.
Alec Bourne
A Doctor's Creed

Meet Brad
Academic Game 1: Fall Behind
The first week of school, students fall behind, and start playing catch-up

The First Stumbling Block of Academic Failure

The Quantity Over Quality Curriculum-Driven Education System

The first stumbling block students encounter is how to keep up with the voluminous academic facts in a "Quantity Over Quality, Curriculum-Driven American Education System." It only takes the first week of school for most students to fall behind and start playing catch up. Some students are not able to catch up and fall behind, flounder, fail, and fall through the cracks of the malfunctioning American education system. Some students fail and go to summer school. Some students fail and change schools. Some students fail and choose homeschooling. Some students fail and dropout. The majority of students are surviving, but not thriving.

Brad's father wishes me luck, as I open the door to his son's bedroom. There is no empty space on the floor. The floor is completely covered with crumpled paper. I have no choice but to step on the paper and find my way to his son's desk and chair.

The avalanche of paper is a result of his son's schoolwork, namely, the class handouts, homework assignments, research papers, quizzes, and tests. Most students stuff the daily assault of loose paper into a messy folder. Most students do not have innate organizational skills. Organization is a learned skill.

Brad is eleven years old. His father told me that he has a problem with organization, as well. It is a "genetic" condition that runs in the family and he can trace it back more than two generations. His wife has given up on him and refuses to pick up after him.

I let them know that organization is a learned skill and that in one session, Brad will learn everything he needs to know about organization.

The first step is to get on our hands and knees and remove the paper from the floor, and put it into separate piles on Brad's bed. We make seven piles: Math, science, history, English, Latin, music, and computers. The second step is to separate each pile into four parts: Handouts, homework assignments, research reports, and tests.

Brad's dad can't believe his eyes. He is able to enter his son's bedroom and walk directly on the floor. As far as he is concerned, that makes me an organizational genius. I then reach for my school supplies and give Brad a new set of lightweight, color-coded, fuss-free, instant-organization **SMARTGRADES** school notebooks with four built-in files for handouts, homework assignments, and tests. We file his schoolwork into his new school notebooks. In less than two hours, Brad is organized.

The next question I am usually asked is:
Q: Is Brad able to stay organized without my intervention?
The answer is a resounding YES.

I spend the next fifteen minutes giving Brad some loose papers to file into his new school notebooks and he files each and every one into the right pocket. He has a brand new organization system in place and it is easy as pie. I reward Brad with a nutritious and delicious study snack (*Yummy in My Tummy: Good Grades Deserve Great Rewards and Great Desserts,* Appendix G).

As is usually the case, I have my work cut out for me because Brad needs a complete academic overhaul. He has fallen behind.

Quantity Over Quality Curriculum-Driven Education System

He is floundering. He is failing. He has been labeled with A.D.H.D. He is taking Ritalin for his "incurable brain disorder." Brad is one of the many senseless casualties of a malfunctioning American education system.

On Brad's bedroom door, I post a sign that says:

THIS STUDY ROOM IS UNDER NEW MANAGEMENT

Grade **A** Students are M**A**DE not Born
Website: www.everydayaneasya.com

ENERGIZE   ORGANIZE   PRIORITIZE

As far as Brad is concerned, the following five academic interventions transform him into an A-grade student.

Step 1. New School Notebooks
SMARTGRADES School Notebooks contain the new learning technology, SMARTGRADES Processing Tools, p. 140.

Step 2. New Study Room
(*Your Study Room Is Under New Management*, p. 56)

Step 3. New Learning Tools for Self-Reliant and Life-Long Learners
SMARTGRADES Processing Tools: New Learning Technology Every Student Earns an A Grade on the Very Next Test
(**EVERY DAY AN EASY A**, p. 56)

Step 4. Rebuild Self-Esteem and Repair Broken Wings
Integration Therapy for Intrapersonal Growth, Development, and Maturity (*Integration Therapy Modality*).

Step 5. Parent Empowerment Skills for Academic Success
(*How to Parent for Academic Success*, p. 56)

Students Earn a Diploma, But Not an Education

What I remember most about transforming Brad into an excellent student was that even the two of us working together were unable to keep up with Brad's schoolwork. For six months, from Monday through Thursday, 7 p.m. to 11 p.m., we would tackle his homework assignments, research papers, and test preparation. We were always lagging behind. There was always an assignment that had to be put on the back burner and left for the weekend. Brad needed the weekends to catch up on his schoolwork. There was no longer anytime left in his schedule for rest, relaxation, and recovery. Schoolwork is a seven day a week chore.

One year ago, Brad had been emotionally disconnected from his schoolwork. After earning good grades, his self-confidence returned and his self-esteem was renewed. He developed a new interest in his schoolwork and was now determined, more than ever, to earn an A grade on every school assignment. But there was another obstacle standing in his way. Brad needed more time for his schoolwork. He decided to pretend that he was sick and stayed home just to have more time to read textbooks, write papers, and prepare to take tests.

I am often asked whether I approve of a student taking the day off from school to read a textbook chapter, write an essay, and prepare to take a test. It doesn't happen often, but when it does, it is a sign that my student needs more "time to learn" the academic material. The learning curve is steep. It takes time to learn. Staying home from school is the imperfect solution to the imperfect problem of needing more "time to learn" to be able to "learn and process" voluminous academic facts to ace exams. Consequently, Brad earned A grades on all of his exams.

As of now, Brad is a self-reliant learner:
1. Brad understands that he first has to "retrieve" the academic facts and then "return" the academic facts to the teacher.

2. Brad has learned how to write an English essay, paraphrase the research material, footnote the sources, and proofread the paper.

3. Brad has learned how to read, extract, condense, associate, convert the academic facts for instant recognition and recall on tests. Once Brad mastered the new learning technology, SMARTGRADES Processing Tools, he was able to ace his exams:

SMARTGRADES 10 Step Processing Tools to Ace Tests
Step 1. Estimation Tool
Step 2. Divide and Conquer Tool
Step 3. Active-Reading Tool
Step 4. Extraction Tool
Step 5. Condensation Tool
Step 6. Association Tool
Step 7. Test-Review Note Tool
Step 8. Conversion Tool
Step 9. Visualization Tool
Step 10. Self-Testing Tool

(**EVERY DAY AN EASY A**, Appendix G).

If the truth be told, there was nothing ever wrong with Brad's brain. Brad had been paying the ultimate price for falling behind, floundering, failing, and falling through the cracks of the malfunctioning American education system. Before the age of puberty, he was misdiagnosed with A. D. H. D., and his powerful brain was placed into a virtual wheelchair for life by a clueless psychiatrist (who has a clue). His powerful brain was taken out of the virtual wheelchair and set free.

Let's Recap: Brad is an A-Grade Student

1. Brain Power: The human brain is the most powerful biological machine in the world. The brain does not come with an instruction manual and Brad does not know how to use it.

2. The Second Universal Gold Standard of Education: Children cannot raise themselves. If a child is failing, it is never the child's fault.

3. Brad needs a healthy breakfast for the energy to learn.

4. Brad needs three daily doses of love to feed his soul, "I love you and I am very proud of you." You don't find love, you create love. There is no such thing as too much love.

5. Brad needs a quiet study space to do his schoolwork.

6. Brad needs color-coded notebooks to keep him organized.

7. Brad needs learning tools, **SMARTGRADES** Processing Tools, to "learn and process" voluminous academic facts.

8. Brad needs a daily reward system to stay motivated.

9. Brad needs a bulletin board to hang up his A grades as a constant reminder that he is an excellent student.

10. Brad needs a regular bedtime for the energy to learn.

11. Brad still needs "time to learn."

Reinventing the American Education System

In America there is only one education agenda, and that is, how do we shove the massive curriculum down the throats of the students. Ready or not, here it comes: Voluminous academic material. At first glance the "Curriculum-Driven" American education system seems like a stimulating and rewarding experience regarding the quantity of information conveyed. In practice, it fails miserably to achieve its educational objectives.

First and foremost, the curriculum-driven system is all about the quantity of information conveyed, with little attention paid to quality. The processes of teaching and learning are sacrificed to maintain the frenetic pace of the stream of academic material flowing to meet the goals set by the "Higher Standards." The term "Higher Standards" means that more and more academic material has to be shoved down the throats of students, at a frenetic pace, even if there is no time to teach the academic facts and no time to learn the academic facts.

The game of quantity over quality gets played out on many fronts: Politicians play the game when they tell the public about more academic standards. School administrators play the game when they tell parents and students that they have to fulfill more academic requirements. Teachers play the game when they tell students that this is a "difficult course" (a code word for there is no time to teach and no time to learn, but there is always time to test), and that students will have to hand in more academic assignments. Students play the game when they have to cut more corners and cheat to pass, survive, and graduate.

Students Earn a Diploma, But Not an Education

Schools Play the Game of Quantity Over Quality

Parents read the course catalog and choose the school with the heaviest course catalog. The game of quantity over quality looks good on paper especially when parents are browsing through the meaty course catalog, and have to decide what is the best school for their child; and where to invest their hard-earned dollars for the hefty-tuition payments.

Teachers Play the Game of Quantity Over Quality

Even teachers are failing to "make the grade" because they can't keep up with their own massive curriculum agendas. They don't have time to teach the voluminous curriculum properly. Students have to fend for themselves and find tutors to teach them the academic material. Teachers have adopted a justification to excuse themselves from having to teach the academic material with the following overwrought cliché, "I refuse to spoon feed students understanding. They have to learn how to think for themselves."

Teachers don't have time to read papers and have learned how to skip and scan papers for required particulars: Title, thesis statement, double spacing, conclusion, and bibliography.

Teachers don't have time to properly grade papers for spelling, grammar, and punctuation are not corrected. When school papers are not properly corrected, it is impossible for students to learn from their mistakes.

Teachers have confided in me that the only teacher who is responsible for correcting spelling, grammar, and punctuation errors is the English teacher. The history and science teacher can ignore writing errors and spend their time grading for the right answers to academic questions.

Most Students Are Surviving, But Not Thriving

Students Play the Game of Quantity Over Quality

Students have learned how to play the game of quantity over quality when they pad their papers with bibliographic reading materials that they have never read. They have learned that it is better to pad their research papers with twenty bibliographic references that they had no time to read, because quantity is what will earn them a better grade. The teachers don't read it, they weigh it. The papers that weigh the most earn the highest grades.

I don't think we could find one single elementary, high school, or college student who has not padded a research paper with unread bibliographic works. This is not even considered cheating by most students; this is considered learning how to play the academic game and survive. Ironically, this practice is analogous to having "street smarts," but it is called having "school smarts."

Students will not only play this outrageous game of quantity over quality, but they will also pay the price for the unrealistic academic expectations that are required of them: They will fall behind the first week of school and start playing catch up. They will feel anxiety, stress, and suffer from "bouts of depression." They will feel the "Pain of Inadequacy" after taking an abusive (tricky) "hotdog" exam. They will escape into mind-numbing activities to seek relief from the "Academic Pressure Cooker." They will learn how to cut corners and cheat to pass, survive, and graduate. They will incur substantial financial debt in student loans, for years to come. The ultimate price paid is that students will graduate bearing the "Scars of Incompetence." American students will earn a diploma, but not an education.

Educators Need Time Management Skills

Educators are always telling students to "learn how to manage your time," and to "study harder." However, it is the educators who need time-management skills. If educators want students to learn how to manage their time, then educators have to learn how to manage the curriculum, so that teachers have time to teach the academic material for in-depth comprehension, and students have "time to learn" and learning tools to "learn and process" the voluminous academic material.

Let's Recap: The Quantity Over Quality Curriculum-Driven Malfunctioning American Education System

(Let's replay my favorite game called "connect the dots")

1. Brain Power: The human brain is the most powerful biological machine in the world. The only thing that is wrong with students is that the brain does not come with an instruction manual and students do not know how to use it.

2. The Second Universal Gold Standard of Education: Children cannot raise themselves. If a child is failing, it is never the child's fault.

3. Educators are clueless as to "How Does Learning Take Place?" Educators do not know how to nurture and cultivate the awesome power of the human brain.

4. Students are enrolled in a malfunctioning "Quantity Over Quality Curriculum-Driven American Education System."

5. Teaching and learning are sacrificed to push the curriculum forward at a frenetic pace to meet the goals dictated by the "Higher Standards."

6. In the first week of school, students fall behind and start playing catch up.

7. Students study for hours, but do not have "time to learn" or learning tools to "learn and process" voluminous academic facts.

8. Parents are asked to fill in the gaps, the gigantic potholes, of a malfunctioning education system: Parents are asked to pay for tuition, tutors, learning specialists, abusive (tricky) standardized "Hotdog" exam courses, and psychological counseling.

a. Parents Pay the Astronomical Cost of Tuition
Parents pay top dollar for the malfunctioning education system where teaching and learning are sacrificed to drive the curriculum forward.

b. Parents Pay for Regular Tutors
Since teachers do not have time to teach for in-depth comprehension; parents have to pay regular tutors to teach students the academic material that teachers do not have time to teach.

c. Parents Pay for Learning Specialists
Since students do not have "learning tools," parents have to pay learning specialists to teach students how to "'learn and process" voluminous academic material to ace "Hotdog" tests.

d. Parents Pay for "Hotdog" Test Preparation Courses
Parents have to pay for expensive preparatory classes for abusive (tricky) standardized "Hotdog" exams that measure a different curriculum that is not taught in school. Albert Einstein, had a disappointing academic setback because he failed a "Hotdog" exam.

e. Parents Pay for Pill-Pushing Prescription Drug Dealers

Bad grades are painful. Students who perform poorly on tests have become disconnected, depressed, distracted, and disgruntled. Parents pay psychiatrists to help heal their emotionally wounded children, "Here is a psychotropic drug, a crutch with a dangerous side effect, to help you mask the symptoms of the internalization of disappointment, pain, and rage that is causing your depression."

f. Parents Pay for the Misdiagnosis of A.D.H.D.

Clueless psychiatrists (with a clue) add insult to injury, and misdiagnose floundering and failing students with A.D.H.D., "This child has a prefrontal lobe cortex problem, because he can't get organized or finish what he starts. You have A.D.H.D., an 'incurable brain disorder.' Here is some Ritalin."

In sum, educators need to acquire time-management skills to learn how to set realistic expectations about curriculum guidelines.

Let's Recap: Teaching is a Time-Intensive Activity

- Teachers need time to teach for in-depth comprehension.

- Teachers need time to teach the craft of writing (ten to twenty rough drafts) and proofreading skills.

- Teachers need time for continuous feedback of strengths and weaknesses until the academic material is mastered.

- Teachers need time to read and correct writing assignments.

Let's Recap: Learning Is a Time-Intensive Activity

It is time to get real, take stock, and do reality checks about how long it takes to read textbooks, write papers, and prepare to take tests. School assignments need realistic-time allotments and detailed step-by-step instructions.

Here is a sample school assignment from the new "Quality Over Quantity Learning-Processing Education System" for in-depth comprehension, long-term retention, and mastery of the academic material:

1. Read and Outline (20% of grade)
   Read the chapter (1x) for a general overview. Write an outline of the main ideas and supporting details: 4 hours

2. Read and Think for In-Depth Comprehension (20% of grade)
   Read the chapter again (2x) for in-depth comprehension. Use your **SMARTGRADES** Critical Thinking Skills: 4 hours

3. Read and Process for Long-Term Retention (20% of grade)
   Read the chapter again (3x), and use your SMARTGRADES Processing Tools to "learn and process" the academic material: 7 hours

4. Read and Write for Mastery of Material (20% of grade)
   • Write a three-page essay: 25 hours
   • Write a five-page research paper: 50 hours

5. Red and Test (20% of grade)
   Prepare to take a test: 20 hours

Estimated Time:
Actual Time:
Hand in a time log with your assignment
Use book, **EVERY DAY, AN, EASY A,** for detailed step-by step instructions, p. 56)

The "Quantity Over Quality Curriculum-Driven Malfunctioning Education System" is the first stumbling block that contributes to the downward spiral of the malfunctioning American system.

Students Earn a Diploma, But Not an Education

Don't Look Down on Another Person
Unless You Are Leaning Over
to Help Them Up.
Anonymous

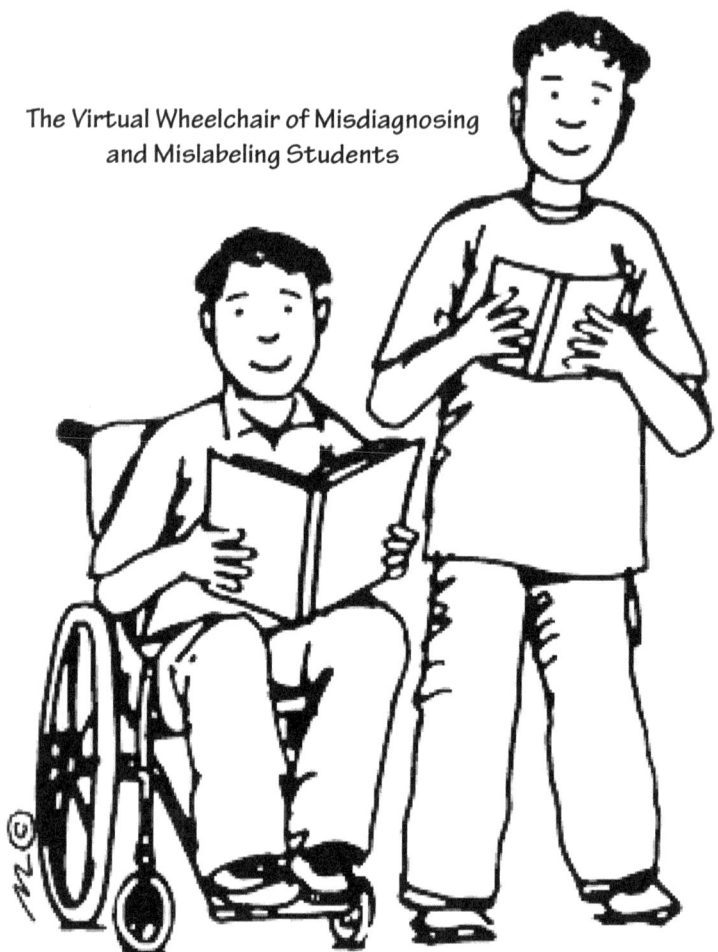

The Virtual Wheelchair of Misdiagnosing and Mislabeling Students

Meet Christopher and Joseph

After a horrible early childhood of emotional and physical abuse; and a bad public school and terrible homeschooling experience, these brothers master the **SMARTGRADES** Processing Tools and are back on track for academic success and a bright future. These brothers are now victors, not victims.

The Second Stumbling Block of Academic Failure

Poor Learning Tools to Process Voluminous Academic Facts

The second stumbling block students encounter is that they do not have "time to learn" or learning tools to "learn and process" voluminous academic facts to achieve academic success: Organization Skills, Time Management Skills, Academic Planner Skills, Critical Thinking Skills, English Essay Skills, Research Paper Skills, Proofreading Skills, and Test Preparation Skills.

Christopher is about to turn eighteen and he dreams of a good job and a girlfriend. In the second grade, Christopher was taken out of school because of an incident that he can't recall. He never again returned to school. During his childhood, Christopher was walloped by his biological father and stepfather. His soul bears the emotional scars of verbal and physical abuse and he has difficulty sitting still and paying attention. His mother has labeled him with A.D.H.D. Christopher purchased some over-the-counter pills that are supposed to help him be able to focus his attention.

His younger brother, Joseph, who is fourteen-years old, has never stepped foot inside a school. Joseph's passion is baseball and he dreams of becoming an All-American baseball player.

Paul, the next door neighbor, is homeschooling the boys. Paul is a staunch Roman Catholic. The boys don't want to hurt his feelings, but they don't want to follow his brand of religious fanaticism. There is a growing rift between Paul and the boys. Paul gives the boys a reading assignment and then spends the rest of his day in church. The boys are able to read, but don't know how to write essays, research papers, or prepare to take tests.

I was riding the Lexington Avenue subway line, gave them my business card, and they were in my office the very next day. They want to go to public school. Joseph wants to attend his local high school. Christopher wants to do the same, however, he does not want to be the only eighteen-year old in the ninth grade. Also, Christopher's writing skills are at a fifth-grade level.

As is usually the case, I have my work cut out for me. Will I accept the challenge of preparing two boisterous teenage boys for the greatest adventure of their lives--their entry into the malfunctioning American education system?

Science was the primary focus of my undergraduate and graduate education: Psychobiology (major) and Philosophy (minor), B.A.; Science Education, M.A.; and an Individualized Study Project, M.A. Soon after, I coauthored a scientific paper at Rockefeller University on brain research. The scientific paper is entitled, "Hyperphagia and Obesity Induced by Neuropeptide Y Injected Chronically Into the Paraventricular Hypothalamus of the Rat."

It now seems as if my office is my science laboratory and my students have become the guinea pigs in my experiments. I am "rewiring" the brains of my students by using my new learning technology, SMARTGRADES Processing Tools, to transform them into excellent students. I decide to accept the Herculean challenge. This case is going to require every learning tool that I have ever developed.

First of all, these boys are used to sleeping in all morning and start their day at 12 p.m. The first challenge will be asking them to wake up at 6 a.m., eat a healthy breakfast of oatmeal pie, ride two subway trains to Manhattan, and be on time for class at 8:30 a.m.

The second challenge is to separate the boys as they are psychologically enmeshed and function like a married couple. At a moment's notice they will bark and bicker at each other, and elbows and fists start to fly. I make the boys sit on opposite sides of the room.

I decide to work with each one separately. The older boy, Christopher, has a history of child abuse, and I will use the new therapy modality, Intrapersonal-Integration Therapy, to develop his internal voice and rebuild his self-esteem. We will begin the healing process that will allow him to regain control of his ability to pay attention and focus. The younger boy, Joseph, does not have a history of abuse, and he is able to focus and concentrate easily.

Whenever Paul walks into the room, Christopher starts to squirm in his seat. The sight of Paul makes the boys anxious. Paul makes unrealistic demands and the boys cannot live up to his unreasonable expectations, e.g., This week, read the complete works of Shakespeare and go to church or you will burn in HELL.

The third academic challenge is to teach the boys how to write standard English essays and research reports.

The fourth academic challenge is to teach the boys the new learning technology, SMARTGRADES Processing Tools. They will be able to retrieve the facts from the teacher and return the facts to the teacher in a homework assignment, essay, research paper, and on a test.

Students Earn a Diploma, But Not an Education

Here is the official list of SMARTGRADES Processing Tools that the boys mastered before their entry into the malfunctioning American education system.

SMARTGRADES SUCCESS STRATEGY STUDY SKILLS

In-Class Skills:
- Active Notetaking Tools
- Active Listening Tools
- Active Questioning Tools
- Fuss-Free Notebook Tools

At-Home Skills:
- Study Room Tools
- Organization Tools
- Time Management Tools
- Daily Planner Tools
- Study Strategy Tools
- Subject Strategy Tools
- Annotating Tools
- Outlining Tools
- Summarizing Tools
- Paraphrasing Tools
- Active Reading Tools
- Processing Facts Tools

On-Test Skills:
- Essay Test Tools
- Multiple Choice Tools
- Standardized Exam Tools
- College Preparation Tools
- Career Preparation Tools

Writing Skills:
- English Essay Tools
- Research Paper Tools
- Proofreading Tools

Thinking Skills:
- Critical Thinking Tools
- Mathematical Thinking Tools
- Scientific Thinking Tools
- Creative Thinking Tools

Test Preparation Skills:
- Memorization Tools
- Self-Test Preparation Tools
- Standardized Exam Tools

3 Editions:
- Elementary
- High School
- College

3 Formats:
- Hardcover
- Paperback
- E-Book

In sum, after two years of hard work with me, Christopher was ready to take the G.E.D. exam. He passed and enrolled in a community college. Most importantly, he can control his attention and focus. He is no longer taking the over-the-counter pills to help him focus. He no longer thinks he has A.D.H.D. His powerful brain was taken out of the virtual wheelchair and set free.

His brother, Joseph, has enrolled in a local public high school and is doing very well. These boys mastered the, SMARTGRADES Processing Tools, and after more than a fifteen-year hiatus from school, they are back on track for a bright academic future.

When I look back at this case, I feel very proud of these boys and I am very happy with myself. I was a parent, teacher, psychologist, and scientist all rolled up into one. I succeeded in each of these roles and I proved once again that, SMARTGRADES Processing Tools, are the most important factor in achieving academic success in school because students will become self-reliant learners.

Reinventing the American Education System

On most high school and college websites there are student support centers that teach study skills. On closer inspection, the study skills listed are quite meager in detail and design. There are no time logs that give the actual time that an assignment takes to complete and no detailed step-by-step instructions for homework assignments, essays, research reports, and test preparation.

1. Manage Your Time. How?
   Most students and teachers have no idea how long it takes to read a textbook, write a paper, and prepare to take a test.

2. **Eat Healthy Food: How?**
   For most students, what constitutes healthy is a can of diet soda instead of a regular can of soda.

3. **Get a Good Night's Rest: How?**
   For most students, going to sleep before the stroke of 12 p.m. is considered early, when, in fact, a 10 p.m. bedtime is what is required to really feel refreshed the next day.

4. **Paraphrase Don't Plagiarize: How?**
   Most students don't know how to paraphrase academic material.

5. **Study for the Test: How?**
   Most students read and reread the academic material, but do not have the learning tools of, estimation, condensation, association, and conversion, for instant recognition and recall to ace their tests.

Students do not receive detailed step-by-step instructions of how to actually perform these tasks. This is a blind spot. Students will not be able to perform these tasks without further specification and elaboration.

Before students can achieve academic success in school, they need to acquire learning tools to process voluminous academic material. The learning curve is steep. It takes time to "learn and process" academic material. Learning requires learning tools, namely, the new learning technology, SMARTGRADES Processing Tools. In 24 hours, educators can place the new learning technology, SMARTGRADES Processing Tools, directly into the hands of every student. As a result, students will become self-reliant and life-long learners.

Quantity Over Quality Curriculum-Driven Education System

If you can send back 80% of the academic facts for a B grade, then you can send back the remaining 20% of the academic facts for an A grade.

SMART POWER IS BACK IN THE HANDS OF ALL STUDENTS

STUDENTS EARN A GRADES ON THE NEXT TEST

EVERY STUDENT IS A SUCCESS STORY!

EVERY DAY AN EASY A

Elementary School Edition: Hardcover, Paperback, E-Book
High School Edition: Hardcover, Paperback, E-Book
College Edition: Hardcover, Paperback, E-Book

Poor learning tools to "learn and process" voluminous academic material constitute the second stumbling block that contributes to the downward spiral of the malfunctioning American education system.

Students Earn a Diploma, But Not an Education

"Half of the freshmen at community colleges and a third of freshmen at four-year colleges matriculate with academic skills in at least one subject too weak to allow them to do college work. Unsurprisingly, the average college graduation rates even at four-year institutions are less than 60 percent."

Harold O. Levy
New York City Schools Chancellor, 2000-2002

(Harold, O. Levy, "Five Ways to Fix America's Schools" New York Times, June 8, 2009)

I Cannot Teach Anybody Anything,
I Can Only Make Them Think.
Socrates

"I am smarter than I thought!"

Meet Pierre

He was a foreign student with marginal grades.
The Step Ahead Program: He prereads all of his
college textbooks during the summer months.
Also, he masters his **SMARTGRADES** Processing Tools
to earn A grades and make the Dean's List.

The Third Stumbling Block of Academic Failure

The Fast Food Restaurant: Cursory Comprehension

The third stumbling block students encounter is that teachers don't have time to teach for in-depth comprehension of the academic material. Teachers only have time to teach a brief overview of the academic material. The teacher's first priority is to stay on schedule and cover the curriculum on time. Sometimes, teachers don't even have time for a brief overview. Parents are asked to fill in the gaps (gigantic potholes) where the teacher left off.

No matter how often I tell Pierre, he will never eat a slice of my oatmeal pie for breakfast. He prefers a chocolate croissant or a slice of Brie cheese on a baguette. He was born in France. He is eighteen years old. He speaks English with a beautiful French accent.

Pierre wants to go to a brand name college in America that has an international reputation. He comes from a wealthy family, so money is not an issue. The director of admissions told him to take the G.E.D. exam and then submit an application.

When he called my office, he had already taken the G.E.D. exam and passed every part except for the English section. There is another problem. The English test is in two weeks.

His father's private secretary, Aimee, wants me to teach him how to write an English essay and pass an English test in less than two weeks. She will send him in for two weeks of English classes every day for four hours a day.

I agree to help Pierre pass his English test. Aimee is delighted that I am going to help him because she has already called ten other teachers and nine out of the ten teachers thought that she was crazy to think that two weeks was enough time to prepare a foreign student for an English test. The tenth teacher simply hung up on her. She let me know that I am the only teacher who is willing to take on the challenge and that she appreciates my help.

At our first meeting I am surprised to find out that Pierre is unable to write a single sentence correctly in English. He also does not have a clue about how to structure an English Essay. The G.E.D. English essay is a five paragraph, 200-word essay.

Last year, he took a college writing class. He shows me his essays, and they are badly written. There is no essay structure. The teacher did not correct the grammar, spelling, and punctuation errors.

On a typical day in an American college classroom, a teacher gives a lesson and expects the students to learn the academic material based on a cursory overview of the material. The teachers don't have time to teach for in-depth comprehension of the academic material. There is no time for students to ask and answer questions in class. The teacher usually runs out of time and can't even finish the general overview of the academic material.

In addition, the teacher has no time to read the essays and correct the errors. The essays are handed out to fellow students who make comments. The students are supposed to learn from the comments made by the other students (the blind leading the blind). The teacher will only read the final draft of the essay and grade it. The 4 credit, $4000 dollar English course was a waste of his personal resources of time, money, and energy.

As is usually the case, I have my work cut out for me as I soldier on with the English essay challenge. In less than one hour, we have a working plan and outline for the English essay.

G.E.D. Standard English Essay: 5 Paragraphs = 200 Words

Step 1. The Title of the Essay

Step 2. The Essay Overview
Paragraph 1. Introduction
Paragraph 2. Body
Paragraph 3. Body
Paragraph 4. Body
Paragraph 5. Conclusion

Rule: One main idea per paragraph with supporting details

Step 3. The Essay Outline
One Topic and Three Supporting Examples
Paragraph 1. One Main Idea and 3 Supporting Examples
Paragraph 2. Supporting Example 1
Paragraph 3. Supporting Example 2
Paragraph 4. Supporting Example 3
Paragraph 5. Restate Introduction and 3 Examples

Step 4. Add Transition Words to Bridge Ideas
For example, In addition, Furthermore, In conclusion

Use 5 Transition Words for Each Body Paragraph

1. According to

2. For example

3. In addition

4. Furthermore

5. In conclusion

College English Boot Camp (Appendix G)

In less than three hours, Pierre understands how to structure an English essay. I now refer to this class as "In 24 Hours, Learn How to Write a Perfect English Essay."

We take a fifteen minute break for a nutritious and delicious study snack and a fresh-fruit smoothie and then continue the lesson.

Clearly in order for Pierre to pass the essay exam in two weeks, he is going to have to use short sentences and simple English words, e.g., "I love soccer. Soccer is a great sport." We agree that Pierre not use more than seven words in any sentence because there will be grammatical errors and he will lose points. We agree that Pierre not use any word he can't spell correctly.

The next two hours are spent writing the English essays according to our plan. Pierre is delighted. He can't believe it. He has finally learned how to write a standard English essay and it only took a few hours. He feels that it may be possible to pass the English section of the G.E.D. exam in two weeks and enroll in the American college of his dreams.

After a month, Pierre receives the official letter. Pierre passes the G.E.D. English exam and we celebrate with some Fromage Ardéchois on a toasted baguette. He decides to work with me for the duration of his academic studies. It turns out that he was a marginal student with C and D grades. Moreover, he still reads English very slowly and will not be able to keep up with his classmates. He has never read a 300-page novel. He has never read a 400-page textbook. He has never written a research paper: Paraphrasing, citations, and proofreading. Also, he feels that he will be culturally out of sync and may not understand what is expected of him.

Politically speaking, France and America were not on good terms as a result of the impending Iraq invasion. Americans were spilling bottles of French wine into the streets. Pierre was uncertain as to whether he would be accepted, ignored, or ridiculed by his peers.

Plan A. College Degree
The American college of his dreams is a pressure cooker. That particular elite private university has a 60% dropout rate after the first year, because it is also a, "Quantity Over Quality, Curriculum-Driven Education System." After the first week of school, most students will fall behind and start playing catch up. More than half of the student body will fall behind, flounder, fail, and drop out.

Academic Insanity: Parents foot the astronomical tuition bill, $50,000 a year, and educators cheat students out of an education. If you can't keep up with the fast paced frenetic curriculum there is something wrong with you. The school system is run like a fast food restaurant. Here's the food. Here's the bill. Chop! Chop! Here's the knowledge. Here's a general overview. Here's the test. Chop! Chop!

Students Earn a Diploma, But Not an Education

Monday through Friday, new academic facts are placed on the blackboard accompanied by a brief explanation of the academic material.

Academic Insanity: There is Always Time to Test Students
Teachers may not have the time to teach the academic material for in-depth comprehension, but they always find the time to test you on academic material that they don't have time to teach. Students are under constant pressure to perform. They are given daily quizzes and weekly exams. Knowledge. General Overview. Test. Chop! Chop!

Academic Insanity: No Time to Teach Critical Thinking Skills
Teachers do not have time to teach for in-depth comprehension but they do expect students to hand in written work with an analysis, synthesis, and evaluation.

I can see that the G.E.D. English Essay exam challenge was small potatoes next to the monumental academic challenge developing on Pierre's wish list. Pierre also wants to earn an M.B.A. at a prestigious American school, Cornell University.

Plan B. Family Business
If Pierre fails and drops out of school he will not be stranded and left out in the cold, because he will go into his father's business and be his apprentice. His father did not have a college education, and Pierre wants to achieve this noble milestone.

The Step Ahead Program
Pierre needs a head start. I decide to proceed with this case by recommending that Pierre go to the school bookstore and purchase his textbooks for the first term. We will spend the

next three months prereading the textbooks. On the first day of class, he will be way ahead and will be able to stay afloat.

My Step Ahead Program
Pierre decides to preread all of his textbooks each and every term until he graduates. He forfeits all of his summer vacations to preread his textbooks. Pierre masters the new learning technology, SMARTGRADES Processing Tools. We read every page of his textbook and we make Test-Review Notes. We estimate, extract, condense, associate, convert, and visualize the academic facts for instant recognition and recall. Pierre now has the learning tools to ace his exams. Pierre is test ready six months before the test. When Pierre actually takes the course, it will be a review of the course material.

SMARTGRADES 10 Step Processing Tools to Ace Tests
Step 1.   Estimation Tool
Step 2.   Divide and Conquer Tool
Step 3.   Active-Reading Tool
Step 4.   Extraction Tool
Step 5.   Condensation Tool
Step 6.   Association Tool
Step 7.   Test-Review Note Tool
Step 8.   Conversion Tool
Step 9.   Visualization Tool
Step 10. Self-Testing Tool

(EVERY DAY AN EASY A, p. 140)

My "Step Ahead Program" is a complete success. Pierre is on the, Dean's List, every term, and graduates with an A minus grade-point average.

I am Pierre's primary teacher. Unlike most students who are anxious and stressed out, Pierre is relaxed knowing that I have his back and will teach him the academic material and prepare him to ace his exams. Simultaneously, he is being homeschooled and he is attending the American university of his dreams. He is able to float through the malfunctioning American education system with ease. Most importantly, his energy is not undermined by anxiety, stress, and depression. His energy is completely channeled into learning.

I have time to teach and Pierre has time to learn. We make a great team. On a weekly basis, I fill in the missing gaps and simultaneously teach him elementary, high school, and college skills. I am teaching college level history, psychology, business, and English literature courses.

Even with his own personal teacher on hand, Pierre was reading, writing, and preparing for exams seven days a week. The academic pressure was unremitting. He hardly ever took a day off. His personal chores were taken care of by his father's private secretary.

Like most students, two weeks after the test, the academic material was virtually gone from his memory bank. Like a fast food restaurant, a day later, you can't remember what you had for lunch the day before. This is because there is only time to process the voluminous academic material for short-term retention: Knowledge. Overview. Test. Chop! Chop!

During his first semester, Pierre was the only student who passed the required remedial English class. The rest of his class failed the course. The students signed a petition and marched into the principal's office demanding academic justice. The teacher told them that they should have learned how to write an English essay in high school and that she is not responsible for the failure of the entire class, minus one (the student with the private-learning specialist). Pierre earned an A minus in the class.

During Pierre's first academic term, he saw first hand how one teacher with a callous attitude and an ax to grind could crush students' dreams.

Clearly the teacher felt justified and would rather fail the students than teach the class how to write English essays. All the students that she had failed had to repeat the course.

Let's Recap: Teacher's Justification for Failing the Whole Class
• Some previous teacher was supposed to teach the students how to write English essays.

Two years later, the English teacher was fired for having a love affair with a student. The firing is true, but the love affair is a rumor — so please don't quote me.

Reinventing the American Education System
Can you imagine asking an entire class (minus one) to repeat a $4000-dollar course. When did the teacher know that her students were failing the course? Why doesn't she fill in the missing gaps in their education? There are gigantic potholes in the malfunctioning American education system, namely, that the teachers drive the curriculum forward at a frenetic pace with no in-depth comprehension; and that students only store the voluminous academic material for short-term retention to pass a test. Two weeks after a "Hotdog" exam, most of the facts disappear into a black hole in the mind and vanish into thin air. Students do not achieve mastery of the academic material: Knowledge. General Overview. Test. Chop! Chop!

If the whole class fails, minus one (the student with the private-learning specialist), then the school must bear some of the responsibility for the failure. The teacher says, "Here is your F grade and here is the next English essay assignment that is due this Friday." The parents are asked to foot the entire bill for a malfunctioning American education system that doesn't have time to teach the craft of writing. Did you ever hear of double taxation? This is an example of double tuition. This is a cut and dry case of "Academic Insanity."

The question that needs to be re-examined is as follows:

Q: Are educators running a school for academic success or an education asylum riddled with academic insanity?

Let's Recap: Academic Insanity
1. Academic Insanity: The Fast-Food Restaurant
Schools are run like fast-food restaurants: Knowledge. General Overview. Test. Chop! Chop!

2. Academic Insanity: No Time for In-Depth Comprehension
Teachers don't have time to teach for in-depth comprehension, but they do have time to test you on academic material that they don't have time to teach.

3. Academic Insanity: No Time to Teach Critical Thinking Skills
Teachers don't have time to teach critical thinking skills, but they do expect students to hand in written work with in-depth analysis, synthesis, and evaluation.

4. Academic Insanity: Fail the Whole Class Minus One
If the whole class fails, minus one (the student with the private-learning specialist), the school is responsible for the failure

because, it bears repeating right here that:

> Children Cannot Raise Themselves.
> If a Child is Failing, It Is Never the Child's Fault.

5. Academic Insanity: No Time to Teach the Craft of Writing

Writing is an art form. Art is created through inspiration, incubation, growth, development, and maturity. A flower cannot be pushed out of a plant. A painting cannot be pushed out of a painter. A sculpture cannot be pushed out of a sculptor. A literary masterpiece cannot be pushed out of a writer.

WRITING IS REWRITING: Learning how to write well requires ten to twenty drafts and continuous feedback of strengths and weaknesses. Students make the same writing mistakes in elementary school, high school, and college because teachers don't have time to properly teach the craft of writing or to correct their errors. As a result, after completing K-12, colleges have required remedial English courses to teach students the lost art of the craft of writing. Too often, college English classes also fail to teach the craft of writing because they also don't have time to teach it properly. Students should be required to reread, revise, and rewrite their papers until literary mastery is achieved (ten to twenty-five rough drafts). Here is a recent news bulletin that speaks volumes about the problem of poor writing skills in one of the best high schools in the nation:

"Writing Across the Curriculum is being created with the idea of improving student writing by giving students more opportunities to write in all of their classes. This is partly a response to faculty complaints that Stuyvesant students do not have sufficient writing skills" (The Editorial Board, "Writers Wanted" *The Spectator,* October 10, 2008).

Students Earn a Diploma, But Not an Education

Students spend far too much time paraphrasing (or plagiarizing) good writing for their research reports, and not enough time learning how to develop their own style of writing, as well as learning how to proofread their papers.

6. Academic Insanity: Limits on Research Papers

There is a tendency for teachers to give out research paper assignments as if they were the only teacher in your life. On a given day, Pierre could receive five research report assignments from five different teachers. Research papers should be limited to five pages and three primary sources, as follows.

1. Write a five-page research paper
a. Use three primary sources
b. The estimated time required is: 53 hours
   - Research: 10 hours
   - Note-taking: 20 hours
   - Write a rough draft: 10 hours
   - Proofreading (read, revise, and rewrite): 10 hours
   - Footnotes and citations: 3 hours
c. The actual time required is:
d. Hand in your paper with a time log
e. For detailed step-by step instructions, see, **EVERY DAY, AN EASY A**

Let's Recap: The Lost Art of the Craft of Writing
1. The learning curve is steep. It takes time to learn.

2. Writing is an art form that requires inspiration, incubation, growth, development, maturation, and proofreading skills.

3. WRITING IS REWRITING. It takes continuous feedback of strengths and weaknesses from a teacher to learn how to write well.

4. Students need "SMARTGRADES Proofreading Tools" to develop a discerning eye and find the writing errors **(EVERY DAY AN EASY A,** Appendix G).

5. English essays require detailed step-by-step instructions

6. Research papers require detailed step-by-step instructions.

7. It takes time to reread, revise, and rewrite written material.

8. It is time to get real, take stock, and do a reality check. It takes ten to twenty rough drafts of literary incompetence to achieve literary competence.

Let's Recap: The Lost Art of In-Depth Comprehension
1. The learning curve is steep. It takes time to learn

2. To do something right, you have to put time into it

3. It takes time to read for a general overview of the subject

4. It takes time to think about what you are reading

5. It takes time to understand what you are reading

6. Understanding requires in-depth comprehension: Analyis, synthesis, and evaluation

7. In-depth comprehension requires "SMARTGRADES Critical Thinking Skills" **(EVERY DAY AN EASY A,** Appendix G).

8. "SMARTGRADES Critical Thinking Skills" enable students to analyze, synthesize, and evaluate the academic material:

   a. Read with a Critical Mind

   b. Separate Facts from Opinions

   c. Evaluate the Underlying Assumptions

   d. Read for Arguments Based on Fallacies

   e. Read for Inductive and Deductive Reasoning

   f. Read Passage for Patterns of Organization
     (*EVERY DAY AN EASY A*, Appendix G).

Do you remember that game called "connect the dots?" You draw a line from one dot to another in the correct order and a picture appears. All of the hard work of connecting the dots, has been done for you. Just sit back and enjoy the ride and see all of the dots connect right before your eyes, and like a magic trick, two pictures are going to appear.

One picture is of the "Quantity Over Quality, Curriculum-Driven American Education System" that is destroying America's Brightest Minds: Students fall behind, flounder, fail, and fall through the cracks of a malfunctioning American education system.

The other picture is of the new "Quality Over Quantity, Learning-Processing American Education System." The new education system is going to catapult the American education system out of the dark ages and into the 21st century. I am going to "Reenvision, Reinvent, and Rebuild" the American education system into one of the greatest education systems in the world, as follows:

The New Education Paradigm
The Quality Over Quantity Learning-Processing Education System

1. Nurture and Cultivate the Awesome Power of the Human Brain

2. In-Depth Comprehension: SMARTGRADES Critical Thinking Skills

3. Long-Term Retention: SMARTGRADES Processing Tools

4. Mastery of Academic Material: Continuous Feedback of Strengths and Weaknesses

5. New Grading System: Grade A or REDO

6. Every Student Is a Success Story

7. Students are able to further the progress of civilization

8. America has the greatest education system in the world

It is time for educators to bring back "In-Depth Comprehension" and "Critical Thinking Skills" to the classroom, so that students, parents, teachers, psychiatrists, and politicians will learn how to connect all of the dots on their own: Knowledge. In-Depth Comprehension. Critical Thinking Skills. Writing Skills. Chop. Chop.

Cursory comprehension of the academic material is the third stumbling block that contributes to the downward spiral of the malfunctioning American education system.

I am entirely certain that twenty years from now we will look back at education as it is practiced in most schools today and wonder how we could tolerated anything so primitive.

John W. Gardner

I took a speed-reading course
and read War and Peace in
twenty minutes.
It involves Russia.

Woody Allen

"I am not as smart as I thought I was!"

Meet Brittany
She was a falling shining star.
She has a powerful brain and is a gifted child.
Her mother feels that sports reduce her
anxiety and stress and keep her sane.
She masters the **SMARTGRADES** Processing Tools
and earns A grades on all of her tests.
She is back on track for academic success.
Brittany is a scholar and an athlete.

The Fourth Stumbling Block of Academic Failure

In One Ear and Out the Other: Short Term Retention

The fourth stumbling block students encounter is that they do not absorb the academic material into their minds for long-term retention. Students cram voluminous academic facts with meager comprehension into their short-term memory and regurgitate the facts onto a stressful time-sensitive "Hotdog" exam. Students spend hours performing the academic exercise of "Read, Cram, Regurgitate, and Test." It is an exercise in futility. Two weeks after the test, the facts disappear into a black hole in the mind and vanish into thin air. Students go into education, but education does not go into the students. Students will not be able to use the academic material to further their own goals, or to make a contribution to mankind and further the progress of civilization. Students are uneducated.

It is 6:30 a.m. and Britney is smack in the middle of her ice-skating lesson. Every morning she will skate for an hour and then go to school. She attends an elite public high school. Brittany is a great athlete and a great scholar.

As of last semester, Britany's grades took a turn for the worse. She still has one A grade and one B grade on her transcript, but the rest of the grades are C grades.

On one hand, her parents who have graduated from, Ivy League schools, feel that she will not be able to gain admission to an Ivy League college because she has C grades on her transcript.

On the other hand, her parents do not want to tell her to give up her love of ice-skating, even if she has no plans to go to the Olympics, or to skate professionally.

This is an easy case for me. Britany is a bright and beautiful young woman. She eats properly. She has tremendous energy. She is disciplined. She takes instruction well. Her academic problem is quite common.

Q: How do you participate in an extra-curricular activity and maintain your academic standing?

Many schools have interesting after-school clubs. These clubs have regular meetings during the week. These meetings take time away from a student's after-school study time. However, a student may discover a meaningful life-long passion and make some great friends.

I have been told by parents that their child cannot give up their extra-curricular activity because that activity maintains their child's sanity, and provides a healthy escape from the stress of the "Academic Pressure Cooker" of homework assignments, research papers, and hotdog tests.

I do give classes on weekends, but some students do not want to spend their weekends taking classes. These parents will learn to live with their child's C grades. Parents who have children with D grades will take a stand and put their foot down and suspend the extracurricular activity until the child's grades improve.

Students do not have to sacrifice their extracurricular activities to attain good grades. I recommend that students take time off from the extracurricular activity and learn the, SMARTGRADES

Processing Tools, and become an "Overnight Academic Success Story." Students can have the best of both worlds. They can achieve good grades and participate in extracurricular activities.

As far as the scholar-athlete, Britany, is concerned, I recommend the following two academic interventions:

YOUR STUDY ROOM IS UNDER NEW MANAGEMENT
Grade **A** Students are M**A**DE not Born

ENERGIZE
ORGANIZE
PRIORITIZE

Step 1. New School Notebooks
SMARTGRADES School Notebooks contain the new learning technology, **SMARTGRADES** Processing Tools.

Step 2. New Learning Technology for Self-Reliant and Life-Long Learners **SMARTGRADES** Processing Tools (**EVERY DAY AN EASY A**, Appendix G).

In sum, Britney is following her bliss and is still ice skating every morning at the crack of dawn, before the start of a school day. She did not stop her extracurricular activity to learn the new learning technology, **SMARTGRADES** Processing Tools. She came to my office after school and had a session from 5 p.m. to 6 p.m. every week for six months. She is now able to process the facts for instant recognition and recall to ace her exams. I am delighted to report that Britney earned A grades on all of her exams. Her parents are thrilled that she is now able to achieve academic success without having to sacrifice her passion for ice skating.

Reinventing the American Education System

On late-night television comedy shows, American students have become the butt of gags designed to show that these students are unable to answer simple academic questions, e.g., Who was the first president of the United States of America? Students are randomly picked on and there is not one student in a random selection of ten students who can answer the question. Students do not process the academic material for long-term retention. The academic facts go into one ear, and out the other ear. Poking fun at how "dumb" (no long-term processing of academic material) American students have become is a regular comedic routine on late-night television.

Let's Recap: In One Ear and Out the Other Ear
(Let's replay my favorite game called "connect the dots")

1. Brain Power: The human brain is the most powerful biological machine in the world. The only thing that is wrong with students is that the brain does not come with an instruction manual and students do not know how to use it.

2. The Second Universal Gold Standard of Education: Children cannot raise themselves. If a child is failing, it is never the child's fault.

3. Educators are clueless as to "How Does Learning Take Place?" They do not know how to nurture and cultivate the awesome power of the human brain.

4. Students are enrolled in a malfunctioning "Quantity Over Quality Curriculum-Driven American Education System."

5. Teaching and learning are sacrificed to push the curriculum forward to meet the goals dictated by the "Higher Standards."

6. Parents are asked to fill in the gaps (gigantic potholes).

7. **Academic Game One:** In the first week of school, students fall behind and start playing catch up.

8. Students study for hours, but do not have "time to learn" or learning tools to "learn and process" voluminous academic material.

9. After a month, many students are floundering.

10. Students have become anxious, stressed, and depressed.

11. **Academic Game Two:** Students are asked to play the futile academic game of "Read, Cram, Regurgitate, and Test."

Short-Term Retention

12. Two weeks after the test, most of the academic facts disappear into a black hole in the mind and vanish into thin air. Students go into education, but education does not go into students. Students are uneducated.

13. Students will not be able to use the academic material to further their own goals, or to make a significant contribution to mankind and further the progress of civilization.

14. At a later date, students will have to make time to relearn the academic material with in-depth comprehension, long-term retention, and mastery of the academic material.

Short-term retention of the academic material is the fourth stumbling block that contributes to the downward spiral of the malfunctioning American education system.

Too Often We Give Our Children Answers to Remember Rather than Problems to Solve.
Roger Lewin

The World Breaks Everyone, and Afterward, Some Are Strong at the Broken Places.
Ernest Hemingway

"I am not as smart as I thought I was!"

Meet Tiffany
She was a falling shining star.
She is suffering from test anxiety.
She has a powerful brain and is a gifted student.
Her creative, lateral-right brain, is under constant assault by, "Read, Cram, Regurgitate, and Test."
She masters the **SMARTGRADES** Processing Tools and earns A grades on her tests.
She is back on track for academic success.

The Fifth Stumbling Block of Academic Failure

The Academic Pressure Cooker: Cram Voluminous Academic Facts with Meager Comprehension, No Learning Tools, and for Short-Term Retention into your Mind. Regurgitate the Facts under Psychological Duress and a Stopwatch onto an Abusive (Tricky) Hotdog Test to Earn a Diploma.

The fifth stumbling block students encounter is that education is measured by "Hotdog" exams. How many hotdogs can you stuff into your mouth in an hour to win the Coney Island Hotdog Contest in Brooklyn? How many academic facts do students have to cram with meager comprehension, no learning tools, and for short-term retention to regurgitate onto a stressful time-sensitive test to earn a diploma? Every student draws at least one blank. Most students draw more than one blank and see the academic facts, their emotional health and American dream vanish into thin air.

Tiffany is an aspiring playwright. Members of her high school class are performing her first play. I ask her for a copy of the play. I want her to sign it. I know that her autograph attached to her first literary manuscript will become a valuable piece of memorabilia. Tiffany is a shining star.

Tiffany is a sensitive artist with a great deal of emotional depth. She studies for hours and feels confident that she knows the academic material. When she takes the exam, her anxiety paralyzes her, and she is unable to perform well.

She attends an elite public high school and the pressure to perform is unremitting, without a rest and recovery period. She has to meet a deadline every week. There is an essay due. There is a research paper due. There is a project due. There is a quiz or a test to take. There is no down time in her schedule.

This is an easy case for me because Tiffany has her act together. She is organized. She has an academic planner. She has a decent book bag and a pencil case that is packed to the brim with pens and pencils, an eraser, tissues, and cherry-flavored lip balm. She has her own study room. She doesn't watch TV. She has a regular bedtime of 10 p.m.

She eats a hearty breakfast. She has a lovely figure and eats the right food and the right amount of food. She doesn't drink caffeinated soda, tea, or coffee.

She has a loving and supportive mother. Her father is unhappy about paying the learning specialist to help his daughter succeed in school. He feels that his daughter is smart enough to stand on her own two feet and resolve her academic problems all by herself.

How can I make a difference and get Tiffany to be less anxious and more confident so that she will be able to ace her exams? It is a very frustrating experience to study for hours and do poorly on an exam. It is infuriating to see your dream destroyed by your inability to regurgitate an academic fact onto a hotdog exam.

Tiffany had to take an admission exam to be accepted to the best high school in the city and she outperformed most students.

Q: Why then is she having trouble taking exams? What has changed over time?

Out-of-Control Academic Facts

First of all, like every one of her gifted and talented peers, Tiffany is overwhelmed from the daily bombardment of voluminous academic material of a "Quantity Over Quality, Curriculum-Driven, Malfunctioning American Education System."

No Time to Learn

Tiffany has some learning tools, but they are inadequate for the difficult academic challenges encountered. In addition, the lack of time to read her textbooks, write her papers, and prepare to take the hotdog tests is undermining her ability to attain academic success and achievement.

Let's Recap: Why is Tiffany Anxious?

1. Tiffany is overwhelmed by voluminous academic facts.

2. Tiffany is pressured to remember everything.

3. Tiffany has no time achieve in-depth understanding.

4. Tiffany won't remember the facts beyond test day.

5. Tiffany studies for hours, but is anxious, draws blanks, and does poorly on her exams.

6. Tiffany does not have sufficient "time to learn" and inadequate learning tools to "learn and process" the voluminous academic material.

As for Tiffany, I recommend the following three academic interventions to reduce her test anxiety, so that she can ace her "hotdog" exams:

THIS STUDY ROOM IS UNDER NEW MANAGEMENT
Grade A Students are MADE not Born
Website: www.everydayaneasya.com

Step 1. New School Notebooks
SMARTGRADES School Notebooks contain the new learning technology, SMARTGRADES Processing Tools.

Tiffany no longer spends her time hole-punching five handouts from five different teachers into her notebooks. In less than thirty seconds, Tiffany can file a new handout into her new SMARTGRADES fuss-free instant-organization school notebooks.

Step 2. Integration Therapy for Self-Esteem
Tiffany has to rebuild her self-esteem "What is wrong with me? I am not as smart as I thought I was." Tiffany learns that doing well in school is not about her, but is all about the academic facts. She has to learn how to "retrieve" voluminous academic facts from her textbook, classnotes, and handouts, and "return" voluminous academic facts to the teacher. (Integration Therapy, Appendix G).

Step 3. New Learning Tools for Self-Reliant and Life-Long Learners
SMARTGRADES Processing Tools: New Learning Technology
Every Student Earns an A Grade on the Very Next Test
(*EVERY DAY AN EASY A,* Appendix G).

Tiffany uses her, SMARTGRADES Processing Tools, to read, extract, condense, associate, visualize, and self-test. She processes the academic facts for long-term retention. Her ability to instantly recognize and recall the facts on a test has increased her confidence and decreased her test anxiety.

Most Students Are Surviving, But Not Thriving

SMARTGRADES 10 Step Processing Tools to Ace Tests
Step 1. Estimation Tool
Step 2. Divide and Conquer Tool
Step 3. Active-Reading Tool
Step 4. Extraction Tool
Step 5. Condensation Tool
Step 6. Association Tool
Step 7. Test-Review Note Tool
Step 8. Conversion Tool
Step 9. Visualization Tool
Step 10. Self-Testing Tool

(**EVERY DAY AN EASY A**, p. 140).

In sum, Tiffany earned an almost Straight-A-Grade report card, except for a B+ in math. Her mom sent me a lovely note thanking me for helping to empower her charming, brilliant, and beautiful daughter, so that she can follow her bliss, fulfill her potential, and achieve her American dream of becoming a playwright. Tiffany's academic star is on the rise.

Reninventing the American Education System
In the "Curriculum-Driven" education system, it only takes the first week of school for students to fall behind and start playing catch up. After a month, many students have begun to flounder. The academic facts accumulate and students are overwhelmed with feelings of anxiety and stress because they are uncertain that the facts will reappear in the nick of time during a test.

Let's Revisit a Critical Question:
Q: Are educators running a school for academic success or an education asylum riddled with academic insanity?

Students Earn a Diploma, But Not an Education

1. Academic Insanity: Faulty Regurgitation of Academic Facts
In a bizarre twist of fate, one bad grade on a test can have dire consequences. A student's American dream can be destroyed in an instant. The stress level is high. Anxiety can paralyze students and send them into a tailspin. A disappointment from a poor grade and the loss of one's childhood dream can spiral out of control: Anxiety, stress depression, suicidal thoughts, attempted suicide, and suicide.

2. Academic Insanity: A 2-Hour "Hotdog" Exam = 80% Grade
Even more ludicrous is the fact that 80% of a student's grade may be based on the two-hour exam and the other 20% of a student's grade is based on daily homework assignments. Six months of hard work is reduced into a two-hour abusive(tricky) hotdog test.

3. Academic Insanity: Students Take Three Tests in One Day
There is no coordination among teachers when it comes to test dates. One time-sensitive hotdog exam is stressful, but three hotdog exams on the same day constitute cruel and inhuman punishment. A simple improvement that puts an end to this academic insanity of a student taking three exams on one day is assigning one day of the week to a subject area.

- Monday is for Math Tests

- Tuesday is for Science Tests

- Wednesday is for English Tests

- Thursday is for History Tests

- Friday is for Language Tests

4. Academic Insanity: Failure to Develop Right-Brain Abilities

Albert Einstein, made the following four remarks about the critical importance of imagination:

1. "The true sign of intelligence is not knowledge but imagination."

2. "Logic will get you from A to B. Imagination will take you everywhere."

3. "Imagination is everything. It is the preview of life's coming attractions."

4. "Imagination us more important than knowledge" ("Albert Einstein," Wikipedia).

The right brain, the "Creative Powerhouse," is under constant assault by the futile daily academic exercise of "Read, Cram, Regurgitate, and Test." This daily academic exercise injures the development of lateral right-brain abilities: Daydreaming, imagination, intuition, inspiration, and creation. That is why, extra-sensitive, intuitive, imaginative, and creative children are the first to fall behind, flounder, fail, and fall through the cracks of the malfunctioning American education system.

5. Academic Insanity: Abusive (Tricky) "Hotdog" Exams

Q: How many hotdogs do you have to stuff into your mouth in an hour to win the Coney Island Hotdog Contest in Brooklyn?

Q: How many academic facts do students have to cram with meager comprehension, no learning tools, and for short-term retention into their mind and regurgitate onto a stressful time-sensitive test to earn a diploma?

Education is not measured by the "Academic Pressure Cooker" of "Read, Cram, Regurgitate, and Test and abusive (tricky) "Hotdog" exams for these nine reasons:

Reason 1. Students Do Not Have Learning Tools
Students study for hours, but do not have "time to learn" or learning tools to "learn and process" voluminous academic facts for instant recognition and recall.

Reason 2. The "Academic Pressure Cooker"
Students are asked to cram voluminous academic facts into the mind with meager comprehension, no learning tools, and for short-term retention, to regurgitate the facts under psychological duress and a stopwatch onto an abusive (tricky) "hotdog" test to measure academic achievement.

Reason 3. Education is Not Measured Under Psychological Duress
During a test, all students are anxious and stressed. All students will draw at least one blank. Most students draw more than one blank.

Reason 4. Pain of Inadequacy: What Is Wrong with Me?
"Why can't I cram one-thousand academic facts into my head and regurgitate them onto a stressful, time-sensitive test? Students' self-esteem plummets because they think that it is their fault that they draw blanks and perform poorly. Their self-talk is: "I am not as smart as I thought I was."

Reason 5. Life-Long Mental Health Problems
One bad grade hurts and is painful. Students who perform poorly on tests have become anxious, stressed, depressed, disconnected, distracted, and disgruntled. Some students have become blocked. In some cases, "bouts of depression" escalate into clinical depression, suicidal thoughts, attempted suicide, and suicide.

Reason 6. The Mental Health Clinic
Therapists cannot help students because they do not teach "learning tools" and cannot remove the stressor of the "Academic Pressure Cooker." Psychotropic drugs, a crutch with serious side effects, do not heal a wounded soul, a broken spirit, or a disintegrated mind. The vacuous pills do not solve emotional problems.

Reason 7. The War Zone
Schools resemble a war zone: Few heroes, heavy casualties, and senseless fatalities. Students lose their emotional health (anxiety disorders), self-esteem ("I am not as smart as I thought I was"), and American dream ("If you work hard, you will prosper").

Reason 8. Students Are Uneducated
Two weeks after the test, the academic facts disappear into a black hole in the mind and vanish into thin air. Students are uneducated. Students earn a diploma, but not an education.

Reason 9. Parents Have Horror Stories
Parents work one, two, or three jobs to pay astronomical tuition, tutoring, and mental health bills, and see a child's American dream vanish into thin air because of an unfair (tricky) test question:
Step 1. Take out school loans, e.g., $160,000
Step 2. Study for hours (no processing tools)
Step 3. Pay for private tutoring, e.g., $50-250 per hour
Step 4. American dream sabotaged by unfair test question
Step 5. Depressed, distracted, and disgruntled students

The "Academic Pressure Cooker" of Read, Cram, Regurgitate, and Test) and "Hotdog" exams constitute the fifth stumbling block that contributes to the downward spiral of the malfunctioning American education system.

Education Is the Only Path to a Peaceful World

This Is What My NYU Professor Said:

"You deserve an A+ grade, but I already gave out my two A+ grades to the students who took the oram exam before you. I am going to give you an A - grade. I hope that you can still be happy with this grade."

Sharon Esther Lampert

> The ability to learn faster than your competitors may be the only sustainable competitive advantage.
>
> Arie de Geus

"I am not as smart as I thought I was!"

Meet Alex

Students have become fierce competitors for the two A grades that a teacher is allowed to hand out. Many student experience competitive isolation. Students cannot work together as a team.

The Sixth Stumbling Block of Academic Failure

The Darwinian Grind of Cut-Throat Competition

The sixth stumbling block students encounter is the Darwinian grind, a contest of the survival of the fittest. Every student is an island unto himself or herself. It is difficult for students to work as a team, cooperate for the good of any individual member, or for the common good of the group. Students have become fierce competitors for admission into the malfunctioning American schools.

Stringy rubber skeletons hang from the lighting fixture in Alex's bedroom. When he closes the light, the gory skeletons glow in the dark, emitting a phosphorescent green light.

Alex is fifteen years old. He loves to roller blade. He is a neat freak. He is well organized and every loose paper is hole-punched and bound in a loose-leaf binder.

Alex is on anti-depressants and sees a psychiatrist once a week. His father had a terrible accident, is handicapped, and is in a wheelchair. His father spends the day watching TV. Even if his father has time to proofread his son's written work, he doesn't want to do it. The father does not have professional proofreading skills and does not want to become responsible for a missed writing error. Most parents that I meet do not want to do any more schoolwork. Moreover, they are graduates from the same malfunctioning American education system and suffer the "Pain of Inadequacy" and bear the "Scars of Incompetence."

Alex's parents are divorced, however, they are still fighting and Alex is still in the middle of it all. His father has custody even though he is wheelchair bound. Alex is a well-mannered child who is living with multiple stresses, one of which is a stressful learning environment.

Alex is earning B and C grades and has many incomplete homework assignments. He goes to school on an empty stomach. Alex does have a regular bedtime. He has his own study room with a good desk and a comfortable chair. He needs better lighting over his desk. A portable desk lamp would suffice. His notebooks are neat, but his single large loose-leaf is too heavy and cumbersome to carry to and from school on a daily basis.

YOUR STUDY ROOM IS UNDER NEW MANAGEMENT
Grade A Students are MADE not Born

ENERGIZE
ORGANIZE
PRIORITIZE

As for Alex, I recommend five academic interventions:

Step 1. New School Notebooks
SMARTGRADES School Notebooks contain the new learning technology, SMARTGRADES Processing Tools, p. 140.

Step 2. Upgrade Study Room
(This Study Room Is Under New Management, p. 56)

Step 3. SMARTGRADES SUCCESS STRATEGY STUDY SKILLS
(*EVERY DAY AN EASY A*, p. 56)

Step 4. Rebuild Self-Esteem and Repair Broken Wings
Integration Therapy for Intrapersonal Growth, Development, and Maturity (*Integration Therapy,* Appendix G).

Step 5. Eat for Energy to Learn
Fiber-rich meals with fresh fruits and vegetables.

As for Alex, he is no longer going to school on an empty stomach. He eats a bowl of oatmeal pie for breakfast and has energy to learn: Listen, think, read, write, research, memorize, and test.

The first two weeks we deal with incomplete school assignments. We mail letters to five different teachers for a comprehensive list of the incomplete school assignments. We complete the missing assignments and his homework requirements are now up-to date.

Alex has a new notebook system that makes it easier for him to manage his daily handouts and loose school papers. He was organized from the start, but he was spending too much time hole-punching every assignment into a loose-leaf binder. He has given up the time-consuming task of hole-punching and has more time for test preparation and roller blading.

Runt of Litter Versus Class Nerd
Alex earns an A grade on his science test. Alex is using the, SMARTGRADES Processing Tools, to "learn and process" academic material for instant recognition and recall and is able to ace all of his exams. Alex, the "Runt of the Litter," is now competing with the "Class Nerd" for the best grades in the class.

Students Earn a Diploma, But Not an Education

SMARTGRADES 10 Step Test-Preparation Tools to Ace Tests
Step 1. Estimation Tool
Step 2. Divide and Conquer Tool
Step 3. Active-Reading Tool
Step 4. Extraction Tool
Step 5. Condensation Tool
Step 6. Association Tool
Step 7. Test-Review Note Tool
Step 8. Conversion Tool
Step 9. Visualization Tool
Step 10. Self-Testing Tool

(EVERY DAY AN EASY A, p. 140).

Alex's self-esteem and confidence are rebuilt thanks to the new therapy modality, Intrapersonal-Integration Therapy, that rebuilds a child's internal emotional resources from "flight to fight." The last time we met, Alex was beaming from ear to ear and gave me a warm and loving farewell hug.

Reinventing the American Education System
It is normal behavior for a disconnected, depressed, distracted, disgruntled, and blocked student to forget to write down a homework assignment or to scribble down a homework assignment incorrectly. It is not a sign of A.D.H.D., the "incurable brain disorder." I recommend that a student call a classmate and ask for the homework assignment. Time and again, many students do not have friends in school. If they are absent from school, then they need to have someone to call to find out what happened in class that day. It is sad to hear that kids are so competitive that they do not have good friends, or want to help each other.

As is the case in many elite schools, the normal learning environment is an unhealthy breeding ground for stress, anxiety, and depression. Students are driven, determined, and goal oriented. Students have become fierce competitors.

School is a competitive battleground. There is hardly ever time to tell a joke and laugh at a joke. And there is little about school that is funny: Homework assignments, research reports, and tests. There is little time to smile, so most of my students have adopted a half-smile to get it over with.

The "Throating" Students
Johns Hopkins Univeristy students are cited for originating the term "throating." The name is short for cutthroat. According to a student blog, "The slang word means to sabotage someone else's coursework to make your own look better. It is the despicable practices of certain members of the pre-med class, who would do anything to up their class standing for their med school applications. A Throat could exist in almost any major, or for that matter doesn't have to be a pre-med, although most are. A Throat is the type of person who borrows notes and "forgets" to give them back, who checks out every single issue of Animal Behavior from the library and keeps them all semester" (everything2.com).

The Cutthroat Parents
Parents always tell me that more than half of the class needs my help but they won't refer me to other parents in the class. Parents do not wish to share my services with other parents. Moreover, they do not want their child to compete with other students who have the new learning technology, SMARTGRADES Processing Tools.

Educate the Whole Student: Mind, Body, and Spirit

It is not enough to educate the mind and body of a student. The spirit, "the light from within" of the student, needs to be educated. Spiritual development is a critical missing piece of the education puzzle. Character development is defined by the following attributes: Caring, kindness, compassion, forgiveness, and helping people in need. There are many kinds of behavior that promote character development: Play by the rules, take turns and share, be open-minded, listen to others, don't take advantage of others, and don't blame others.

Spiritual Education: My Daily Gratitude Journal

Every day, students should be required to keep a gratitude journal of their spiritual development to show how doing good deeds for others enriches their own life and the lives of people around them.

Date: Monday April 10th, 2009

My Daily Gratitude Journal

1. I am thankful that mom is a great cook and made a delicious dinner.

2. I am thankful that my good friend, Bobby, had an extra ticket and invited me to the baseball game.

3. I am thankful that, Grandma Rose, only has a cold and not a flu.

4. I am thankful that my school does not make us wear uniforms.

5. I am thankful that my teacher always gives us a fair test.

My Good Deeds: Self, Family, Friends, and Community

1. My Good Deed for Myself
   a. I ate the fresh fruit salad instead of eating junk food
   b. I proofread my English essay for writing errors.

2. My Good Deed for My Family
   a. I took out the trash since Dad was helping Grandma.

3. My Good Deed for My Friends
   a. John is sick. I called him to see how he was feeling.

4. My Good Deed for My Community
After school, I visited with Grandma's friend, Trudy, who is living in the old-age home on the corner. She saved the cookies from her lunch to give me a present. They were my favorite frosted black and white cookies. Mom told me to put them away until after dinner. I told Mom that Trudy will be disappointed if I don't eat at least one cookie. Mom agreed. I ate one cookie and put the rest away for after dinner. I thanked Trudy and gave her a hug and a kiss. The nursing home only has frosted black and white cookies on Mondays. I will visit Trudy on the first Monday of every month.

The Class-Buddy System
One simple example of caring and kindness is the establishment of a buddy system that would be mutually beneficial if one student gets sick, or forgets to write down his homework, or loses his memo pad on the bus. He could call his class-buddy and get an update on what happened in school that day.

The Darwinian grind of cutthroat competition is the sixth stumbling block that contributes to the downward spiral of the malfunctioning American education system.

I was thrown out of college for cheating on the metaphysics exam; I looked into the soul of the boy sitting next to me.

Woody Allen

Note: Woody Allen was expelled from N.Y.U., and wrote more than one joke about it.

I was thrown out of N.Y.U. for cheating-with the deans wife.

Woody Allen

A student hands a professor an essay.
The professor states, "It still gets an A."
The student says, "What do you mean?"
"When I wrote it in 1945, it got an A,
and its been getting one ever since."

Morris Stoler

Senator Edward M. Kennedy
Expelled from Harvard for Cheating

The youngest member of the famous Massachusetts political family, Kennedy prepped for Harvard at Milton Academy and entered the College in the fall of 1950. At the end of his freshman year, Kennedy was suspended for having another student take a Spanish exam in his place.

Lauren D. Kiel, Harvard Crimson, November 30, 2008

The Seventh Stumbling Block of Academic Failure

Student Survival Strategies: Cutting Corners and Cheating to Pass, Survive, and Graduate

The seventh stumbling block students encounter is that students don't learn how to succeed; they only learn how to cut corners and cheat to pass, survive, and graduate. The learning curve is steep. Learning takes time. Students don't have "time to learn" and learning tools to read their textbooks, write and proofread their papers, and prepare for tests. Teachers also cut corners and cheat students out of an education: No in-depth comprehension, long-term retention, and mastery of academic material.

There is an adorable kids' clothing store in my neighborh- ood. I thought I would stop in and see whether I would be able to leave some of my promotional education flyers on the counter.

The owner of the store says, "We could use your writing services. My daughter has a research paper due next week. Go ask her if she wants to take some lessons."

Her teenage daughter, Lindsay, is sitting on the floor of the store folding t-shirts. Lindsay overhears her mom chatting with me, and says, "Mom, I hate writing. I don't want to take classes. I just buy my papers on-line."

This took me by surprise because buying papers on-line has become pervasive, like buying Cliff's Notes, so that you don't have to read the dense and difficult 300-page novel.

After a brief pause to reflect on her admission and confession, I said, "Lindsay, if you change your mind and want to learn how to write, I would be delighted to help you."

The problem of students cutting corners and cheating is composed of five distinct, but overlapping problems:

Problem 1. Teaching and learning are sacrificed to push the curriculum forward to meet the goals dictated by the "Higher Standards." Teachers give a brief overview of the academic material and sometimes even run out of time to even give a brief overview. Teachers use quizzes to force kids to do the reading assignment, even if the academic material is untaught.

e.g., Monday: Read Chapter One
   Tuesday: Quiz on Chapter One

Problem 2. Students do not have "time to learn" and learning tools to "learn and process" voluminous academic material.

Problem 3. Educators do not have time to properly teach the craft of writing English essays, research reports, and proofreading skills.

Problem 4. Teachers cut corners and cheat the students out of an education: No in-depth comprehension, long-term retention, and mastery of academic material.

Problem 5. In return for teachers cheating students out of an education, students also learn how to cut corners and cheat to pass, survive, and graduate.

The following examples illustrate how the second problem, "time to learn" contributes to the problem of cutting corners and cheating. Students don't have enough time to read their textbooks, write their papers, and prepare to take their tests.

The Reading Assignments
Do you want students to read their textbooks or do you want them to skip and scan and read the end-of-chapter summaries?
Read Chapter in Textbook 5 hours
Skip and Scan Textbook 30 minutes

The Essay Assignments
Students do not have learning tools to write a standard English essay. Q: How long does it take to write an essay?
Write an Original Essay 25 hours
Rework an Online Essay 2 hours

The Academic Research Paper
Students do not have learning tools to write a research paper.
Q: How long does it take to write a research paper?
Write an Original Research Paper 80 hours
Rework an Online Research Paper 5 hours

Paraphrase or Plagiarize
Students do not know how to paraphrase academic sources and have poor writing skills.
Q: How long does it take to paraphrase a source?
Paraphrase a Source 10-15 minutes
Copy a Source 1-3 minutes

Test Preparation

Students do not have learning tools to memorize voluminous facts for instant recognition and instant recall. Q: How long does it take to memorize one-thousand academic facts for a two-hour time-sensitive, stressful hotdog exam?

Memorize Facts	25 hours
Black Market of Recycled Exams	2 hours

Student Survival Strategies

Robert
"I don't have time to read this dense and difficult 400-page novel. The teacher said that the test will only be on the classnotes."

Susan
"I don't have time to read this complicated and tough 300-page novel. Cliff's Notes summarize the essential facts of the story."

Steve
"I don't have time to write the 10-page research paper. There are on-line essays and research papers that you can buy and rework."

Michael
"I don't have time to read the ten required books that are in the bibliography. The teacher doesn't have time to ask questions about these books."

Robin
"There is a black market of recycled exams. You have to be in the loop to have access to these recycled exams. If you're not in the loop, you may not survive the course."

Most Students Are Surviving, But Not Thriving

Schools complain about plagiarism, but don't offer a lesson on "How to Paraphrase Source Material." Students learn how to plagiarize academic material in elementary school. Students answer homework questions by copying the answers verbatim out of their textbooks. Students practice plagiarizing for years and become good at it. In high school, students are asked to stop plagiarizing and start paraphrasing. Students are told to "write in out your own words and keep the meaning intact." There are no detailed step-by-step instructions for learning how to paraphrase. In college, students are told that they will be expelled if they are caught plagiarizing academic material.

Teachers Cut Corners and Cheat Students Out of an Education
It is within reason to argue that if teachers don't have time to teach, then they cheat the students out of an education:

- No time to teach for in-depth comprehension of academic material

- No time to teach for continuous feedback of strengths and weaknesses for mastery of the academic material

- No time to teach the craft of writing (ten to twenty-five rough drafts) and proofreading skills

- No time to read papers and correct writing mechanics

- There is time to test students with abusive (tricky) hotdog exams on facts that they don't have time to teach

- Students earn a diploma but not an education

The teachers are blameless. It is not their fault. The teachers are also innocent victims of the "Quantity Over Quality Curriculum-Driven Malfunctioning American Education System."

Let's Recap: Cutting Corners and Cheating
(Let's replay my favorite game of "connect the dots")

1. Brain Power: The human brain is the most powerful biological machine in the world. The only thing that is wrong with students is that the brain does not come with an instruction manual and students do not know how to use it.

2. The Second Universal Gold Standard of Education: Children cannot raise themselves. If a child is failing, it is never the child's fault.

3. Educators are clueless as to "How Does Learning Take Place?" Educators do not know how to nurture and cultivate the awesome power of the human brain.

4. Students are enrolled in a malfunctioning "Quantity Over Quality Curriculum-Driven American Education System."

5. Teaching and learning are sacrificed to push the curriculum forward at a frenetic pace to meet the goals dictated by the "Higher Standards."

6. Parents are asked to fill in the gaps (gigantic potholes).

Academic Game One: Catch Up
7. In the first week of school, students fall behind and start playing catch up.

8. Students study for hours, but do not have "time to learn" or learning tools to "learn and process" voluminous academic material.

9. Students suffer from the "Pain of Inadequacy." Students think "What is wrong with me? Why don't I have time to read the textbooks, write the papers, and prepare to take the tests?

10. After a month, many students are floundering. A disgruntled student calls the principal's office and threatens a bomb scare and the entire school is locked down until the threat is investigated.

Academic Game Two: The Academic Pressure Cooker
11. Students are asked to "Read, Cram, Regurgitate, and Test" to earn a diploma.

Academic Game Three: Abusive (Tricky) "Hotdog" Exams
12. Students try to stuff one-thousand academic facts into their mind with meager comprehension, no learning tools, and for short-term retention and regurgitate them under psychological duress and a stopwatch onto an abusive (tricky) hotdog test.

13. All students have become anxious and stressed. Every student draws at least one blank on a test. Most students draw more than one blank on a test.

14. The students' self-esteem plummets, "I am not as smart as I thought I was!"

15. Disappointments build up and so does the pain. In some cases, stress, anxiety, and "bouts of depression" escalate into clinical depression (debilitating psychological paralysis), suicidal thinking, attempted suicide, and suicide.

16. Broken American Psychiatric System: The Vacuous Pills

In some cases, students suffering from clinical depression will be given a brain scan, misdiagnosed with a brain disorder, and given psychotropic drugs, a crutch with serious side effects, to treat their emotional problems. In some cases, disconnected, depressed, distracted, and disgruntled students will be misdiagnosed with A. D. H. D., an "incurable brain disorder" and their powerful brain will be placed into a virtual wheelchair for life.

17. Malfunctioning Education System: The Vacuous Test Scores

Educators cut corners and cheat students out of an education, destr[oy] their emotional health (anxiety, stress, and depression), and undermi[ne] their American dream ("If you work hard, you will prosper"):

- No time to teach to teach for in-depth comprehension

- No time to teach the craft of writing (twenty rough drafts)

- No learning tools for instant recognition and recall on tests

- No time for continuous feedback of strengths and weaknesses

- No long-term retention and mastery of academic material

- Educators do make time to test students on significant and trivial details.

- Students earn a diploma, but not an education

Academic Game Four: Students Cut Corners and Cheat
18. In return for cheating students out of an education, students also learn how to cut corners and cheat to pass, survive, and graduate from a malfunctioning American education system.

"When 4,500 high school students were asked by Don McCabe of Rutgers if they'd ever cheated on tests or exams, roughly three-quarters admitted they had. When McCabe asked them if they'd ever cheated on homework, 97 percent said yes. That's not a typo. Ninety-seven percent" (Bob Ivry, "The Culture of Cheating Pervades Our Society" *The Record*, June 10, 2003).

"In a survey of nearly 62,000 undergraduates on 96 campuses over the past four years, two-thirds of the students admitted to cheating. The survey was conducted by Don McCabe, a Rutgers professor who has studied academic misconduct and helped found the Center for Academic Integrity at Duke" (Jonathan Glater, "Colleges Chase as Cheats Shift to Higher Tech" *The New York Times*, May 18, 2006).

University of Nevada, Las Vegas
"After students photographed test questions with their cellphone cameras, transmitted them to classmates outside the exam room and got the answers back in text messages, the university put in place a new proctoring system (Jonathan D. Glater, "Colleges Chase as Cheats Shift to Higher Tech," *The New York Times*, May 18, 2006).

You Tube Videos
"YouTube has dozens of student-made videos teaching how, for example, to scan a Coke bottle label into a computer, replace the nutrition information with physics notes, and paste the label back onto a bottle to create a cheat aid unlikely to be caught by teachers" (Kim Clark, "Professors Use Technology to Fight Student Cheating" *U.S. News & World Report*, October, 2008).

Here is another mind-boggling news bulletin from the prestigious Stuyvesant High School:

"A recent Stuyvesant graduate has been accused of plagiarizing her winning submissions to three writing contests. The alumna also published the poem under her name in the 2007 spring issue of Caliper, the Stuyvesant literary magazine. She was an editor of that publication. Pudding House, the publisher of 18-year-old Eva Della Lana's poem "Menarche in Rural Ohio," said that the Stuyvesant alumna submitted that poem under her own name to the three contests and won a total of 5,200 dollars (Prameet Kumar and Noah Rayman, "Stuyvesant Graduate Accused of Plagiarism" *The Spectator,* February 15, 2008).

Here is the question that needs exploration:
Q: Why did one of America's Brightest Minds, submit another poet's verse under her own name?

I want to look at this problem by making a comparison from the point of view of, Marion Jones, one of the greatest female track athletes in America.

Q: Why did America's greatest female track star, Marion Jones, use athletic-enhancing drugs to cut corners and cheat her way to eight Olympic-gold medals?

In a video-taped interview, Marion Jones, said that when she looks back at the situation, her confidence in herself had been undermined. The "Pain of Inadequacy" had reared its ugly head. She said: "I truly believe that the reason I made the awful mistake and a few thereafter was because I didn't love myself enough to tell the truth (Disgraced Track Star Marion Jones tells Oprah About Lying to the Feds (Michael Okeeffe, *Daily News,* October 28, 2008).

Olympic athletes make use of every possible advantage:
1. Good genetics and the best trainer are an advantage.
2. Steelcut oatmeal and coffee for breakfast are an advantage.
3. Drinking water and taking multivitamins are an advantage.
4. A good night's sleep is an advantage.
5. Good weather on the outdoor track is an advantage.
6. Eating the right food is an advantage.
7. Illegal athletic-enhancing drugs are an advantage.
8. Illegal drugs: Rewards are great and risks are low.
9. Many athletes take drugs, only a handful get caught.

Let's try to connect the invisible dots ... as to why a student plagiarized a poem. Conversely, it is within reason to assume that this student cut corners and cheated based on a long laundry list of disadvantages:

1. Students spend too much time paraphrasing or plagiarizing the the work of others, and far too little time learning how to write.

2. Pain of Inadequacy: "I am not as smart as I thought I was."

3. The lateral creative right-brain is under assault by the daily academic grind of, "Read, Cram, Regurgitate, and Test."

4. Students learn how to cut corners and cheat and only a handful of students get caught.

Cutting corners and cheating by educators who cheat them out of an education, and by students to pass, survive, and graduate from a malfunctioning education system constitute the seventh stumbling block that contributes to the downward spiral of the malfunctioning American education system.

Students Earn a Diploma, But Not an Education

The First and Most Important Step Toward Success Is the Feeling that We Can Succeed!

Nelson Boswell

"I am not as smart as I thought I was!"

Meet Spencer
Disconnected, Depressed, Distracted,
Disorganized, Disgruntled, and Disobedient
He does not have an incurable brain disorder.

He is seeking refuge from the "Pain of Inadequacy."
His mind-numbing escape is pornography.
Spencer has a powerful brain and is really
a straight-A-grade student and gifted child.

The Eighth Stumbling Block of Academic Failure

Escapism: Seeking Refuge from the Pain of Inadequacy

The eighth stumbling block students encounter is the constant feeling of inadequacy that permeates their every academic endeavor. Students study for hours, but they can't read fast enough, write fast enough, or memorize fast enough. Students can't seem to catch up. The "Academic Pressure Cooker" is unremitting: Voluminous academic facts, essays, research papers, projects, and tests. Students seek relief from the "Academic Pressure Cooker" and the "Pain of Inadequacy" by escaping into mind-numbing activities: TV, movies, internet, mp3, video and computer game addictions, shopping addiction, chain smoking and caffeine addiction, overeating and obesity, dangerous drugs, college binge-drinking, gambling, promiscuous sex, teenage pregnancy, and pornography.

Spencer has a great arm and can hit a home run. He is almost thirteen years of age. He spends his weekly allowance on pornographic magazines. Blonde, brunette, and redhead pin-ups occupy every inch of the wall in his cluttered bedroom. He likes them all and doesn't play favorites. Every month, like clockwork, he changes the naked girly photos. He has great time management and organizational skills, except when it comes to his schoolwork.

He attends an elite boys' private school. He is barely passing and surviving with D grades. He is stubborn, argumentative, and depressed. The clueless psychiatrist (who has a clue) is going to label him with A.D.H.D., and prescribe Ritalin. His parents don't want to put him on psychotropic drugs, a dangerous crutch with serious side effects.

Spencer is Raging and Acting Out

When Spencer misbehaves in school, he reports to the principal's office and is placed on detention. Detention is a form of punishment that requires that a student spend extra time in school by sitting in a room with no amenities. The first level of punishment is detention, the second level of punishment is suspension, and the third and final punishment is expulsion.

Spencer thinks school is a waste of his time because he wants to be a baseball player. I think that he can be both a great scholar and a great baseball player. He decides to give me a chance. I was hired for two reasons. The first reason is that I can transform Spencer into a Straight-A-Grade student with the new learning technology, SMARTGRADES Processing Tools. The second reason is that I am attractive and look like one of those pin-up playmates on his bedroom wall, and this gives me an advantage. He just might pay attention to me and listen to what I have to say to him.

I know from day one that there is nothing whatsoever wrong with Spencer's brain, and for three very good reasons: First, Spencer's brain is the most powerful biological machine in the world. Second, Spencer does not have "time to learn." Third, Spencer does not have learning tools to "learn and process" academic material.

Spencer fell behind and can't catch up. Spencer is floundering. Spencer is failing. Spencer has become disconnected. Spencer has become depressed. Spencer has become distracted. Spencer has become disgruntled. Spencer has become blocked. Spencer has shutdown. He does not know why he is floundering and failing and neither do his parents and teachers. They are completely clueless. If a child is failing, there must be something wrong with the child.

His parents want to know, "What is wrong with Spencer?"

Most Students Are Surviving, But Not Thriving

His teachers want to know, "What is wrong with Spencer?" The clueless psychiatrist is the only professional who thinks he has a clue, "He has A.D.H.D., "the incurable brain disorder."

Q1: "Are you inattentive (can't focus)?"
Q2: "Are you impulsive (acts out)?"
Q3: "Are you hyperactive (can't sit still)?"

The clueless psychiatrist thinks that he can fix Spencer's emotional and academic problems with some Ritalin. We will never know the actual statistics of just how many bright, brainy, and beautiful children are misdiagnosed with A.D.H.D. Many hospitals have opened a special psychiatric wing to treat the rising epidemic of A.D.H.D. Adding insult to injury, the treatment plan is to misdiagnose children with A.D.H.D., and put children on psychotropic drugs, a dangerous crutch with serious side effects, and place their powerful brains into virtual wheelchairs. As long as students fall behind, flounder, fail, and fall through the cracks of the malfunctioning school system, and parents and educators refuse to take responsibility for their part in a student's downfall, then this tragedy will continue. It bears repeating right here, ad nauseum, that: Children cannot raise themselves. If a child is failing, it is never the child's fault.

Educators need to make sure that their third-grade students have learning tools before they start overloading them with unreasonable school assignments with no realistic-time allotments and no detailed step-by-step instructions, and ask them to cram hundreds of academic facts into their mind and regurgitate them onto an abusive (tricky) "Hotdog" test.

Once again, I have my work cut out for me, because Spencer needs a complete academic overhaul. Here is the game plan that transforms Spencer into an A-grade student:

YOUR STUDY ROOM IS UNDER NEW MANAGEMENT
Grade **A** Students are M**A**DE not Born

ENERGIZE
ORGANIZE
PRIORITIZE

Step 1. New School Notebooks
SMARTGrades School Notebooks, p. 56 and p. 140.

Step 2. 10 Step SMARTGRADES Processing Tools
(**EVERY DAY AN EASY A**, p. 56)

Step 3. Rebuild Self-Esteem and Repair Broken Wings
Integration Therapy for Intrapersonal Growth, Development, and Maturity (*Integration Therapy Modality*).

Step 4. Parent Empowerment
Parenting Skills and Strategies for Academic Success
(*Your Study Room Is Under New Management,* p. 56)

Step 5. Eat for the Energy to Learn
It takes tremendous energy to read, write, and test. Students need fiber-rich meals with fresh fruits and vegetables for ENERGY.

Step 6. New Study Room
The first week is spent cleaning Spencer's bedroom to transform it into an efficient and effective study room.

Spencer's Self-Talk Self-Esteem Affirmation
Spencer looks at himself in the mirror and learns self-talk:

"I love you Spencer. I will do everything in my power to help you to achieve your dreams. My dream is to become a baseball player. Everything else that I say to myself is just NOISE."

Spencer's Study Desk and Chair
Spencer has a new modern desk that is equipped to hold a computer and a printer. Spencer needs a comfortable chair to be able to sit for hours while he prepares his homework, research papers, and gets ready to take a test.

Spencer's Bulletin Board
Spencer's academic achievements are showcased. As soon as Spencer earns an A grade, I hang the A grade on the bulletin board and make a big fuss.

Spencer's Bookcase
First Shelf: School Textbooks and Notebooks
Second Shelf: Self-Help Reference Books
Third Shelf: Old School Papers
Fourth Shelf: Pornographic Magazines

Spencer's Book Bag
Spencer forgets (he is disconnected, depressed, and distracted) to bring his book bag to school and sometimes he forgets to bring his book bag home. At the bottom of his book bag are crumpled pieces of paper that need to be filed.

Spencer's SMARTGRADES School Notebooks
Spencer receives color-coded, lightweight, fuss-free, instant organization SMARTGRADES school notebooks. In less than ten seconds, Spencer can file his handouts, homework assignments, and tests.

Spencer's Book Bag: New Pencil Case
5 Pens
5 Pencils
5 Highlighters
1 Sharpener
2 Erasers

Spencer's Academic Planner
Spencer does not know how to use a homework planner. He writes down his homework assignments on scraps of paper. Spencer's homework gets done only if he can locate his scrap of paper with the homework assignment.

Spencer's Healthy Eating Habits
Spencer goes to school on an empty stomach. Spencer likes to eat greasy fast food for dinner. He is overweight and needs to develop healthy eating habits, namely, fresh fruits, steamed vegetables, and whole grains. He needs to cut out caffeinated soda before he goes to bed.

Spencer's Fast Food Diet
Monday: Take-out burgers, fries, and soda
Tuesday: Take-out chinese and soda
Wednesday: Take-out pizza and soda
Thursday: Take-out tacos and soda
Friday: Take-out frankfurters and soda

Spencer did not have to slowly climb the ladder of success and show improvement from a D to a C, and then to a B grade. As a result of the new learning technology, SMARTGRADES Processing Tools, Spencer earned an A grade on the very next test.

New Learning Technology: SMARTGRADES Processing Tools
Step 1. Estimation Tool
Step 2. Divide and Conquer Tool
Step 3. Active-Reading Tool
Step 4. Extraction Tool
Step 5. Condensation Tool
Step 6. Association Tool
Step 7. Test-Review Note Tool
Step 8. Conversion Tool
Step 9. Visualization Tool
Step 10. Self-Testing Tool
EVERY DAY AN EASY A, Appendix G).

What is most astonishing to everyone, including Spencer, is that he earned a 98 on his history test, a 95 on his science test, and a 90 on his Latin exam.

If the truth be told, Spencer is a gifted child. There was nothing whatsoever wrong with Spencer's brain. He earned grades that were higher than Robert, the official class nerd.

I make it clear to his parents that Spencer takes his exams without me by his side. When he earned a 98 on his exam, Spencer can take full credit for his achievement. He is empowered with learning tools, SMARTGRADES Processing Tools, to achieve academic success. Spencer has a bright academic future ahead of him.

Spencer's brain had been misdiagnosed with A.D.H.D., which placed his powerful brain into a virtual wheelchair for life. Spencer does not have an "incurable brain disorder." Spencer does not have learning deficits. Spencer does not have learning disabilities. Spencer's powerful brain was taken out of the virtual wheelchair and set free.

Spencer's self-esteem diminishes with each and every person in his life who finds fault with him and makes him the fall guy for his academic failure. Spencer had internalized the blame. His self-talk was, "I am stupid!"

Guidance counselors think that I am a miracle worker and want to know the secret to my success. As you can see from reading this book, the secrets to my success are now public record. My students earn A grades and outperform the top students in the class, and Spencer is a prototypical example.

Let's Recap: What Really Happened to M.V.P. Spencer?
(Let's replay my favorite a game of "connect the dots")

1. Brain Power: The human brain is the most powerful biological machine in the world. The brain does not come with an instruction manual and Spencer does not know how to use it.

2. The Second Universal Gold Standard of Education: Children cannot raise themselves. If a child is failing, it is never the child's fault.

3. Spencer is enrolled in a malfunctioning "Quantity Over Quality Curriculum-Driven American Education System."

4. Teaching and learning are sacrificed to push the curriculum forward at a frenetic pace to meet the goals dictated by the "Higher Standards."

5. Parents are asked to fill in the gaps (gigantic potholes).

6. Spencer does not have "time to learn" or learning tools to "learn and process" academic material.

7. Academic Game 1: In the first week of school, Spencer falls behind and starts playing catch up.

8. Spencer falls behind, flounders, and fails. One bad grade hurts and is painful.

9. Spencer has become disconnected, depressed, distracted, disgruntled, and disobedient. Spencer has become blocked.

> 10. Spencer suffers from the "Pain of Inadequacy" and seeks relief in the mind-numbing escape of pornography.

11. Spencer is raging and acting out. He gets weekly detentions. The clueless educator adds insult to injury with more pain, humiliation, and punishment.

12. The clueless psychiatrist (with a clue) adds insult to injury by misdiagnosing Spencer with A.D.H.D. The psychiatrist asks Spencer's parents three questions:

Q1: Is he inattentive? (can't focus)   Disconnected, Depressed, Distracted, and Blocked

Q2: Is is impulsive? (acts out)   Rages, Acts Out, Disgruntled

Q3: Is he hyperactive? (can't sit still)   Escapism

13. Spencer does not have learning deficits, learning disabilities, or A.D.H.D., the "incurable brain disorder."

> 14. Biology 101: Spencer is a child in "flight" because he does not have the learning tools to "fight."

Students Earn a Diploma, But Not an Education

16. Spencer needs three daily doses of love to feed his soul, "I love you and I am very proud of you." You don't find love, you create love. There is no such thing as too much love.

17. Spencer needs a quiet study space to do his schoolwork.

18. Spencer needs, color-coded notebooks, to keep him organized and an Academic Planner, to map out his day.

19. Spencer needs, SMARTGRADES Processing Tools, to "learn and process" voluminous academic material.

20. Spencer needs a daily reward system to stay motivated.

21. Spencer needs a bulletin board to hang up his A grades as a constant reminder that he is an excellent student.

22. Spencer needs a regular bedtime for the energy to learn.

23. Spencer is an A student and won M.V.P. for baseball.

24. Spencer still needs "time to learn."

Reinventing the American Education System
If I were a farmer and 50% of my tomatoes were not growing properly, would I find fault with the tomato seeds? I would look at my planting procedures and make the necessary changes in the soil, water, fertilizer, and sunlight that would ensure a bountiful crop of beautiful, delicious, and nutritious tomatoes. If 50% of my students were dropping out of high school (e.g., New York City), I would make the changes necessary in the school system for these kids (seeds) to grow, develop, and mature properly. Q: When will America's children become America's first priority?

Ivy League Students in Need of Academic Help

When I receive a call to help a student at an Ivy League university, the problem is the same problem as in any other school in the country, the "Quantity Over Quality Curriculum-Driven American Education System." These cream-of-the-crop students fall behind, can't catch up, and do not have "time to learn" or learning tools to "learn and process" voluminous academic material. These students will tell me that they are not as smart as the smartest students in their class. They also feel that something is wrong with them. These students suffer from the "The Pain of Inadequacy." The fault never lies within the school system because they are in the best schools in the country.

Elite Private and Public Schools Have Unpublished Dropouts

In the cream-of-the-crop private and public schools, students have to pass a difficult test to gain admission.
Q: How is it possible that elite schools have students who are dropping out? These students don't really drop out of school; instead, they fall behind, flounder, fail, and quietly change schools. That is why is seems as if elite schools do not have dropouts--but they do--and for the same reasons that other schools have dropouts, "The Fifteen Stumbling Blocks of Academic Failure." Elite private and public schools have an unpublished population of students who drop out and change schools.

America's Brightest Minds: The Pain of Inadequacy

These gifted and talented students have developed feelings of inadequacy and have begun to belittle themselves without the help of a parent, teacher, or psychiatrist, "I am not as smart as I thought I was." In fact, their parents keep reminding them of how smart they used to be, and how they should get back on the bicycle and ride after taking a spill.

Students Earn a Diploma, But Not an Education

But the damage has been done to their minds, hearts, and spirits because of a multiple-choice hotdog exam that more than half of the class failed. Parents are often relieved to hear that more than half of the class has failed the test, because then it was probably a "Hotdog" test that was too hard (unfair).

Pain of Inadequacy, Escapism, and Distractions
Students suffering senselessly from the "Pain of Inadequacy," inflicted by the "Academic Pressure Cooker," will seek refuge in mind-numbing escapes: TV, movies, internet, mp3 players, video and computer game addictions, shopping addiction, chain smoking and caffeine addiction, overeating and obesity, dangerous drugs and college binge drinking, promiscuous sex, teenage pregnancy, and pornography.

The Mental Health Clinic: Academic Insanity
It is absurd to tell students to seek counseling for their psychological problems, e.g., anxiety, stress, depression, and suicidal thoughts, especially when their emotional problems are in part, exacerbated by a malfunctioning "Quantity Over Quality Curricum-Driven American Education System" that is riddled with "Academic Insanity."

Educators ask students to play four academic games:
Academic Game 1. It only takes the first week of school to fall behind and start playing the game of catch up

Academic Game 2. The "Academic Pressure Cooker" of, "Read, Cram, Regurgitate, and Test"

Academic Game 3. Abusive (tricky) "Hotdog" exams

Academic Game 4. Students learn how to cut corners and cheat to pass, survive, and graduate

Quantity Over Quality Curriculum-Driven Education System

Students suffer from the "Pain of Inadequacy":

Q1: "Why don't I have time to read my textbooks, write my papers, and prepare to take my tests?"

Q2: Why can't I cram voluminous academic facts into my mind and regurgitate the facts onto a test in an hour?

Q3: "Why am I anxious, stressed, depressed, and suicidal?"

Q4: "How come I don't remember the facts two weeks after a test?"

Q5: "I not as smart as I thought I was! "What is wrong with me?"

Let's Recap: Educators Cheat Students Out of an Education:
1. No time for in-depth comprehension of academic material
2. No learning tools for long-term retention
3. No time for continuous feedback of strengths and weaknesses for mastery of the academic material
4. Abusive "Hotdog" exams that do not measure education
5. Students suffer the "Pain of Inadequacy"
6. Students graduate bearing the "Scars of Incompetence"
7. Students earn a diploma but not an education

The Rising Rate of College Binge-Drinking

College binge-drinking is the number one problem on college campuses across the country. In part, college binge-drinking is a mind-numbing escape from the "Pain of Inadequacy." Distinguished, but clueless college administrators are still perplexed by the problem. They don't understand the problem, so they can't solve or resolve the problem. This book will shed some light on the problem of college binge-drinking and make a concerted attempt to explain the problem and solve and resolve the problem once and for all.

Academic Insanity: Amethyst Initiative, August 2008

With all due respect: One hundred distinguished, but clueless college professors, want to see the legal drinking age lowered to eighteen from twenty-one years of age. They think that this will change the biggest social problem on college campuses: College binge-drinking. These clueless college professors are unable to connect the dots ... that define the problem of college binge-drinking:

Q: Do you solve overspending by giving shoppers more credit cards? No.

Q: Do you solve obesity by giving overeaters more greasy fast food? No.

Q: Do you give sexual addicts more pornography and sex toys? No.

Q: Do you solve the college binge-drinking problem by lowering the drinking age to eighteen and giving immature, anxious, stressed, and depressed young adults a license to drink and drive? No.

Q: Why do college students engage in college binge-drinking?

Let's look at the problem and try to connect most of the dots. Like most real-world problems, there are no quick fixes and problems are composed of compound and complex equations. In the real world, every problem under the sun is a problem of nature. There are only imperfect solutions to imperfect problems.

1. "Pain of Inadequacy": Indelible wounds of imperfect childhoods

2. "Pain of Inadequacy": Students find a mind-numbing escape from the "Academic Pressure Cooker" by drinking alcohol.

3. High School Habit: Students begin experimenting with smoking, drugs, alcohol, and sex in high school.

4. Party Culture: A real party needs an alcoholic beverage.

5. Male Bonding Ritual: The lowering of inhibitions, the flow of real emotional intimacy and conversation (more difficult for men than it is for women).

6. Copycat of adult behavior

> Here is the complex and compound equation:
> "Pain of Inadequacy" + High School Habit + Party Culture + Male Bonding Ritual + Copycat = College-Binge Drinking

To solve the problem of college binge-drinking, educators should ask incoming freshman to sign a form that states that they have been informed of the university policy on college binge-drinking:

> The Official University Policy on College-Binge Drinking
> During your four years at our university, we will show zero tolerance for college-binge drinking. Any college student enrolled in our school who is found imbibing alcohol and intoxicated anywhere on our campus or off-campus will be expelled from school and subject to a $10,000 fine and penalty.
>
> Sign here: _____

I am certain that statisticians will argue that deterrents don't work in every case. This is true. In the real world, there are no perfect solutions to imperfect problems. In the real world, there are only imperfect solutions to imperfect problems. This imperfect solution of a $10,000 fine and penalty, and expulsion from school, will lessen the college binge-drinking problem on college campuses across the country and save the lives of victims: Intoxicated college students and injured bystanders.

I can't help thinking — how would a lazy, beer-drinking, chain-smoking, pot-bellied alcoholic vote? I bet you could not find even one alcoholic, sober or plastered out of his mind, who would vote to give himself the right to drink at age eighteen, because even he knows that alcohol has a mind of its own.

Here are the binge-drinking conundrums that need analysis:
- The student's mind is at the mercy of the alcohol.
- There is no such thing as thinking, binge-drinking alcohol, and driving responsibly.

Q: What is the rationalization of these distinguished, but clueless college professors? Their website is: amethystinitiative.org.

They think that if an eighteen year old can join the military and die for his country, then he is mature enough to drink alcohol. If the truth be told, asking men in the prime of life to die for their country should also be prohibited. War as a means of solving social problems is another "human animal" behavior that should be outlawed, just like pissing in public. Most men don't mature emotionally until age forty. Age forty sounds like the right age to allow men to drink alcohol responsibly. Moreover, when men reach the ripe old age of sixty-five, they should be voluntarily recruited into the American army, and spend the final years of their life taking their heart medication and fighting the "Evil Ones." If the truth be told, young men in the prime of life "sit on their asses" in American prisons and should be rehabilitated into "fighting dogs" and serve the country, and let loose on the Taliban.

Here is another college-binge drinking conundrum:
With all due respect: These distinguished, but clueless college professors have not had any alcohol, and they still can't think straight Q: What is their excuse?

Q: Do these distinguished professors really want to be driven off the road and into a ditch by a stressed-out college student on anti-depressants, who is plastered out of his mind, because his dream was to go to Harvard, but he only got into Yale because of an unfair tricky test question, and spent his evening drowning out his sorrow ("Pain of Inadequacy") in alcohol?

Here are two more college-binge drinking conundrums worthy of analysis. Distinguished, but clueless professors can't control the college binge-drinking problem on their own campuses.

Q: Are they really in a position to take a stand on an issue that will effect the rest of society?

Q: Do they want to open the alcoholic flood gates and let loose their college binge-drinking problem on the rest of society?

These college professors should keep their college binge-drinking problem on their college campuses, where it belongs, and try to solve the problem by offering students a diploma and an education: In-depth comprehension, long-term retention, and mastery of the academic material. In addition, students need required business skills to earn a living, so that they can pay off their astronomical school loans. Consequently, students will then understand why they want to drink themselves under the table and onto the floor and into an early grave: "How the HELL am I ever going to pay off my astronomical school loans?"

Let's Recap: Escapism: Seeking Relief from the "Pain of Inadequacy" (Let's replay my favorite game of "connect the dots")
1. Students are enrolled in a malfunctioning "Quantity Over Quality, Curriculum-Driven American Education System."

2. Teaching and learning are sacrificed to push the curriculum forward to meet the goals dictated by the "Higher Standards."

3. Parents are asked to fill in the gaps (gigantic potholes).

4. **Academic Game One:** It only takes the first week of school for students to fall behind and start playing catch up.

5. Students study for hours, but do not have "time to learn" or learning tools to "learn and process" voluminous academic facts for instant recognition and recall on hotdog tests.

6. **Academic Game Two:** Students are in an "Academic Pressure Cooker." Every day, they have to play the academic game of, "Read, Cram, Regurgitate, and Test" to pass, survive, and graduate from a malfunctioning education system.

7. **Academic Game Three:** Students are asked to cram voluminous facts into their mind with meager comprehension, no learning tools, and for short-term retention and regurgitate them in an hour under psychological duress and a stopwatch.

8. During a hotdog test, all students are anxious and stressed. Every student draws at least one blank. Most students draw more than one blank. The faulty regurgitation of academic facts destroys students' emotional health and American dream.

9. Hotdog exams are an exercise in futility, because two weeks later, most of the academic facts disappear into a black hole in the mind and vanish into thin air. Students are uneducated.

10. Students' self-esteem plummets because they think that it is their fault that they draw blanks and perform poorly. Their self talk is, "I am not as smart as I thought I was!"

11. Students suffer from the "Pain of Inadequacy." Students' self-talk is: What is wrong with me? Why don't I have time to read textbooks, write papers, and prepare to take tests?

12. Students have become anxious, stressed, and depressed.

13. Students visit the mental health clinic for their anxiety, "bouts of depression," clinical depression, and suicidal thinking.

14. To treat emotional problems, psychiatrists hand out psychotropic drugs, a dangerous crutch with serious side effects, like happy-go-lucky Halloween candy.

15. Educators cut corners and cheat students out of an education: No time for in-depth comprehension, long-term retention, and mastery of the academic material.

16. **Academic Game Four:** In return, students also learn how to cut corners and cheat to pass, survive, and graduate.

17. Escapism and Distractions: Students seek relief from the "Pain of Inadequacy," inflicted by the "Academic Pressure Cooker" in mind-numbing escapes: TV, movies, internet, mp3, video and computer game addictions, shopping addiction, chain smoking and caffeine addiction, overeating and obesity, dangerous drugs, college binge-drinking, gambling, promiscuous sex, teenage pregnancy, and pornography.

18. Students graduate bearing the "Scars of Incompetence" because there is no time for continuous feedback of strengths and weaknesses, and no mastery of the academic material.

19. Here's a C grade. Students earn a diploma, but not an education.

Students Earn a Diploma, But Not an Education

College Binge-Drinking Update
February 9, 2009
Princeton Says 13 Intoxicated Students Taken to Hospital
"Princeton University officials said 13 intoxicated students were taken to a hospital during an initiation weekend for off-campus eating clubs." (Associated Press, myfoxphilly.com, February 9, 2009).

October 29, 2009 (largest arrest ever made for underage drinking)
103 Students from Sacred Heart and Fairfield College Arrested
"65 fake driver's licenses and other phony IDs were confiscated" (John Burgeson, Connecticut Post, October 29, 2009).

Philip Markoff: Is His Downfall Really Incomprehensible?
One of America's Brightest Minds, Philip Markoff, is the 23-year-old suspended Boston University medical school student who is allegedly accused of robbery and murder. He is also known as a heavy drinker and gambler. When this story is looked at through the fractured lens of just another cutthroat (cold-blooded), binge-drinking college student who is abusive to women, his downfall comes into focus. Other out-of-control, college binge-drinking students, abuse women sexually, and kill innocent people.

Let's Recap: College Binge-Drinking and Violence
"Drinking to excess by college students contributes to 1,400 deaths, 500,000 injuries, and 70,000 cases of sexual assault and date rape each year" (NIAAA, 2008).

It is not uncommon to hear horror stories about male college students who dangerously dabble in drugs or gambling or of women college students who have become prostitutes to pay their college-tuition bills.
Updates:
- "21 U of Illinois Students Arrested for Dealing Drugs (5/2009)
- Drug Sting Nabs 75 Students at San Diego State U. (5/2008)

Phillip Markoff is innocent until proven guilty. The hard evidence against him is mounting: The handgun and matching bullets, duct tape and plastic ties, hotel cameras and e-mails, and interviews with men and women who have crossed his path. Markoff's e-mail address was "sexaddict5385." Based on the video-taped interview with the prostitute, Trisha Leffler, Markoff took her cash and underwear. If Markoff is found guilty of all charges, his motive for murder is a classic-textbook case. At first, he used the gun only to instill fear into his victims. In this case, it will probably be the prostitute, Trisha Leffler, who survived the robbery, who will put him behind bars (48 Hours, "Exclusive: Craigslist Victim Speaks Out," April 25, 2009).

Let's Make Some Hypothetical Unsubstantiated Assumptions:
1. **PAIN:** Childhood pain from parent's bitter divorce
2. **PAIN:** Did not really want to be a doctor, family pressure
3. **PAIN:** Did not really want to get married at age 23
4. **PAIN:** Academic Pressure Cooker, every day is a competition
5. **PAIN:** Astronomical medical school tuition loans and debt
6. **ESCAPISM** from pain: Drinking, gambling, and prostitution
7. As is often the case, disappointment, rage, pain, escapism from pain, and distractions spiral out of control: Food, shopping, drugs, alcohol, gambling, or sex addiction. Concurrently, he was out of control, having found mind-numbing escapes from his emotional pain in drinking, gambling, and sex; and he owned a handgun to be able to exercise a modicum of control. If found guilty, Phillip Markoff, one of America's Brightest Minds, may very well become the next fallen academic star.

Escapism and Distractions: Students seeking refuge in mind-numbing activities from the "Pain of Inadequacy," inflicted by the "Academic Pressure Cooker," make up the eighth stumbling block that contributes to the downward spiral of the malfunctioning American education system.

#1 Poetry Website for School Projects

The Greatest Poems Ever Written on Extraordinary Events
www.WorldFamousPoems.com

Poetry Analysis: The Prescription-Drug Pushers

1. Patients seek a quick fix and instant relief. Grieving the loss of a loved one can take three years of tears.

2. Life is a bumpy road of setbacks, delays, detours, and disappointments and patients need to learn how to "FEEL to HEAL" (grieve their losses) as well as life strategies to climb over life's inevitable obstacle course.

3. Doctors hand out psychotropic drugs to heal emotional pain as if they are handing out happy-go-lucky Halloween candy.

4. Psychotropic drugs, a dangerous crutch with serious side effects, do not heal a patient's emotional pain.

5. The patient is now suffering from emotional pain and the adverse side effects of the psychotropic drugs.

6. Patients in emotional pain think that if they pop the pills, they will heal their pain. Patients in emotional pain, keep popping the vacuous pills, overdose, and die, or they use the pills to commit suicide.

A poem about the broken American psychiatric system

The Prescription-Drug Pushers

disappointment (emotional pain)

disconnection (flight from pain)

depression (internalization of pain)

distraction (escape from pain)

diagnosis (brain scan)

disorder (label)

deficits (condition)

drugs (mask the pain)

dangerous crutch with side effects

disintegration (emotional pain and side effects)

drugs (to treat the side effects of drugs)

death (Michael Jackson is a recent fatality)

By Sharon Esther Lampert

More than any other time in history,
mankind faces a crossroads.
One path leads to despair and utter hopelessness.
The other, to total extinction.
Let us pray we have the wisdom to choose correctly.

Woody Allen
My Speech to the Graduates

See Hear Kid,
Tragically in This World,
They Many Times Break You Down,
Before They Sometimes Build You Up.

Sharon Esther Lampert
Poet, Philosopher, Paladin of Education

Meet Samantha
She does not have an incurable brain disorder.
She has a powerful brain and is a gifted child.
She masters the **SMARTGRADES** Processing Tools
and is back on track for academic success.

The Ninth Stumbling Block of Academic Failure

The Downward Spiral of Academic Failure

The ninth stumbling block students encounter is the "Downward Spiral of Academic Failure." Most students are surviving, but not thriving. A bad grade hurts. Failure is painful. Students have become anxious, stressed, disconnected, depressed, distracted, and disgruntled. Some students have become blocked. Some students have shutdown. Some students will change schools, choose homeschooling, or drop out. In some cases, psychiatrists misdiagnose students with learning deficits, learning disabilities, and A. D. H. D. Born in perfect health, the brain, the most powerful biological machine in the world, is placed into a virtual wheelchair for life. These students will not be able to grow, develop, and mature properly because they internalize the label, A. D. H. D., and their self-talk is, "I can't do this, and I can't do that, because I have A.D.H.D., the incurable brain disorder"

Samantha wants to become a veterinarian and save animals. She is eleven years old. She has a dog-named Bubbles who only wears designer duds. She loves to read whodunit novels and is good at solving the mystery before the ending is revealed.

She lives in the penthouse apartment on Fifth Avenue and has a bedroom window looking out over Central Park. She has a maid who cleans her room, cooks her meals, and prepares her Juicy-designer wardrobe for school. She attends an elite private school. She is dropped off and picked up from school in a black stretch limousine. She has a private tutor who comes to her home and helps her with her daily homework assignments.

Samantha has a staff on hand to help her with each and every task, including lugging her book bag to and from school. Many parenting duties are delegated to the live-in help.

Samantha's Report Card is littered with C and D grades. She is a poor test-taker. Samantha is the one who has to go to school and take her exams. Test taking is one of the tasks in life that cannot be delegated to her housekeeper, driver, or tutor.

Last year, Samantha took a battery of psychological tests. The test results concluded that Samantha had "learning deficits." Samantha was diagnosed with A.D.H.D., the "incurable brain disorder" and is taking Ritalin. These psychological tests can cost between 2500-5000 dollars. **[Please note: The test results will never conclude that your child does not have the required learning tools to achieve academic success.]** Moreover, your child may not be able to write because your child was not taught how to write, not because your child has "learning deficits." College students are required to take remedial English courses after a K-12 education.

As is usually the case, I have my work cut out for me. Samantha's brain has been placed into a virtual wheelchair for life. I know I can turn the game around and take her brain out of the virtual wheelchair and give her back her powerful brain and a bright academic future. Samantha is a another senseless casualty of a malfunctioning American education system and a broken American psychiatric system because educators and psychiatrists find fault with the child and blame the child for her academic failure, as follows:

Q: "What is wrong with Samantha?"

Q: Why can't Samantha learn how to organize the daily assault of five handouts and five homework assignments from five different teachers? What is wrong with Samantha?

Q: Why can't Samantha learn how to manage her time to read the textbooks, write the papers, and prepare to take the tests? What is wrong with Samantha?

Q: Why can't Samantha cram one-hundred academic facts into her brain and regurgitate them onto a stressful time-sensitive abusive hotdog test? What is wrong with Samantha?

Let's Recap: The only professional who has a clue is the clueless psychiatrist who misdiagnosed her with A. D. H. D., the "incurable brain disorder." Many of my students have been misdiagnosed with A. D. H. D. These growing children will not be able to develop properly as the label of A. D. H. D. undermines their self-esteem, self-confidence, and self-reliance. Their self-talk is "I can't do this and I can't do that, because I have A. D. H. D., an incurable brain disorder."

As is usually the case, Samantha fell behind, floundered, and failed because she does not have "time to learn" and learning tools to "learn and process" voluminous academic material to achieve academic success.

As for Samantha, I recommend the following six academic interventions to transform her into an A-grade student:

YOUR STUDY ROOM IS UNDER NEW MANAGEMENT

Grade **A** Students are M**A**DE not Born

Step 1. New Study Room (Appendix G)

Step 2. New School Notebooks
SMARTGRADES School Notebooks, p. 56 and p. 140.

Step 3. New Learning Tools for Self-Reliant and Life-Long Learners
SMARTGRADES Processing Tools: New Learning Technology
Every Student Earns an A Grade on the Very Next Test
(*EVERY DAY AN EASY A*, p. 56).

Step 4. Rebuild Self-Esteem and Repair Broken Wings
Integration Therapy for Intrapersonal Growth, Development, and Maturity (*Integration Therapy Modality*).

Step 5. Parent Empowerment
Parenting Skills and Strategies for Academic Success
(*How to Parent for Academic Success*, p. 56).

Step 6. Eat for Energy to Learn
It takes tremendous energy to read, write, and test. Students need fiber-rich meals with fresh fruits and vegetables for ENERGY!

Reinventing the American Education System

It bears repeating right here, ad nauseam, and as many times as is necessary throughout this book, until the message is internalized (processed for long-term retention) into the hearts, minds, and spirits of parents, educators, psychiatrists, and even politicians, and if need be, written into, The Constitution of the United States of America, that:

The Second Universal Gold Standard of Education

Children Cannot Raise Themselves
If a Child is Failing, It Is Never the Child's Fault

Students' Self-Talk

John
Q: Why can't I read fast enough? What is wrong with me?

Roberta
Q: Why don't I understand what I am reading? What is wrong with me?

Tom
Q: Why can't I write fast enough? What is wrong with me?

Harry
Q: Why do I make the same writing mistakes over and over again? I don't know how to proofread my paper. What is wrong with me?

Lucy
Q: Why can't I memorize one-hundred academic facts for instant recognition and recall and regurgitate them onto a two-hour hotdog exam? What is wrong with me?

Tiffany
Q: Why can't I remember any of the academic material two weeks after the test? What is wrong with me?

Steven
Q: Why am I anxious, stressed, and depressed? What is wrong with me?

Samantha
Q: Why was I labeled with A.D.H.D., the "incurable brain disorder," that put my powerful brain, the greatest biological machine in the world, into a virtual wheelchair for life?

Teachers' Self-Talk

Q: Why don't I ever have time to cover the curriculum?

Q: Why don't I have time to teach the academic material for in-depth comprehension?

Q: Why don't I have time to read papers and correct the writing errors: Spelling, grammar, and punctuation?

Q: Why don't I have time to answer questions in class?

Q: Why don't I have time for continuous feedback of strengths and weaknesses, so that a student can master the material?

Most Students Are Surviving, But Not Thriving

Parents' Self-Talk

Get a Clue: Nurture and Cultivate Brain Power
Q: When will educators understand that knowledge is brain food and that students come to school to eat facts and build their brain muscles? Students cannot stuff a whole sandwich into their mouth. They have to take small bites and chew, chew, chew, and digest. Learning requires small amounts of information that have to be chewed and digested for In-depth comprehension, long-term retention and academic mastery of the material, for students to become educated.
Q: What is wrong with them?

Get a Clue: Set New Education Priorities
Q: When will educators put students first, the learning tools second, in-depth comprehension third, and the curriculum last?
Q: What is wrong with them?
Priority 1. How Do You Nurture and Cultivate Brain Power?
Priority 2. How Does Learning Take Place?
Priority 3. Learning Tools to Process Academic Material
Priority 4. In-Depth Comprehension
Priority 5. The Lost Art of the Craft of Writing
Priority 6. Mastery of the Academic Material

Get a Clue: In-Depth Comprehension
Q: When will educators understand that learning requires time for in-depth comprehension? Q: What is wrong with them?

Get a Clue: Learning Tools for Long-Term Retention
Q: When will educators understand that students need learning tools to process academic information for instant recognition and recall on abusive (tricky) hotdog exams.

Get a Clue: The Learning Environment
Q: When will educators create a learning environment that is conducive to the love of learning that is free of anxiety, stress, depression, and suicide? Q: What is wrong with them?

Get a Clue: Time to Get Real
Q: When will educators understand that it takes time to do something well. If you want to achieve excellence, you have to put time into it. The learning curve is steep. Learning takes time. Teaching is a time-intensive activity. Learning is a time-intensive activity. Education is a time-intensive activity. Q: What is wrong with them?

Get a Clue: Develop The "Light From Within"
Q: When will educators understand that you have to educate the whole student: Mind, body, and spirit ("Light from Within").
Q: What is wrong with them?

Get a Clue: Abusive "Hotdog" Exams
Q: When will educators understand that the "Academic Pressure Cooker" of hotdog exams does not measure education. Q: What is wrong with them?

Q: When will educators understand that test scores have no value if students can't remember the academic facts two weeks after a test? Q: What is wrong with them?

Q: When will educators realize that even their top students don't process facts for long-term retention and don't remember most of the academic facts two weeks after the test. Q: What is wrong with them?

Get a Clue: The Maldevelopment of Right-Brain Abilities
Q: When will educators see that the most sensitive, creative, and imaginative children are the first children to be wounded? The "Academic Pressure Cooker" of "Read, Cram, Regurgitate, and Test," is a barbaric academic daily exercise that is destroying the lateral right-brain development of students. It is the right brain that has the ability for lateral thinking and thinking outside the box. It is the right brain that will find cures for Cancer, A.I.D.S., and "Academic Insanity."

Q: Why do they first slash the ARTS education budget?
Q: What is wrong with them?

Get a Clue: Measuring Academic Achievement
Q: When will educators understand that education can only be measured by in-depth comprehension, long-term retention, and mastery of the academic material. Q: What is wrong with them?

Author's Self-Talk:
When will educators stop the destruction of America's Brightest Minds? It bears repeating right here and again that:

> The Second Universal Gold Standard of Education
> Children Cannot Raise Themselves
> If a Child is Failing, It Is Never the Child's Fault

Diagnosing disconnected, depressed, distracted, disgruntled, and disobedient students who fall behind, flounder, and fail with learning deficits, learning disabilities, and A.D.H.D., the "incurable brain disorder" is the ninth stumbling block that contributes to the downward spiral of the malfunctioning American education system.

"To those of you who received honours, awards and distinctions, I say well done. And to the C students, I say you, too, can be president of the United States!"

President George W. Bush
43rd President

You know, a lot of people say this too,
if you're the smartest and the brightest,
we won't need affirmative action.
We can get rid of affirmative action.

They say this as if the whole country is
run by the smartest and the brightest.

I was in black schools and white schools,
so you can't fucken tell me shit, ok.

When you go to a class, there are five smart,
five dumb, and the rest are in the middle.
That's all America is, a nation in the middle.
A nation of B and C students. That's all the
fuck there is, a nation of B and C students.

Let's keep it fucken real:
A black C student can't run no-fuckin company.
A black C student can't even be the
manager of a Burger King.

Meanwhile, a white C student just happens to be
the president of the United States of America.

Chris Rock

"I am not as smart as I thought I was!"

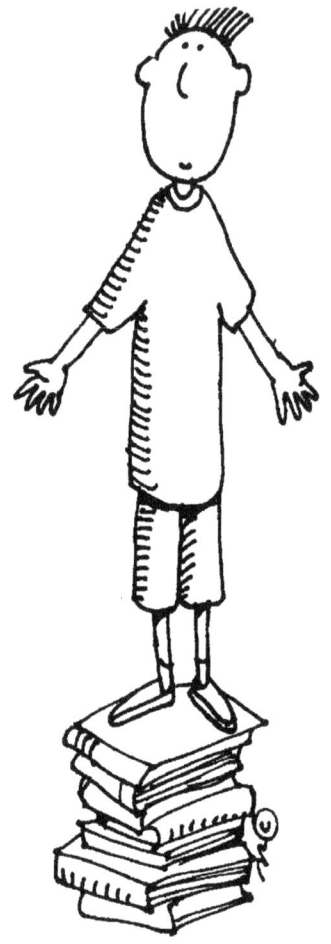

Meet Jonathan
Expulsion, Resurrection, Reincarnation
He has a powerful brain and is a gifted child.

The Tenth Stumbling Block of Academic Failure

The War Zone: Few Heroes, Heavy Casualties, and Senseless Fatalities

The tenth stumbling block students encounter is that their school resembles a "War Zone" with a few heroes, heavy casualties, and senseless fatalities. Students have not learned how to achieve academic success in school, or in life. Students have only learned how to survive the malfunctioning American education system. Students suffer from the "Pain of Inadequacy" and bear the "Scars of Incompetence." The students go into the education system, but education does not go into students. Every student has a horror story to tell about an injustice suffered.

Jonathan loves loud rock music and speedy race cars. He is fifteen years old. He is tall and handsome with a wry smile and a mischievous laugh. He has a comic book collection that is the envy of his friends. He loves to read the funnies in the newspaper. He finds the rest of the paper depressing and wonders why his teacher makes the class read the front page of the newspaper every morning. The front page of the newspaper puts him in a bad mood. Is the teacher going to ruin his good mood every day of the week?

Jonathan attended an all boys' elite private school. He was expelled for attacking another student with the cork screw from his mother's lacquered Chinese wine-bottle opener. He has three viable options: Change schools, home schooling, or earn a G.E.D. and go to college. The private schools won't admit him. His parents are concerned that the public school learning environment will only exacerbate his rage and violent outbursts.

All is not lost. Homeschooling and earning his G.E.D. are the best and only viable options. He will then be able to apply to a community college, earn a college degree and get a decent job.

His parents have invested more than, $500,000 in his K-12 private school education, and have received little to no return on their financial investment:

• $35,000 dollars for the annual private school tuition payment.

Their investment in Jonathan's education was compounded by psychological tests, treatment, and tutoring services, as follows:

• Academic Intervention: $ 20,000 for Regular Tutoring Services
Regular tutors do not teach students learning tools required for academic success in school.

• Academic Intervention: $ 5,000 for Psychological Testing
These tests will NEVER return the result that your child does not have the learning tools to achieve academic success.

• Academic Intervention: $ 30,000 for Psychiatric Treatment
Psychiatrists do not teach learning tools for academic success. In some cases, psychiatrists misdiagnose children with a learning deficit, learning disability, or A.D.H.D., and prescribe psychotropic drugs, a crutch with dangerous side effects.

• Last but not least, his parents had to pay the medical bills of the student who was assaulted by their son. As is usually the case, I have my work cut out for me. Jonathan was expelled from school.

He fell behind, floundered, failed, and fell through the cracks of the, "Quantity Over Quality Curriculum-Driven Malfunctioning American Education System." I accept the challenge of preparing Jonathan for the G.E.D. As for Jonathan, I recommend the following six academic interventions:

YOUR STUDY ROOM IS UNDER NEW MANAGEMENT

Grade **A** Students are M**A**DE not Born
Website: www.everydayaneasya.com

ENERGIZE
ORGANIZE
PRIORITIZE

Step 1. New Study Room, p. 56

Step 2. New School Notebooks
SMARTGRADES School Notebooks, p. 56 and p. 140

Step 3. SMARTGRADES Study Skills
(**EVERY DAY AN EASY A**, p. 140.)

Step 4. Rebuild Self-Esteem and Repair Broken Wings
Integration Therapy for Intrapersonal Growth, Development, and Maturity (*Integration Therapy Modality*).

Step 5. Eat for the Energy to Learn
It takes tremendous energy to read, write, and test. Students need fiber-rich meals with fresh fruits and vegetables for ENERGY!

Students Earn a Diploma, But Not an Education

General Educational Development tests are a group of five tests which certify that the taker has American or Canadian high school level academic skills. The five tests that comprise the G.E.D. are: Writing, social studies, science, reading, and mathematics.

I have a large stuffed yellow pillow in the shape of the sun hanging in my office. I tell my students that the sun is always shining in my office. I promise students that I will transform them into A-grade students, and I always keep my promise. Jonathan is no exception to the rule. Jonathan is going to be an A-grade student.

Until the underlying emotional problems of depression, disconnection, and distraction are treated, Jonathan cannot get back on track for academic success. In this case, he was also raging and acting out.

Parents use a series of punishments that don't work because punishment humiliates a child who was already humiliated by failing a test after studying for hours. Punishment adds insult to injury, and the damage to the psyche of the child has life-long consequences.

Schools also use a series of punishments such as detention and suspension as warnings and then when warnings fail, expulsion is the final solution to the problem.

In many elite private schools in this country, there are brilliant students, some of, America's Brightest Minds, who are about to be expelled for misconduct, because of clueless parents and educators. Most parents are winging it, and have inadequate or abusive parenting tools. In addition, educators do not have psychological tools to rebuild the student's self-esteem and the learning tools to empower the student for academic success.

Using Intrapersonal-Integration Therapy, Johnathan learned how to develop his internal voice and begin an internal dialogue between his strengths and his weaknesses. The development of his inner voice is the emotional tool that will enable him able make decisions that are in his best interest. Of course, he also received, SMARTGRADES Processing Tools, for academic success.

SMARTGRADES Processing Tools
Step 1. Estimation Tool
Step 2. Divide and Conquer Tool
Step 3. Active-Reading Tool
Step 4. Extraction Tool
Step 5. Condensation Tool
Step 6. Association Tool
Step 7. Test-Review Note Tool
Step 8. Conversion Tool
Step 9. Visualization Tool
Step 10. Self-Testing Tool
(**EVERY DAY AN EASY A**, Appendix G)

In sum, Jonathan earned a G.E.D. and is a freshman in a community college. He is doing very well. School is all about "retrieving facts" from the teacher, textbook, and handouts and "returning facts" to the teacher in a written assignment, or on a test. Jonathan has learned how to play the academic game, "Read, Cram, Regurgitate, and Test." Jonathan is able to put his unruly past behind him. He understands that he is not to blame for his academic failure of the past, because he did not have, SMARTGRADES Processing Tools, to "learn and process" the academic material. He is one of the many senseless casualties of a malfunctioning American education system.

Q: What really happened to Jonathan before he was expelled from one of the best private schools in the country?

Jonathan's Downward Spiral of Expulsion

(Let's replay my favorite game of "connect the dots")

1. Brain Power: The human brain is the most powerful biological machine in the world. It does not come with an instruction manual and Jonathan does not know how to use it.

2. Educators are clueless as to "How Does Learning Take Place?" They do not know how to nurture and cultivate the awesome power of the human brain.

3. Jonathan is enrolled in the, Quantity Over Quality Curriculum-Driven Malfunctioning American Education System.

4. In the first week of school, Jonathan falls behind and can't catch up.

5. Jonathan studies for hours, but does not have "time to learn" or learning tools to "learn and process" voluminous academic facts.

6. Jonathan is floundering and fails a test. A bad grade feels like a punch in the face. Failure hurts and is painful.

7. Jonathan has become disconnected, depressed, distracted, and disgruntled, and disobedient.

8. Jonathan's teachers are aware that he has C grades but do not help him. The C grade is a warning sign that a student needs help A.S.A.P.

9. Jonathan's parents do not pay attention to his grades until the report card period and then become upset with him, when it is too late to help Jonathan make the changes required for academic success.

10. The advice, "Be a good boy and study harder" is inadequate advice. Jonathan studies for hours, but does not have learning tools, SMARTGRADES Processing Tools, for academic success.

11. Jonathan's next report card is littered with D grades. He is still not receiving help, namely, the learning tools to achieve academic success.

12. Jonathan is raging and acting out in class and at home. His parents, teacher, and psychiatrist want to know: "What is wrong with him?" Jonathan is criticized, blamed, and labeled. It is his fault that he is failing.

13. Jonathan does not have learning deficits, learning disabilities, or A.D.H.D., "the incurable brain disorder."

14. Jonathan is punished and is sent to detention once a week for acting out in class.

15. Jonathan is suspended for using a cork screw to attack another student. Jonathan is expelled from an elite private school.

16. Jonathan's parents are clueless. The educators are clueless. The clueless psychiatrist has a clue, A.D.H.D., "the incurable brain disorder."

Jonathan's Upward Spiral of Education

17. Jonathan's mother calls the learning specialist, Ms. Sugar. In three months, his self-esteem is rebuilt. In six months, he masters the, SMARTGRADES Processing Tools, and passes the G.E.D. exam. In one year, he is a college student with a transcript of A grades and is on the Dean's List.

18. Jonathan is back on track for a bright future filled with promise, purpose, passion, prosperity, and peace. Jonathan wants to be a surgeon. He has good hands. He was good with a cork screw, and perhaps he will be great with a doctor's scalpel.

Reinventing the American Education System

There are a small number of parents who have walked away from it all. This is the homeschooling crowd. They refuse to subject their children to the "Academic Insanities" of the malfunctioning American education system. The problem is too big, it won't be changed overnight, and by the time the necessary changes are implemented, their children will have had their own great grandchildren.

Most American schools, private, public, and parochial, resemble a war zone: Few heroes, heavy casualties, and senseless fatalities.

Few Student Heroes

The heroes are the students who master the weekly academic exercise of "Read, Cram, Regurgitate, and Test." Two weeks after the test, even the heroes will not remember most of the academic facts.

Heavy Student Casualties

1. Most students will suffer from the "Pain of Inadequacy" and graduate bearing the "Scars of Incompetence."

2. Students who constantly change schools, e.g., The Republican \ Vice Presidential Nominee, Sarah Palin.

"Sarah Palin received her bachelor's degree (B.A.) in journalism after transferring five times in six years: Hawaii Pacific University, North Idaho College, University of Idaho, Matanuska-Susitna College, University of Idaho again" (ABC News, 2008).

3. Students who fall behind, flounder, and fail, go to summer school, and then pass, survive, and graduate (The first C grade is a warning sign that a student needs help).

Most Students Are Surviving, But Not Thriving

4. Students who fall behind, flounder, and fail, and are misdiagnosed with A.D.H.D., "the incurable brain disorder."

5. Students who fall behind, flounder, and fail, dropout, and are homeschooled.

6. Students who fall behind, flounder, and fail, dropout, and earn a .E.D.

7. Students who fall behind, flounder, and fail, dropout, and get a job.

Senseless Student Fatalities

1. The number one cause of death among college students is college binge-drinking and driving. College students seek relief from the "Pain of Inadequacy" from the "Academic Pressure Cooker," and find a mind-numbing distraction and escape in alcohol.

2. Suicide is the second leading cause of death among college students. Students have become anxious, stressed, and depressed. Disappointments build up and so does the pain. "Bouts of depression" escalate into clinical depression, suicidal thinking (the ticking-time bomb), attempted suicide, and suicide.

3. Students who have lost their lives in school shootings and massacres by disgruntled students on psychotropic drugs.

4. Students who fall behind, flounder, fail, drop out, commit a crime, and go to prison.

The war zone of a few heroes, heavy casualties, and senseless fatalities make up the tenth stumbling block that contributes to the downward spiral of the malfunctioning American education system.

When I look back on all the crap
I learned in high school it's a wonder
I can think at all... but my lack of
education hasn't hurt me none,
I can see the colors on the wall.

Paul Simon

The difference between school and life?
In school, you're taught a lesson and then
given a test. In life, you're given a test
that teaches you a lesson."

Tom Bodett

Meet Richard
He found his passion and purpose in life.
He masters the **SMARTGRADES** Processing
Tools and earns A grades on tests.
He is now a scholar and an artist.

The Eleventh Stumbling Block of Academic Failure

The Desert:
Wander Aimlessly with No Direction

The eleventh stumbling block students encounter is that most students do not have an opportunity to explore an area of study that is interesting, engaging, and meaningful to them. There is little time during their formative years to develop their natural affinities, talents, or gifts. Students do not find a purpose and passion that will give meaning to their short-term existence.

His father, the doctor, wants him to be a doctor. His mother, the lawyer, wants him to be a lawyer. His name is Richard and he loves music and wants to become a musician.

He thinks that school is a waste of his time. He wants to spend his time creating original music compositions and wants to make a living playing his music. He threatens to leave home and join a band. Richard is one of the lucky ones because he has found his passion early in life and wants to pursue it.

Every parent has a dream for a child and it is often the case that the parent's dream is different from the dream the child is dreaming. Quite often, they are both wrong. The child achieves a different dream than either of them could have ever imagined.

I convince Richard that he can be both a great musician and a great student, and that he needs both skill sets to be a successful person in life. I suggest that we start and end every session with a mini-concert of one of his original compositions. He likes the idea. After the mini-concert, we decide to first tackle his science test and then work on his history research paper that is due in two weeks.

This is not a difficult case because Richard has fallen behind and is floundering, but he is not failing. His report card is sprinkled with B and C grades. He is wounded, but he is passing. Richard's innate musical gift nourishes his soul and keeps him happy.

As for Richard, I recommend the following five academic interventions to transform him into an excellent student.

YOUR STUDY ROOM IS UNDER NEW MANAGEMENT

Grade **A** Students are M**A**DE not Born

Step 1. New Study Room
(*Your Study Room Is Under New Management,* p. 56)

Step 2. New School Notebooks
SMARTGRADES School Notebooks contain the new learning technology, SMARTGRADES Processing Tools (p. 56).

Step 3. New Learning Tools for Self-Reliant and Life-Long Learners
SMARTGRADES Processing Tools: New Learning Technology Every Student Earns an A Grade on the Very Next Test
(**EVERY DAY AN EASY A**, p. 56)

Step 4. Rebuild Self-Esteem and Repair Broken Wings
Integration Therapy for Intrapersonal Growth, Development, and Maturity (*Integration Therapy,* Appendix G).

Step 5. Parent Empowerment
Parenting Skills and Strategies for Academic Success (How to Parent a Child for Academic Success, Appendix G).

Artistic creation is a time consuming endeavor. Artists are extra-sensitive beings, who are inspired by the world around them. When an artist gives birth to an idea, the idea has to be raised to maturity, as if it were a child: Sensitivity, inspiration, impregnation, incubation, birth, growth, development, and maturity.

Composing music is one of the greatest gifts that can be conferred on a child. No one knows the breadth and depth of the gift until the artist and the gift are nurtured and brought to fruition. The artist has to be nurtured to bring forth the gift of music, and then the music composition has to be nurtured to bring it to maturity.

I convince Richard's parents to let him off the hook with family chores so that he has more time to work on his music. They decide to hire a part-time housekeeper to walk the dog, do the laundry, and clean his room.

I also recommend having a weekly after-dinner concert in the home. Richard performs his music while his parents sip tea and eat dessert. To feed his soul, they should end the concert with an enthusiastic applause and a standing ovation. Richard receives a bear hug from dad and a mushy kiss from mom. As far as I am concerned, there is no such thing as too much love.

Let's Recap: Nurturing Artistic Gifts
1. All children have unique minds and natural affinities.

2. The artist has to be nurtured to bring forth the gift.

3. The artistic creation has to be nurtured to bring it to maturity.

4. The artist and the artistic creation need support.

In sum, Richard masters the new learning technology, SMARTGRADES Processing Tools, and earns A grades on his science test and history research paper. To ace the science test, Richard learns how to process the voluminous academic facts for instant recognition and recall. To ace the history research paper assignment, Richard learns how to properly research, paraphrase, quote and footnote sources, and proofread his paper. Richard is no longer feeling torn between his passion for music and his academic chores. As promised, he can be both an academic scholar and a musician.

Good Grades Deserve Great Rewards
Richard's parents are delighted with the change in his attitude and his good grades, and buy him a new blue electric guitar as a reward for his academic achievements.

Reinventing the American Education System
The students have survived. They have graduated. Paradoxically, their schooling has sidetracked them into a ditch. They still have no idea of who they are and who they want to be. They have not found their purpose or passion in life. Little attention was given to the student's unique mind, personality, and career aspirations. Students don't know how to develop their talents and pursue their dreams in the real world.

Conversely, there are many students who found their passion early in life and dropped out of high school or college to pursue dreams in the real world: 8 U.S. Presidents, 25 Billionaires, 1 Astronaut, 10 Nobel Prize Winners, 8 Olympic Medal Winners, 62 Oscar Nominees, 55 Best-Selling Authors, and 14 Presidential Medal of Freedom recipients (U.S.'s highest civilian honor). On one hand, the list of illustrious high school dropouts is quite long and fascinating (www.angelfire.com/stars4/lists/dropouts.html).

On the other hand, there is a much longer list of high school dropouts who have committed crimes and are incarcerated in prison.

There is also the list of students whose parents pointed them in a definite direction and got it all wrong, and then they had to pay for their costly mistake with multiple academic degrees. There are countless horror stories about doctors who went back to school to become lawyers. There are lawyers who went back to school to become doctors. There are teachers who went back to school to become chefs.

Most people are dissatisfied with their career choices because they were unable to develop their unique gifts and talents at an early age. It seems as if students were mismatched with their professions and were unable during their formative years to align their gifts and talents with their career goals and professional aspirations.

As early as the third grade, schools need to open the "Department of American Dreams" that is focused on helping students find their passion, develop their talents, and pursue their goals. These simple questions begin the process of finding out who the students are and how best to help them:

Q: What is your favorite school subject?
Q: Which school subject is easy for you?
Q: Which school subject is difficult for you?
Q: What are your strengths and weaknesses?
Q: What do you like to do in your free time?
Q: What person in the world do you admire and why?
Q: Name a person who is living a personal dream?
Q: What problem in the world do you want to solve?
Q: How do you make your American dream come true?
Q: How do you make an action plan and breakdown one big dream into a thousand, one-foot-in-front-of-the-other, baby steps?

Expose students to a whole host of professional careers, and introduce them to the people who solve problems, make significant contributions, and leave the world in better shape. Here are examples of people who make a big difference each and every day of their lives:

Steve Jobs, a college dropout, is my favorite hero. The Mac computer shifted the creativity paradigm and put the power to create back into the hands of artists. Students who think "outside the box" have the power to move the world in new directions.

Ms. Suze Orman: The financial therapist/guru who is teaching business skills that need to be taught in elementary school. Teaching basic business skills in elementary school will be the first step toward growing a prosperous American economy. Elementary school business teachers--not--politicians will fix the American economy.

Ms. Oprah Winfrey: The master teacher who uses her talk-show platform to inspire, educate, and change the world. First, Oprah sounds a wake-up call. Second, Oprah sounds a call to action.

Oprah uplifts the minds and hearts ("Light from Within") of millions of people all around the world.

Musicians have used concerts as a means to build bridges of peace among warring nations, e.g., the New York Philharmonic in North Korea. We saw arch enemies sit down with each other, break bread and rice, and sing the same tune in harmony (Daniel J. Wakin, "North Korea Welcomes New York Philharmonic," N.Y.T., February 26, 2008).

Mayor Michael Reuben Boomberg: He is perhaps the sole politician in America who has education on his list of priorities. He made a dent and a difference, but there is still a 50% dropout rate in the N.Y.C. high schools. He missed the boat on the problem of social promotion. Get a clue: SMARTGRADES Processing Tools. Also, please take down the pathetic education subway ads (p. 332).

President Barack Hussein Obama: He has empowered Americans with his spiritual manifesto of hope: "YES WE CAN."
1. "YES WE CAN" make America's children and the education system America's top priority: In-depth comprehension, long-term retention, and mastery of academic material, "Every Student Is a Success Story!"

2. "YES WE CAN" teach basic business skills in elementary school and entrepreneurial business skills in high school, that will ensure a prosperous American economy.

3. "YES WE CAN" nurture the "Creative Powerhouse," the right brain, of our students: Intuition, Insight, imagination, and ingenuity.

Students wandering aimlessly for years without direction make up the eleventh stumbling block that contributes to the downward spiral of the malfunctioning American education system.

Please Don't Waste My Time, My Dime, or My Mind!

Sharon Esther Lampert
Prodigy, Philosopher, Poet, Peacemaker

Meet Thomas
He masters the **SMARTGRADES** Proce
Tools and earns A grades on tests.
His journey from academic failure to
academic success was a financial
hardship for his father. Parents are
asked to fill in the gigantic potholes
of a malfunctioning education system

The Twelfth Stumbling Block of Academic Failure

The Wasteland:
One Size Does Not Fit All or Any

The twelfth stumbling block students encounter is that the one size fits all education system does not serve the needs of teachers, students, or parents. Teachers don't benefit because there is no time to teach for in-depth comprehension. Teachers are then scapegoated for being poor teachers and blamed for poor test scores. Students don't benefit because they don't have "time to learn" or learning tools. Parents don't benefit because they are asked to fill in the gigantic potholes with tutors, learning specialists, and psychiatrists.

His name is Thomas. He is fourteen years old. He failed his history class. He is enrolled in summer school and is taking the class again. The summer school course condenses six months of academic material into six weeks. To be able to pass this class, Thomas has to read, cram, and regurgitate more than five hundred academic facts on the history of China onto a time-sensitive hotdog test. There are no writing assignments. If he passes the test, he will be promoted to the next grade.

The Summer School Hotdog Exam on Chinese History
Thomas needs learning tools, namely, SMARTGRADES Processing Tools, for instant recognition and recall of more than five hundred academic facts on the history of China. In addition, he needs "dumb and dumber elimination strategy" to ace his multiple choice exams (**EVERY DAY AN EASY A**, p. 56.).

In sum, Thomas mastered the new learning technology, SMARTGRADES Processing Skills, and aced his exams. His parents were delighted with his perfect tens on quizzes. His parents decided that he should continue to work with me during the school year.

As is usually the case, I have my work cut out for me because Thomas needs a complete academic overhaul. His report card is littered with D grades. He is barely staying afloat.

As for Thomas, I recommend the following six academic interventions to transform him into an excellent student.

THIS STUDY ROOM IS UNDER NEW MANAGEMENT
Grade A Students are MADE not Born

Step 1. New Study Room (Your Study Room Is Under New Management, p56)

Step 2. New School Notebooks
SMARTGRADES School Notebooks contain the new learning technology, SMARTGRADES Processing Tools (p. 56).

Step 3. New Learning Tools for Self-Reliant and Life-Long Learners
SMARTGRADES Processing Tools: New Learning Technology
Every Student Earns an A Grade on the Very Next Test
(**EVERY DAY AN EASY A**, p. 56)

Step 4. Rebuild Self-Esteem and Repair Broken Wings
Integration Therapy for Intrapersonal Growth, Development, and Maturity (Intrapersonal-*Integration Therapy Modality*).

Most Students Are Surviving, But Not Thriving

Step 5. Parent Empowerment
Parenting Skills and Strategies for Academic Success
(*Your Study Room Is Under New Management*, p. 56)

Step 6. Eat for Energy to Learn
It takes tremendous energy to read, write, and test. Students need fiber-rich meals with fresh fruits and vegetables.

There is trouble brewing at home. His father is a policeman who is losing his patience with his son. His father does not want to foot the bills for the learning specialist.

One evening, his father lets loose and beats him up. Thomas is admitted to the local hospital for evaluation. In less than one hour, Thomas is sent into a tailspin by his father, a policeman, the one person who is supposed to be there to protect him and the city at large.

Thomas is released from the hospital and returns to school. Thomas writes an English essay that says that he wants to kill himself and die. His English essay is his suicide note. I read the essay and correct the misspelling, punctuation, and grammar. I try to work with Thomas to rebuild his fragile self-esteem that was partially restored when he had aced his summer-school exams.

Finally, his father abandons the family and moves to Florida. His mother is no longer able to pay for the, SMARTGRADES Processing Tools, to help Thomas. She also has to move into a smaller apartment to reduce her expenses. Thomas takes a medical leave of absence from school. He is readmitted into the psychiatric hospital for further evaluation.

Reinventing the American Education System

This is a common scenario: The mother wants to help the child and the father does not want to foot the bills for the learning specialist. The father wants the child to go into his room and "study harder." His teachers also want Thomas to "study harder" so that he will be able to ace the hotdog exams.

You cannot tell a depressed person to "cheer up and develop a positive attitude." You cannot tell a failing student who is disconnected, depressed, and distracted to "study harder." First, the student needs to rebuild his self-confidence. Second, the student needs to acquire learning tools for academic success.

Students go into their rooms, open their textbooks, read the chapters, and do not have "time to learn" and learning tools to "learn and process" voluminous academic facts. They do not know how to extract, condense associate, and convert voluminous academic facts for instant recognition and recall to ace the hotdog exams.

Many parents don't pay attention to the grades until the report card period and then start to yell and scream at the child for poor grades. The child makes a promise to study harder and it is a promise that will soon be broken because the child does not have the learning tools to achieve academic success. The child does not know why he is failing. His parents do not know why he is failing. The educators are clueless as to, How Does Learning Take Place?

Educators know that students are falling behind and floundering, but they don't pay attention, until the child is failing. Most public and private schools allow students to pass with C and D grades until the student earns an F grade. Most failing students live on on three battlefields with three war fronts:

Most Students Are Surviving, But Not Thriving

1. Students have to do battle at home with clueless parents:
Q: "What is wrong with Thomas?"

2. Students have to do battle in school with clueless educators:
Q: "What is wrong with Thomas?"

3. Students have to do battle with a clueless psychiatrist who has a clue: "Thomas has A.D.H.D., the incurable brain disorder."

Academic Insanity: Summer School Programs
If a student fails a class, at the end of the year, the student goes to summer school and takes the class again. Summer school classes condense six months of academic facts into six weeks. Summer school is a complete waste of time, energy, and money. It only takes the first test to know if a student is on track for academic success. The C grade is a warning sign that a student needs help A. S. A. P.

Academic Insanity: No Beneficiaries
The definitive academic insanity is that there are no beneficiaries in the malfunctioning American education system. The teachers don't benefit because there is no time to teach for in-depth comprehension. The students don't benefit because they don't have "time to learn" or learning tools to process the voluminious facts for long-term retention. The parents don't benefit because they are asked to fill in the gigantic potholes by teaching what teachers don't have time to teach and helping their kids learn.

1. Academic Insanity: Teachers Do Not Benefit
Teachers don't have time to teach the academic material for in-depth comprehension. Teachers are then scapegoated for being poor teachers and blamed for poor test scores.

Students Earn a Diploma, But Not an Education

2. Academic Insanity: Students Do Not Benefit

a. Students study for hours, but don't have "time to learn" and learning tools to "learn and process" voluminous academic material for academic success.

b. American dreams are destroyed by faulty regurgitation of academic facts or sabotaged by abusive (tricky) hotdog exams.

c. Students suffer from the "Pain of Inadequacy" and graduate bearing the "Scars of Incompetence."

d. Two weeks after a test, the facts disappear into a black hole in the mind. Students go into education, but education does not go into students. Students earn a diploma, but not an education.

e. Students will not be able to use the knowledge to enhance their own lives or to further the progress of civilization.

3. Academic Insanity: Parents Do Not Benefit

Parents are asked to fill in the gigantic potholes of the "Quantity Over Quality, Curriculum-Driven" malfunctioning American education system. They are asked to pay astronomical tuition bills and incur the hefty bills associated with psychiatrists, learning specialists, regular tutors, and preparatory classes for abusive (tricky) standardized exams. In some cases, there will be little to no return on their financial investment. Students will pass, survive, and graduate, but will not learn how to achieve academic success in school, or in life.

The one size fits all education system does not fit all or any is the 12th stumbling block that contributes to the downward spiral of the malfunctioning American education system.

When I went to school, Larry, you didn't go to a private bank to get a loan for 20 years. You went to the financial aid office. And in that office, you got a grant, or a scholarship, or work study. Maybe you had to work at the library ten hours a week. Or maybe there was a low-interest loan for one or two percent from the college. You pay it back when you can.

That's the way it was. If you lived in New York or California, at many of the colleges, you went to school for free. Now this young man, what he has ahead of him is if is going to have to — if he has to get a student loan, for instance, for four years of college, 20,000 dollars a year, 80,000 dollars, that means that by the time he actually pays it off in 20 to 30 years, he will have paid that bank at least a half a million dollars just to go to school.

Michael Moore, Documentary Filmmaker
September, 23, 2009
CCN, Larry King Live

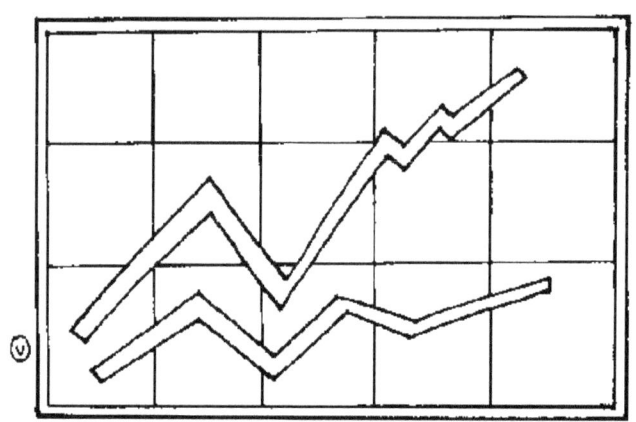

"Not Everything that Counts Can Be Counted, and Not Everything that Can Be Counted Counts."
Albert Einstein

Studies show that twenty percent of high school
dropouts are actually gifted children.
Winston Churchill was the last in his class.
Albert Einstein didn't read until he was
seven and struggled in high school.
Guiseppe Verdi was denied admission to the
Milan conservatory on the way to becoming
one of Italy's greatest composers.
We are all much brighter than we think.

Professor Claude Olney

Meet Rosemary

She was a falling shining star.
She has a powerful brain and is a gifted child.
She masters the **SMARTGRADES** Processing Tools
and is back on track for academic success.

"I am not as smart as I thought I was!"

Game 1. Fall Behind and Play Catch Up
Game 2. Read, Cram, Regurgitate, and Test
Game 3. Abusive (tricky) Hotdog Exams
Game 4. Cut Corners and Cheat to Survive
Game 5. Suffer from the "Pain of Inadequacy"
Game 6. Bear the "Scars of Incompetence"
Game 7. Anxiety, Stress, Depression, and Suicide
Game 8. Escapism from Pain with Mind-Numbing Distractions
Game 9. Earn a Diploma, but Not an Education

The Thirteenth Stumbling Block of Academic Failure

American Dreams: Deferred, Denied, and Destroyed

The thirteenth stumbling block that students encounter is that before the age of puberty, their childhood dreams have vanished into thin air. Students study for hours. They promise their parents and teachers that they will work harder. Students are unable to keep their promise because meager comprehension, no learning tools, abusive hotdog exams, the "Pain of Inadequacy," and the "Scars of Incompetence" undermine their best effort and destroy all hope of a bright future filled with an American dream that really will come true. The malfunctioning American education system has hindered or destroyed their dreams, aspirations, and ambitions.

Her name is Rosemary. She is habitually prepared for class. When the teacher asks a question, her hand is the first one up in the air, and Rosemary always has the right answer. She was always the brightest student in her class until she entered an elite public high school. Rosemary's admission into the very best high school in the city was supposed to buttress her big dream of becoming a doctor and support her ambition to find the cure for cancer. Instead, her American dream has been sidetracked by a poor performance on abusive (tricky) hotdog tests and mediocre grades on her report card. Rosemary is suffering from the "Pain of Inadequacy" and she finds relief from her pain by eating comfort foods. Rosemary is overeating and has become obese.

Her parents do not understand why their shining academic star has become a fallen star. They call the guidance counselor and receive my name, phone number, and website. Parents of academically gifted students always let me know that their child scored in the 90th percentile of every standardized exam ever taken, since nursery school. These parents are dumbfounded as to why their children have begun to flounder academically.

When I first met Rosemary, she told me that she had to run one mile around the school track to fulfill her 9th grade athletic requirement. She is so out of shape, that it is hard for me to believe that a gym teacher would ask an obese student to perform this athletic feat. Even if it took her longer than most students, she ran and walked around the track and passed the gym requirement. Rosemary also told me about her after school extracurricular activity, the Student Government Club. It is a wonderful opportunity to make new friends, but it was taking too much time away from her studies.

As for Rosemary, I recommend the following four academic interventions to transform her back into an academic star:

Step 1. New School Notebooks
SMARTGRADES School Notebooks contain the new learning technology, SMARTGRADES Processing Tools, p. 56.

Step 2. New Learning Tools for Self-Reliant and Life-Long Learners
SMARTGRADES Processing Tools: New Learning Technology Every Student Earns an A Grade on the Very Next Test
(EVERY DAY AN EASY A, p. 56)

Step 3. Rebuild Self-Esteem and Repair Broken Wings
Integration Therapy for Intrapersonal Growth, Development, and Maturity (*Integration Therapy Modality p. 56*)

Step 4. Eat for Energy to Learn
It takes tremendous energy to read, write, and test. Students need fiber-rich meals with fresh fruits and vegetables.

In sum, in less than two weeks, Rosemary was back on track. She earned an A grade on her very next test. She loves her new school notebooks because she no longer has to hole-punch her loose handouts and can file them in less than ten seconds without a fuss. This saves Rosemary at least one hour a week. Every day Rosemary receives two types of loose paper from five different teachers and ten loose papers have to be filed each week. In addition, weekly quizzes, tests, essays, and research reports have to be filed, as follows:

1. File: Five daily homework assignments
2. File: Five daily handouts
3. File: Quizzes, tests, research reports, and school projects

Most importantly, Rosemary is losing weight and regaining her health. She is no longer eating emotionally and is able to see the connection between the stress of academic failure, the "Pain of Inadequacy," and her out-of-control eating habits.

Let's Recap: What Really Happened to Darling Rosemary?
1. Rosemary is enrolled in an elite public high school and is destined for a bright future.

2. Rosemary is enrolled in a malfunctioning Quantity Over Quality Curriculum-Driven American Education System.

3. Rosemary does not have "time to learn" or learning tools to "learn and process" voluminous academic material.

4. After the first week of school, Rosemary falls behind and can't catch up.

5. After a month, Rosemary is floundering and earns mediocre grades.

6. Rosemary suffers from the "Pain of Inadequacy" and her self-talk is "I am not as smart as I thought I was."

7. Rosemary seeks an escape from her "Pain of Inadequacy." Food fills the void. She overeats and becomes obese.

8. Rosemary's parents seek help immediately when they see C grades.

9. Rosemary masters the **SMARTGRADES** Processing Tools, and aces her hotdog exams:
Step 1. Estimation Tool
Step 2. Divide and Conquer Tool
Step 3. Active-Reading Tool
Step 4. Extraction Tool
Step 5. Condensation Tool
Step 6. Association Tool
Step 7. Test-Review Note Tool
Step 8. Conversion Tool
Step 9. Visualization Tool
Step 10. Self-Testing Tool
(**EVERY DAY AN EASY A**, Appendix G)

10. Rosemary masters the academic game of "Read, Cram, Regurgitate, and Test" and earns an A grade on the test.

11. Rosemary understands that two weeks after the test, most of the academic facts will disappear into a black hole in her mind, because there is only time to process the voluminous academic facts for short-term retention.

12. Rosemary, the fallen star, is back on track for a bright academic future and an American dream that may come true.

Reinventing the American Education System

The malfunctioning American education system is a runaway train with no one manning the control booth. Students are decapitated without warning. Before the age of puberty, students, like young seedlings, are uprooted, displaced, and lose their way and their American dream.

There are only a handful of heroes in every school. Most students are wounded casualties and senseless fatalities. The few heroes will be able to achieve their American dream and this is quite a remarkable achievement, because even the heroes can't remember most of the academic facts two weeks after the test.

Timing is everything. The academic heroes are able to cram the voluminous facts for short-term retention in the nick of time to ace their hotdog exams. They have learned how to play the academic game of "Read, Cram, Regurgitate, and Test." Consequently, the heroes can achieve academic success in the malfunctioning American education system.

An American dream deferred, denied, and destroyed is the thirteenth stumbling block that contributes to the downward spiral of the malfunctioning American education system.

Students Earn a Diploma, But Not an Education

What happens, as we get older,
to this extraordinary capacity
for learning and intellectual growth?
What happens is that it is destroyed,
and more than by any other one thing,
by the process that we misname
education – a process that goes
on in most homes and schools.
We adults destroy most of the intellectual
and creative capacity of children
by the things we do to them
or make them do.

John Caldwell Holt

Education: The Inculcation of the Incomprehensible into the Indifferent by the Incompetent.
John Maynard Keynes

We learn more by looking for the answer to a question and not finding it than we do from learning the answer itself.

Alice Wellington Rollins

Being ignorant is not so much a shame, as being unwilling to learn.

Benjamin Franklin

Live as if you were to die tomorrow.
Learn as if you were to live forever.

Mahatma Gandhi

The Fourteenth Stumbling Block of Academic Failure

Get a Clue: How Does Learning Take Place

The fourteenth stumbling block that students encounter is that educators are clueless as to "How Does Learning Take Place?" School is a restaurant and facts are on the menu. Children eat facts and build their brain muscles. You cannot stuff a whole sandwich into your mouth. You have to take small bites, chew, chew, chew, and digest. You cannot stuff voluminous academic facts into your brain. The human brain is the most powerful biological machine in the world, and educators have not yet learned how to nurture, cultivate, and mine its extraordinary depths and infinite possibilities.

A guidance counselor from a distinguished private school calls my office and invites me to visit her school. She is trying in vain to write a book that will help students learn. I recommend that she show the book to me and she declines the offer. She becomes agitated and wants to have a list of the students in her school that have been helped by my services. I tell her that I sign confidentiality agreements with parents and I can't give her that proprietary information.

She becomes more agitated and wants to know why earning an A grade matters. She is losing her cool. She has been a guidance counselor for over thirty-five years. She is frustrated by the fact that she can't get the same results as I do and there is a hint of professional envy displayed in her conversation. After the visit, I find myself questioning the reason why she asked me into her office in the first place.

Most guidance counselors are delighted and surprised to find out that the borderline students they sent to my office earned A grades on the very next test. They want to know how it is possible to transform an F grade student into an A grade student without a slow climb up the ladder of academic success by first earning C and B grades along the way.

Q: What is Wrong with that Student?
Educators do not want to take on any of the responsibility for failing students, and prefer to find fault with the seemingly "lazy student," or the seemingly "ineffectual parents." When students fall behind, flounder, fail, and fall through the cracks, educators are remiss at understanding why this is happening. Educators want to know, "What is wrong with that student?" and "Why can't that student cram one-thousand academic facts into his mind and regurgitate them onto a hotdog test in an hour to earn a diploma and graduate?"

Educators do acknowledge that more than 80% of their student body do not have learning tools to achieve academic success. Fast asleep at the steering wheel, educators do not connect the dots ... between the lack of learning tools and their borderline and failing students because they have learned how to shift the blame to the student or parent; and conversely, the parents and students shift the blame to the teachers and the education system. Ironically, educators are unable to answer the critical question that is at the heart of education: "How Does Learning Take Place?"

1. Facts are food for the brain. You cannot stuff a whole sandwich into your mouth. You have to take small bites and chew, chew, chew and digest. You cannot stuff voluminous facts into your mind. You have to take small amounts of knowledge and chew (in-depth comprehension), chew (long-term retention)), and chew (mastery of the academic material) and digest.

2. The learning curve is steep. It takes time to learn.

3. Learning requires time to teach for in-depth comprehension.

4. Learning requires "time to learn" and learning tools to "learn and process" academic material for long-term retention.

5. Writing is an art form that requires time for ideas to grow, develop, and mature. Learning how to write well requires that students reread, revise, and rewrite ten to twenty rough drafts. Also, writing requires classes on basic, intermediate, and advanced proofreading skills.

6. Learning requires time to practice.

7. Learning requires time for trial and error.

8. Learning requires time for continuous feedback of strengths and weaknesses until mastery is achieved.

9. Learning requires realistic-time allotments for school assignments.

10. Learning requires detailed step-by-step instructions for school assignments.

11. Learning requires a stress-free environment that is conducive for the love of learning.

Educators are clueless as to, "How Does Learning Take Place?" This is the thirteenth stumbling block that contributes to the downward spiral of the malfunctioning American education system.

Recently a young mother asked for advice.
What, she wanted to know, was what to do
with a 7-year-old who was obstreperous,
outspoken, and inconveniently willful?
"Keep her," I replied....
The suffragettes refused to be polite
in demanding what they wanted or grateful
for getting what they deserved.
Works for me.

Anna Quindlen

Michael Phelps
8 Olympic Gold Medals in Swimming

"Before traveling here from Baltimore, Phelps's mother, Debbie, received a letter from Barbara Kines, who had taught Phelps in the third grade.

Before he found an outlet for his abundant energy in swimming, Phelps had immense difficulties concentrating and sitting still, leading one of his grade-school teachers to wonder if he would ever be able to focus on anything.

Kines, recalling those days, wrote about how proud she was of Phelps and how, perhaps, it had never been focus he lacked, but, rather, a goal worthy of his focus."

By Reporter Karen Crouse

August 16, 2008, N.Y. Times

Meet Robert
He does not have an incurable brain disorder.
He has a powerful brain and is a gifted child.

The Fifteenth Stumbling Block of Academic Failure

Unintentional Institutionalized Child Abuse (blind leading the blind)

The fifteenth stumbling block students encounter is unintentional child abuse from a parent, teacher, or psychiatrist. You used to be a brainy, creative, happy-go-lucky kid with a very bright future ahead of you. It is all your fault that you are falling behind, floundering, failing, and falling through the cracks of the, "Quantity Over Quality, Curriculum-Driven Malfunctioning American Education System."

Robert has one dog named Sallie, and two cats named, Brice and Buttons, at home. He is seven years old. He was diagnosed with A. D. H. D. and is taking Ritalin for his "incurable brain disorder."

His mother knows of another child in the community who has committed suicide and feels that her child's diagnosis of A. D. H. D., by contrast, is a comparatively minor problem.

His mother is waiting at a bus stop and calls me on her cell phone to tell me that she may be late for her appointment. Her son is fighting with her and does not want to visit the learning specialist. I ask her to put him on the phone so that I can speak to him. I tell Robert that my cat, Schmaltzy, is looking forward to meeting him and that he is all dressed up in his bright blue bow tie and is waiting at the door. Robert changes his mind and is now looking forward to our visit and to meeting his new feline friend named Schmaltzy. When I open the door, the first words out of Robert's mouth are, "Where is Schmaltzy?"

Schmaltzy and Falafel are the most famous cats in the world. Schmaltzy is a working cat who wears bow ties, plays a piano, and has a famous long-haired Exotic feline girlfriend named Falafel. He has his own website and movie at schmaltzy.com and an international fan club on You-Tube. The high profile animal magazine, Animal Fair, featured Schmaltzy and called him a "Feline Prodigy." The New York Post featured, Schmaltzy, as one of the "Most Eligible Pets in the World," and as a "Celebrity In His Own Right," because he does not need to be owned by a celebrity to have his adorable face printed in the newspaper.

Schmaltzy is also a study buddy. When he hears the door buzzer, he quickly runs to the door and waits for Robert and greets him by rubbing his head on Robert's shirt. He then follows Robert to the desk, and curls his body around his schoolbooks and takes a nap while he has his lesson. When Robert is ready to leave, Schmaltzy is already at the door waiting to say goodbye to him.

Schmaltzy plays his piano and entertains, Robert, with one of his original music compositions. Robert can't believe his eyes. His mom is also in awe of the piano-playing cat. Schmaltzy listens to instructions, he is focused, and does not take his eyes off the keyboard. He is the PURRfect role model for students because he practices his piano three times a day and receives a reward of bonito tuna flakes for every great performance. Schmaltzy is an excellent student and a super-cool cat.

I have seen students who are staunch dog lovers and hate cats develop an affinity for cats because of Schmaltzy's very big-hearted personality. All of my students enjoy his comforting companionship when he wraps his long orange tail around their schoolbooks.

Quantity Over Quality Curriculum-Driven Education System

As is usually the case, I have my work cut out for me. Robert fell behind, floundered, failed, and fell through the cracks of the malfunctioning American education system. He is one of the brightest, most creative, and imaginative children I have ever met. Like most students, he does not have "time to learn" and learning tools to "learn and process" voluminous academic material. Robert is seven years old and he is already a senseless casualty because he is on the road to ... HELL. He has been labeled with A.D.H.D., and is taking Ritalin for his "incurable brain disorder."

The First Red Flag: Energy to Learn
"What did you have for breakfast today?" I ask Robert. "I don't eat breakfast" he replies. Robert goes to school on an empty stomach.

The Second Red Flag: Energy to Concentrate
"What time do you go to sleep?" I ask Robert. "I don't have a regular bedtime? he says. In addition, Robert drinks caffeinated soda at dinner. Robert stays up late and does not get enough sleep.

The Third Red Flag: Study Room
"Where do you study?" I ask Robert. "I do my homework in the kitchen" he says. Robert does not have a quite study area that is free of distractions to complete his homework assignments, write his research papers, and prepare for tests.

The Fourth Red Flag: School Notebooks
"May I see your school notebooks?" I ask Robert. All of his schoolwork is undifferentiated by subject area and is stuffed into one very messy green folder that is splitting at the seams.

The Fifth Red Flag: TV

"What television shows do you like to watch?" I ask Robert. He lists five shows that are broadcast on weeknights. He is spending too much time watching television.

As far as Robert is concerned, I recommend the following three academic interventions:

YOUR STUDY ROOM IS UNDER NEW MANAGEMENT

Grade A Students are MADE not Born
Website: www.everydayaneasya.com

Step 1. New School Notebooks
SMARTGRADES School Notebooks contain the new learning technology, SMARTGRADES Processing Tools, p.56.

Step 2. New Learning Tools for Self-Reliant and Life-Long Learners
SMARTGRADES Processing Tools: New Learning Technology
Every Student Earns an A Grade on the Very Next Test
(**EVERY DAY AN EASY A**, p. 56)

Step 3. Rebuild Self-Esteem and Repair Broken Wings
Integration Therapy for Intrapersonal Growth, Development, and Maturity (*Integration Therapy Modality*).

In sum, his mother spoke to the psychiatrist and he was slowly weaned off Ritalin and put back on the A-grade track for academic success and achievement. Every morning, he eats a nutritious breakfast and every night he goes to sleep at 9:30 p.m.

He has his own study area to do his homework that is free of noise and distractions. He has a new set of fuss-free, instant-organization school notebooks and each subject is filed in its own folder. In less than ten seconds, he can file a loose handout into a subject specific notebook. The television was removed from his bedroom and was moved to the family room. Most importantly, he was taught the new learning technology, SMARTGRADES Processing Tools, and has test preparation skills for instant recognition and recall to ace his tests.

Let's Recap: What Really Happened to Darling Robert?
1. Robert goes to school on an empty stomach, has no energy to learn, and can't focus on his studies.

2. Robert goes to sleep too late, has no energy to learn, and can't focus on his studies.

3. Robert watches too much TV and has no time to do his home work.

4. Robert does not have his own study area to do his homework and is using the kitchen table as a desk. The kitchen is noisy and full of distractions and Robert is not able to focus and concentrate on his homework assignment.

5. Robert gets too much negative attention and too little positive attention from his mother. His mother yells at him for every mistake. This negative attention further humiliates Robert and undermines his self-esteem.

6. Robert's mother takes him to see a psychiatrist and complains that he is unable to sit still and can't focus. He also can't finish what he starts.

7. The clueless psychiatrist (with a clue) misdiagnoses Robert with A.D.H.D., the "incurable brain disorder" and prescribes Ritalin.

8. Robert still needs help with his schoolwork, and his mother finds Ms. Sugar, the learning specialist and education warrior. Ms. Sugar transforms Robert into a A-grade student. Robert is back on track for academic success and a bright future.

9. His mother talks to the psychiatrist and Robert is slowly weaned off Ritalin. Robert's self-esteem is rebuilt with, Integration Therapy. He learned, self-talk, and how to negotiate "fight" or "flight." He is no longer disconnected, depressed, and distracted. He is now receptive to learning. His brain is taken out of the virtual wheelchair and set free.

Reinventing the American Education System

Every call is an emergency. I feel as if my tutoring office has become like an emergency room in a hospital because many of my students are in critical condition, diagnosed with "incurable brain disorders."

"There is nothing seriously wrong with your child, Mrs. Williams." I tell this to every parent who tells me that his or her child was misdiagnosed with A.D.H.D., the "incurable brain disorder."

"Mrs. Williams, I have good news for you. Your child is probably one of the brightest children in the class, because linear right-brain creative children are the first to fall through the fifteen jagged-edged cracks of a malfunctioning American education system."

The problem of misdiagnosing children who fall behind, flounder and fail in school with A.D.H.D., the "incurable brain disorder," is made up of three distinct but interrelated problems:

Problem 1. Parents with Inadequate Parenting Skills
The first problem is the lack of supervision in the home. Most often, a child goes to school on an empty stomach and does not have a regular bedtime. Parents use the television as a babysitter. Children have been placed in front of a noisy and violent television for more than five hours a day. Some of these kids play on noisy and violent computer games for more than four hours a day. Some of these kids are raised on caffeinated drinks, and cakes and cookies loaded with processed sugars. Simply stated, this generation of boob-tube couch potatoes, computer-game players, and sugar-addicted kids cannot sit quietly and read a book from cover to cover. These kids have short attention spans and crave dramatic action. Many of these kids will be misdiagnosed with A. D. H. D. In some cases, the parents would rather excuse their kids misbehavior by justifying it as a medical disorder, "My kid has A. D. H. D., and that is why he can't sit still and read a book."

Problem 2. The Malfunctioning American Education System
I used to tell parents that students without learning tools will start to flounder in the fifth grade, but I was wrong. According to the education initiative in New York City to end social promotion in 2004, 10,000-15,000 children in the third grade were going to be left back because they did not pass a citywide "hotdog" test. I was livid, when I read about this "Academic Insanity" taking place as early as the third grade. Children do not mature at the same rate.

Q: How many academic facts do third-grade students have to cram into their mind with meager comprehension, no learning tools, and for short-term retention and regurgitate, under duress and a stopwatch, onto a time-sensitive stressful citywide "hotdog" test to graduate and be promoted to fourth grade?

Here is your proof positive that before the age of puberty, namely, the third grade, age eight, there is institutionalized destruction of **A**merica's **B**rightest **M**inds.

The third grade students who don't pass the hotdog test think, "What is wrong with me?" These eight-year-old students will suffer from the "Pain of Inadequacy." Their self-esteem plummets and they will become anxious, stressed, depressed, distracted, and disgruntled, "What is wrong with me? Why can't I cram five-hundred academic facts into my brain, with meager comprehension, no learning tools, and for short-term retention, and regurgitate the facts in two hours, under psychological duress and a stopwatch onto a tricky "Hotdog" exam?

Mayor Bloomberg's head and heart are in the right place and he always puts 500% into everything that he does for New York City, but this one his administration got wrong, and for these eight reasons:

1. "Social Promotion" is a better problem than the "Pain of Inadequacy" (disconnected, depressed, distracted, disgruntled, and disobedient students).

2. Children are enrolled in a "Curriculum Driven" malfunctioning education system: No in-depth comprehension, long-term retention, and mastery of academic material. Academic Insanity: Educators want students to be able to remember voluminous facts that they barely comprehend. Knowledge, General Overview. Test. Chop! Chop!

3. Citywide "Hotdog" tests do not measure education. Regurgitating voluminous facts under psychological duress and a stopwatch does not measure education. Under stress, every student draws at least one blank. Under stress, most students draw more than one blank.

4. It only takes the first test to know if a student is on track for academic success. The C grade is a warning sign that a student needs help (If the truth be told, 75% of the student body needs help). Educators wait until students fail before they help them--by telling them to go to summer school.

Most Students Are Surviving, But Not Thriving

5. Third grade students return home to parents with inadequate parenting tools, who will find fault with them for their failure.

6. If you fix the bigger problem of a "Curriculum Driven" malfunctioning education system, then the little problem of "Social Promotion" will cease to exist.

7. Information changes so rapidly that no one can make decisions based on yesterday's hard facts. The facts have to be reexamined on a day to day basis, as new facts come to light and shine a brighter ray of hope on intransigent problems.

8. Educators can't remember what they had for lunch yesterday

Problem 3. Clueless Psychiatrists Who Add Insult to Injury
Psychiatrists tell parents to praise their children for good behavior. Too often, good behavior is ignored. Parents tend to give children too much negative attention for bad behavior. Children will seek out any kind of attention from a parent. Even bad attention from a parent is better than no attention. If the truth be told, paradoxically, the psychological damage done to children by psychiatrists who misdiagnose children with A.D.H.D., is even worse than the damage that is done by the parents. I am going to use the worst-case scenario to support my argument that the most cruel and humiliating remark from a parent is still the lesser of the two evils. What would you rather hear? that, "You are a lazy piece of shit," from a parent or that "You have A.D.H.D., the incurable brain disorder" from a clueless psychiatrist who has a clue? Personally, I would rather hear that I was "a lazy piece of shit" from a parent than hear from a psychiatrist that I have A.D.H.D., the "incurable brain disorder." The psychiatrist adds insult to injury, doing more harm than good to the child. In fact there is nothing to be gained, and everything to be lost.

Children who are branded with A.D.H.D., cannot grow, develop, and mature properly. Their daily self-talk is: "I can't do this, I can't do that, because I have A.D.H.D., an incurable brain disorder." It causes permanent damage to the child's self-esteem which has already been beaten down by the clueless parents and teachers by the following destructive remarks:

Parent: "You are a lazy kid with a bad attitude!"

Teacher: "You are unmotivated and apathetic!"

Psychiatrist: "You have A.D.H.D., an "incurable brain disorder."

Q: Why is this happening to very smart, sensitive, and creative children?

Because in 99.9 % of all cases of academic failure, it is always the child's fault. If a child is failing, there has to be something wrong with the child.

Q: "What is wrong with that student?"

Let's revisit the critcal question:

Q: Do you want to put your child's brain, the most powerful biological machine in the world, into a virtual wheelchair for life?

I hope that the psychiatric establishment will open their eyes and begin to see the light and the unintended lie. They are all in deep denial of the deepest truth of biological behavior. Children who exhibit these three symptoms of inattention, impulsivity, do not have the learning tools to "fight." When these children are empowered with the learning tools to "fight," they will no longer be in "flight." The truth is simple. The truth is elegant. The truth will set these children free. It is time to stop misdiagnosing children with A.D.H.D., and placing the human brain, the most powerful biological machine in the world, into a virtual wheelchair for life.

Unintentional child abuse (blind leading the blind) by clueless parents, educators and psychiatrists (who have a clue) make up the fifteenth stumbling block that contributes to the downward spiral of the malfunctioning American education system.

Schmaltzy
The Study Buddy
ww.schmaltzy.com

Schmaltzy's Study Tip:
"Always Look Before You Leap!"

Schmaltzy and student are having a study snack

Schmaltzy wraps his big orange tail around a student's schoolbooks. He sits right between the computer and the student. One eye is cat napping and one eye is on the student.

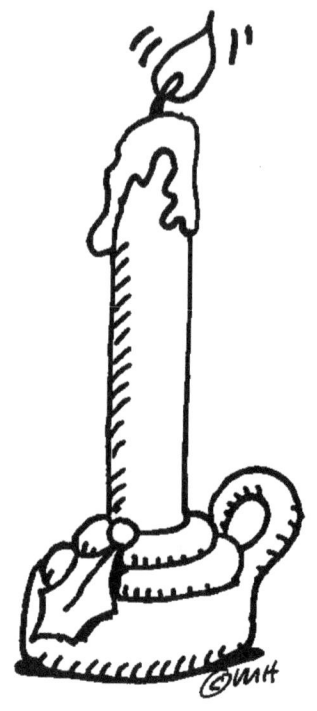

Tell Me and I'll Forget;
Show Me and I May Remember;
Involve Me and I'll Understand.
Chinese Proverb

Don't Curse the Darkness,
Light a Candle.
Chinese Proverb

An error doesn't become a mistake until you refuse to correct it.

Orlando A. Battista

Part Three
Reinventing the American Education System

(1)
THE FIFTEEN STEPPING STONES OF ACADEMIC SUCCESS

(2)
The Quality Over Quantity
Learning-Processing
American Education System

SOLVE ONE PROBLEM
EDUCATION
SAVE ENTIRE WORLD

Children Use the Fist Until They Are of Age to Use the Brain

Elizabeth Barrett Browning

To repeat what others have said,
requires education;
To challenge it, requires brains.

Mary Pettibone Poole

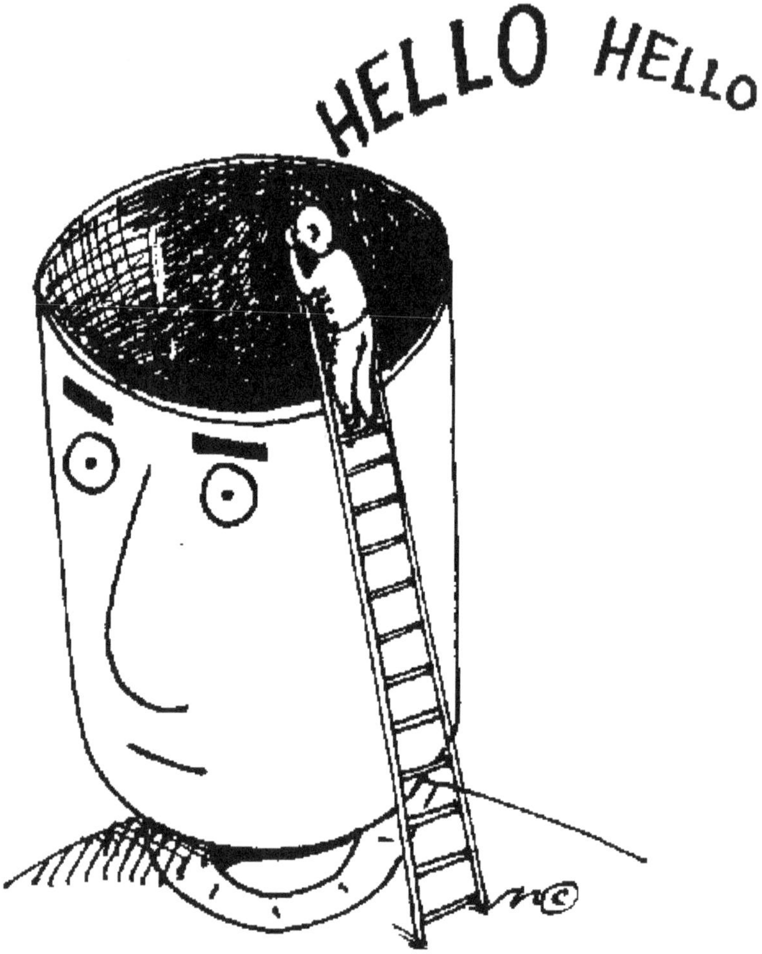
HELLO HELLO

Reenvision, Reinvent, and Rebuild

The First Stepping Stone of Academic Success

BRAIN POWER
The Most Powerful Biological Machine in the World

"Every Student Is a Success Story": The first stepping stone for academic success is understanding how the human brain works. The human brain is the most powerful biological machine in the world. The human brain must be nurtured and cultivated to fulfill its potential. The only thing that is wrong with students is that the brain does not come with an instruction manual and students do not know how to use it. Educators do not know how to nurture and cultivate the awesome power of the human brain.

The human brain is the most powerful biological machine in the world, and the educational challenge before us, is to unlock its potential, cultivate its power, and set free its promise. The brain is the hardware and the mind is the software.

The first question I ask every student is "Put your hands on your head and tell me what you feel?" Most students reply, "I feel nothing." I inform my students that the "nothing," that they feel is their brain, and it is the most powerful biological machine in the world. You already own it. You don't have to go to the department store to buy one. Fortunately, you can never leave your brain at home and forget to take it with you to school.

Facts Are Brain Food
The school is a gym to build your brain muscles. School is also a restaurant where facts are on the menu. Facts are food for your brain. Students spend their entire day eating facts and building their brain muscles: Math muscle, English muscle, history muscle, science muscle, computer muscle, art muscle, and music muscle.

> There is a familiar refrain echoed in the schools that "Drill is Kill." Drilling with no rest, recovery, and rewards is what kills the drill.

The Brain Requires Small Amounts of Digestible Facts
You cannot stuff a whole sandwich into your mouth. You have to take small bites, and chew, chew, chew, and digest. Students have to take small amounts of academic information and chew (in-depth comprehension), chew (absorption), and chew (mastery of academic facts) the facts into their brain (mind). Students have to learn how to break down the voluminous academic facts into bite-size pieces and process the academic facts for in-depth comprehension, long-term retention, and mastery of academic material. Every student is asked to perform three academic tasks:

READ, WRITE, AND TEST

Students Retrieve Facts and Return Facts
Doing well in school is about learning how to "retrieve the facts" from the blackboard, handouts, and textbooks, and learning how to "return the facts" to the teacher in an essay, research paper, and on a test.

Step 1. Retrieve the Academic Facts

Step 2. Return the Academic Facts

The Superhighway of Academic Success
The voluminous academic facts move on a continuum called "The Superhighway of Academic Success." The academic facts move from a teacher's blackboard into a student's notebook, and then, into an essay or research paper, and then, into a student's brain(mind) and onto a test:

THE SUPERHIGHWAY OF ACADEMIC SUCCESS

(1)
The Academic Facts move
from a Teacher's Blackboard into a School Notebook

(2)
The Academic Facts move
from a Textbook, Notebook, and Handouts
into a Homework Assignment, Essay, or Research Paper

(3)
The Academic Facts move
from a Textbook, Notebook, and Handouts
into the Brain and onto a Test

Education Is the Only Path to a Peaceful World

Dr. Norman Doidge and Severe Brain Injuries

A close friend, Richard, shared a book with me that was written by Dr. Norman Doidge, who treats patients afflicted with brain trauma. Richard told me that similar techniques that I had developed to heal students who have broken wings are some of the same strategies that are used by doctors to treat patients with severe brain injuries.

Dr. Jill Bolte Taylor and Severe Brain Injuries

A few months later, Richard, recommended another book, a personal memoir, that was written by the neuroanatomist, Dr. Jill Bolte Taylor, who had survived a stroke. She made a list of what she needed most to heal from her traumatic brain injury. And again, I found myself instinctively on the right path, because I use similar techniques to rebuild a students' self-esteem and repair their broken wings.

Twelve Therapeutic Techniques: No Psychotropic Drugs

Here is a list of twelve therapeutic techniques that are recommended by, Dr. Jill Bolte Taylor, to treat patients who suffer with severe brain injuries. These twelve techniques can also help heal students who suffer from the "Pain of Inadequacy," and have become anxious, stressed, disconnected, depressed, distracted, disgruntled, disillusioned, blocked, shutdown, and suicidal.

1. I am not stupid. I am wounded. Please respect me.

2. Repeat yourself-assume I know nothing and start from the beginning, over and over.

3. Be as patient with me the 20th time you teach me something as you were the first.

4. Approach me with an open heart and slow your energy down. Take your time.

5. Do not assess my cognitive ability by how fast I can think.

6. Cheer me on. Expect me to recover completely, even if it takes twenty years.

7. Break all actions down into smaller steps of action.

8. Look for what obstacles prevent me from succeeding on a task.

9. Clarify for me what the next level or step is so I know what I am working toward.

10. Remember that I have to be proficient at one level of function before I can move onto the next level.

11. Focus on what I can do, rather than bemoan what I cannot do.

12. Celebrate all of my little successes. They inspire me.

(Jill Bolte Taylor, *My Stroke of Insight*, 2006, Viking, 181-183).

Brain Power and Superpowers

As a result of globalization, developing countries, namely, China and India, are mobilizing their economic resources and massive workforce to meet the social, economic, scientific and technological challenges of the 21st century. Without question, the country who learns how to develop their human capital by nurturing and cultivating brain power and reinventing the education system will become the world's next superpower. The term superpower needs to be redefined as the country which will have the first civilization who will close down their prisons and mental institutions, and retire their armies.

If the truth be told, before the age of puberty, most children's lives go way off track because of a home that is a war zone, inadequate parenting skills, and a malfunctioning education system.

To get a driver's license, citizens have to take a class and first get a learner's permit and then a driver's license. This simple, but effective system needs to be implemented to get married and bear children.

Marriage License: More than 50% of Marriages End in Divorce

Step 1. Couples have to take a 6-week course on marriage to get a marriage license.

Step 2. The marriage license has to be renewed every year by a class on marriage.

Parenting License: More than 50% of Families are Broken Homes

Step 1. Parents have to take a parenting course and get a license to have children.

Step 2. The parenting license has to be renewed every year by a class on parenting.

Step 3. Every child receives a $100 dollar birthday gift certificate from the government that can only be cashed in to help pay for college.

Education

Step 1. Cultivate the awesome power of the human brain

Step 2. Get a clue: How Does Learning Take Place?

Step 3. "Quality Over Quantity Learning-Processing Education System: In-Depth Comprehension, Long-Term Retention, and Mastery of the Academic Material"

Step 4. Feed the whole student: MIND, BODY, AND SPIRIT

Step 5. As early as the fourth grade, students need required basic business skills and entrepreneurial skills.

Step 6. Solve the "PROBLEM OF EDUCATION" and save the world: famine, poverty, illiteracy, domestic violence, religious strife, and war

Step 7. Close down the prisons

Step 8. Shut down the mental institutions

Step 9. Retire the armies

Step 10. World Peace Is Coming to Planet Earth

Nurturing and cultivating the awesome power of the human brain constitute the first stepping stone of academic success that will reenvision, reinvent, and rebuild the American education system to meet the challenges of the 21st century and bring us all one step closer to a peaceful world.

Education Is the Only Path to a Peaceful World

Education Is What Remains When One has Forgotten Everything He Learned in School.

Albert Einstein

The Significant Problems We Face Cannot Be Solved at the Same Level of Thinking We Were at When We Created Them.

Albert Einstein

What We Want to See Is
the Child in Pursuit of Knowledge, and
Not Knowledge in Pursuit of the Child.
G. B. Shaw

Reenvision, Reinvent, and Rebuild

The Second Stepping Stone of Academic Success

NEW EDUCATION PARADIGM
Shift Education Paradigm from a Quantity Over Quality, Curriculum-Driven Education System to a Quality Over Quantity Learning-Processing Education System

The second stepping stone for academic success is to shift the education paradigm to a "Quality Over Quantity Learning-Processing Education System." Teachers will have time to teach for in-depth comprehension. Students will have "time to learn" and learning tools to "learn and process" academic material for in-depth comprehension, long-term retention, and mastery of academic material. The new grading system will ensure that, "Every Student is a Success Story." Students will be able to use their education to enhance their own lives, further the progress of civilization, and meet the challenges of the 21st century.

According to Thomas Kuhn, "The historian of science may be tempted to exclaim that when paradigms change, the world itself changes with them" (Thomas S. Kuhn, *The Structure of Scientific Revolutions,* University of Chicago Press, 1996). A paradigm shift causes one to see the same information in an entirely different way. In this chapter, two education paradigms are examined side by side to analyze the inherent strengths and weaknesses. The first education paradigm is the prevailing, Quantity Over Quality Curriculum-Driven American Education System: Fall behind, flounder, fail, and fall through the cracks. The second education paradigm is the new, Quality Over Quantity Learning-Processing Education System, that ensures that, "Every Student Is a Success Story."

Quality Over Quantity Learning-Processing Education System

1. The Curriculum: All school assignments have realistic-time allotments and detailed step-by step instructions.

2. Teachers have time to teach for in-depth comprehension of academic material. Students have "SMARTGRADES Critical Thinking Skills" to analyze, synthesize, and evaluate academic material for in-depth comprehension.

3. Students have "SMARTGRADES Processing Tools" to "learn and process" academic facts for long-term retention.

4. There are only two grades: Grade A and REDO. Teachers have time for continuous feedback of strengths and weaknesses. Students REDO their school assignments until they master the academic material and earn an A Grade: "Every Student Is a Success Story."

5. There is time to teach the craft of writing. Students are required to write as many rough drafts as is necessary to earn an A Grade: "Every Student Is a Success Story."

6. Spiritual Education: Spiritual growth is the development of the "Light From Within." Students keep a daily gratitude journal to foster appreciation, fulfillment, contentment, and inner peace.

7. Education is measured by in-depth comprehension, long-term retention, and mastery of the academic material.

8. Students earn a diploma and an education.

9. Students are able to use their knowledge to further the progress of civilization.

Quantity Over Quality Curriculum-Driven Education System

Teachers only have time to teach a general overview

In the first week of school students fall behind

Students do not have learning tools to process academic material

Students "Read, Cram, Regurgitate, and Test"

The "Academic Pressure Cooker" Education is measured by abusive (tricky) "Hotdog" exams

Teachers do not have time to teach the craft of writing

Students cut corners and cheat to pass, survive, and graduate

Students earn grades of A, B, C, D, and F

Students are anxious, stressed, depressed, disconnected, distracted, disgruntled, blocked, and suicidal

Students suffer "Pain of Inadequacy" Students graduate with "Scars of Incompetence"

THE WAR ZONE
Few Heroes, Heavy Casualties, and Senseless Fatalities

DROP OUT NATION
Students fall behind, flounder, fail, and fall through the cracks of broken education system

Quality Over Quantity Learning-Processing Education System

Teachers have time to teach for in-depth comprehension

The school assignments have realistic-time allotments and detailed step-by-step instructions

Students have New Learning Technology, SMARTGRADES Processing Tools, in their Hands and at their Fingertips.

Students earn a Grade A or REDO

Teachers provide continuous feedback of strengths and weaknesses

Students REDO assignment until mastery is achieved and an Grade A is earned

No "Hotdog" Exams
No "Read, Cram, Regurgitate, and Test"

Writing is Rewriting:
Students learn how to write, edit, and rewrite until mastery is achieved.

Spiritual Education
Students develop mind, body, and spirit

School environment is conducive to the love of learning

Education is measured by in-depth comprehension, long-term retention, and mastery of academic material

Students earn a diploma and an education

Every Student Is a Success Story

Education Is the Only Path to a Peaceful World

Strengths and Weaknesses

We live in an imperfect world. There are only imperfect solutions to imperfect problems. The most that we can ever hope for, President Obama's "Audacity of Hope," is an imperfect solution to our imperfect problem. The best example of this is found in medicine because every medication that alleviates one medical problem has side effects that can create a new medical problem. As a result, when making a decision, we have to weigh advantage and disadvantage, strength and weakness, good and bad, and right and wrong.

The new education paradigm the, "Quality Over Quantity Learning-Processing Education System," can save the lives of millions of American children:

- The Silent Crisis Destroying America's Brightest Minds

- The Misdiagnosis of A.D.H.D.

- The Rising Rate of High School Dropouts

- The Rising Prison Population

- The Rising Rate of School Shootings and Massacres

- The Rising Rate of School Bomb Scares

- The Rising Rate of College Binge-Drinking and Driving

- The Rising Rate of College Depression and Suicide

- The Rising Rate of Childhood Obesity and Illness

- The Destruction of Lateral Right-Brain Creative Students

- The Rising Rate of Students Bullied at School and Suicide

Inadequate/Abusive Parenting
Each of the above problems is exacerbated by the problem of inadequate/abusive parenting practices in the home. Too many parents resort to humiliation and punishment for misbehavior and justify it as teaching a child a lesson for his/her own good.

Notes of Gratitude
Educators who read this book always find something in it that added value to a student, a classroom, and a school. I am delighted to read letters from educators and parents who have thanked me for this book. It is difficult to read a letter from a parent who has lost a brilliant child to suicide. Even before the book was published, I received emails about kids who were lost to suicide. In time, I know this book will save the lives of millions of American children, as well as children around the world because, "Education Is the Only Path to a Peaceful World."

The question that needs analysis is:
Q: Should implementing the new education paradigm be a government initiative or a grass-roots effort on the part of educators?

A Grass-Roots Education Initiative is Required
I recommend that every school in America begin the education paradigm shift, at a grass-roots level, from the "Quantity Over Quality Curriculum-Driven Education System" to the "Quality Over Quantity Learning-Processing Education System."

Shifting the education paradigm to the, Quality Over Quantity, Learning-Processing education system, is the second stepping stone of academic success that will reenvision, reinvent, and rebuild the American education system to meet the challenges of the 21st century and bring us all two steps closer to a peaceful world.

The trouble with the world is not that people know too little, but that they know so many things that ain't so.

Mark Twain

In religion and politics, people's
beliefs and convictions are
in almost every case gotten
at second hand, and
without examination.

Mark Twain

When the President Decides Something on Monday,
He Still Believes it on Wednesday...
No Matter What Happened Tuesday.

Stephen Colbert

Reenvision, Reinvent, and Rebuild

The Third Stepping Stone of Academic Success

IN-DEPTH COMPREHENSION
Give Teachers Time to Teach for
In-Depth Comprehension

The third stepping stone for academic success is in-depth comprehension. In the "Quality Over Quantity Learning-Processing Education system" teachers have time to teach academic material for in-depth comprehension. Students will obtain the "SMARTGRADES Critical Thinking Skills" to analyze, synthesize, and evaluate academic material for in-depth comprehension. Students will have time to ask interesting questions, and teachers will have time to examine questions and explore answers: "Every Student Is a Success Story."

According to a rabbinical saying, "Don't limit a child to your own learning, for he was born in another time" (unknown). It is not enough to ask students to parrot back academic material. Students need to develop their own capacity to think and argue for or against the academic issues based on their own powers of intellectual discernment. Controversial issues are most often the ones that threaten traditional belief systems that were ingrained at an early age and transmitted from one generation to another without question, understanding, or reason, e.g., faith vs. reason. Once in-depth comprehension and "SMARTGRADES Critical Thinking Skills" are brought to bear on the issues, kernels of truth can be culled from preconceived biases, prejudices, and outright lies.

In-Depth Comprehension: SMARTGRADES Critical Thinking Skills
SMARTGRADES Critical Thinking Skills, sharpen the mind and teach students not what to think, but how to think about what they are reading. They are no longer passive receptacles who assume that a written word is flawless and without imperfection. Students learn how to locate an imperfection and find a kernel of truth. To meet the academic challenges of the 21st century, students need to learn how to comprehend the complex variables of a problem and find an imperfect solution to an imperfect problem.

Here is a sample school assignment from a Quality Over Quantity Learning-Processing education system, with critical thinking skills, realistic-time allotments, and detailed step-by-step instructions:

1. Read Only (1x)
Read for a general overview of the main ideas and supporting details: 2 hours.

2. Read Again (2x) and Outline
Read again for in-depth comprehension. Make an outline of the main ideas and supporting details: 4 hours.

3. Read Again (3x) and Think
Use your, SMARTGRADES Critical Thinking Skills, to analyze, synthesize, and evaluate academic material for in-depth comprehension: 4 hours.

Step 1. Read with a Critical Mind
Step 2. Separate Facts from Opinions
Step 3. Evaluate the Underlying Assumptions
Step 4. Read for Arguments Based on Fallacies
Step 5. Read for Inductive and Deductive Reasoning
Step 6. Read Passage for Patterns of Organization

Total estimated time: 10 hours
Total actual time:
Hand in a time log with your assignment
List a minimum of five questions for class discussions
Date due: April 3rd

Let's Recap: In-Depth Comprehension

1. Teaching is a time-intensive activity. Teachers need time to teach for in-depth comprehension of academic material.

2. Learning is a time-intensive activity. It takes time to learn. The learning curve is steep. Students need "time to learn."

3. Students need, SMARTGRADES Critical Thinking Skills, to analyze, synthesize, and evaluate academic material for in-depth comprehension.

4. To meet the challenges of the 21st century, students need to learn how to sift through the academic mountains of, intellectual bullshit, to find the small molehill of discernible academic truth. On a daily basis, the public is assaulted with these news bulletins: "Eating Broccoli Could Prevent Bladder Cancer" or "Add Broccoli to Your Dog's Food to Help Prevent Cancer." In these two examples, the discernible kernels of truth are: Broccoli is a healthy vegetable, broccoli does not prevent cancer, and broccoli will not prevent cancer in your dog.

Giving teachers time to teach for in-depth comprehension and SMARTGRADES Critical Thinking Skills, make-up the third stepping stone of academic success that will reenvision, reinvent, and rebuild the American education system to meet the challenges of the 21st century, and bring us all three steps closer to a peaceful world.

"Academic Insanity:" Special Education Students

"Jessica Shyu is tired of testing kids. She wants to teach, and not to the test. She is also 'tired of watching my students in special education feel like losers for failing a seventh grade test, when in fact they have already made two years of growth to reach the third grade reading level this year. I am tired of watching all that confidence we built up over the past eight months be blown away by a single state-mandated test.'"

Jessica Shyu
Special education teacher at an elementary and
middle school on the Navajo Nation in New Mexico
Teach For America, Second Year
Blog: http://blogs.edweek.org/teachers/jshyu/

Teachers are expected to reach unattainable goals with inadequate tools. The miracle is that at times they accomplish this impossible task.

Dr. Haim Ginott

2009 Subway Ads from the N.Y.C. Board of Education

The New York City education subway ads are embarrassing. Respectively, 20% and 34% improvement ratios in seven years are pathetic. Get a clue: When America's children become America's first priority, these education problems will be resolved.

N.Y.C. Subway Advertisement One
Because finishing high school is the start of a better future, N.Y.C. Public High Schools have increased their graduation rates by more than 20% since 2002.
KEEP IT GOING, NYC

New York City's high school drop out rate hovers around 50%. If you were a farmer and 50% of your tomatoes failed to grow, would you blame the bad tomato seeds, or change your planting techniques? To solve this problem, students need learning tools, SMARTGRADES Processing Tools. Most students are surviving, but not thriving. The 50% of students who graduate will earn a diploma, but not an education because they graduate bearing the "Scars of Incompetence."

N.Y.C. Subway Advertisement Two
Because every student deserves a safe learning environment, N.Y.C. public schools have achieved a 34% drop in major school crimes since 2002.
KEEP IT GOING, NYC

To solve this problem, before the age of puberty, educators have to educate the whole student: Mind, body, and spirit. Spiritual education, "the light from within" is the key to socializing a human animal into a human being. Big kids rob little kids for their lunch money and iPods. Without love, education, law, and a job, the human animal is the nastiest animal on the planet. On Planet Earth, biological survival is the only game in town. In Africa, the human animal has murdered a herd of elephants just for their tusks, or murdered gorilla mothers to sell their babies to a circus. When nasty nature is compounded by nasty nurture, a genocide, as in Darfur, is splattered across the front page of the newspaper. Right here in America, there are puppy mills. Man's best friend, the dog, is caged and crippled, used and abused for breeding puppies. I am a cat lover and I am appalled.

Reenvision, Reinvent, and Rebuild

The Fourth Stepping Stone of Academic Success

NEW LEARNING TECHNOLOGY
Give Students **SMARTGRADES** Processing Tools for Long-Term Retention

The fourth stepping stone for academic success is the new learning technology, **SMARTGRADES** Processing Tools. In a "Quality Over Quantity Learning-Processing Education System" students will have "time to learn" and obtain learning tools to "learn and process" academic material for in-depth comprehension, long-term retention, and mastery of academic material:

- **SMARTGRADES** Organization Tools
- **SMARTGRADES** Time Management Tools
- **SMARTGRADES** English Essay Tools
- **SMARTGRADES** Research Report Tools

According to Abraham Lincoln, "Give me six hours to chop down a tree and I will spend the first four sharpening the axe" (brainyquote.com). The right tools to get the job done is the secret to the successful completion of the task at hand. Moreover, preparation for a task, ensures the successful execution of a task.

I ask every student, "Do you want to be an A student?" Every student answers the question with an enthusiastic "Yes." All students want to do well, they just don't know how. If you want something to come out of a child, you have to put something into a child.

If you want good grades to come out of a child, you have to put learning tools, SMARTGRADES Processing Tools, into a child. In the third grade, students should be required to learn the ten SMARTGRADES Processing Tools, before they are asked to cram voluminous academic facts into the mind and onto a test.

Here is a sample school assignment from the, Quality Over Quantity Learning-Processing Education System, with SMARTGRADES Processing Tools, realistic-time allotments, and detailed step-by-step instructions:

1. Read Only (1x)
Read for a general overview of the main ideas and supporting details: 2 hours

2. Read (2X) and Process "Digestion"
Use your, SMARTGRADES Processing Tools, to "learn and process" academic material for long-term retention: 5 hours
SMARTGRADES 10 Step Processing Tools
Step 1. Estimation Tool
Step 2. Divide and Conquer Tool
Step 3. Active-Reading Tool
Step 4. Extraction Tool
Step 5. Condensation Tool
Step 6. Association Tool
Step 7. Test-Review Note Tool
Step 8. Conversion Tool
Step 9. Visualization Tool
Step 10. Self-Testing Tool

Total estimated time: 7 hours
The actual time:
Write down five questions for class discussions
Hand in a time log with your assignment

NEW! SMARTGRADES School Notebooks
SMARTGRADES Processing Tools are placed directly into the hands of all students. School notebooks are no longer just two pieces of blank cardboard with one-hundred pieces of blank paper. The new school notebooks contain SMARTGRADES Processing Tools.

SMARTGRADES BRAIN POWER REVOLUTION
www.smartgrades.com

Let's Recap: Learning Tools for Academic Success
1. The human brain is the post powerful biological machine in the world, and therefore, "Every Student Is a Success Story"

2. Education is measured by in-depth comprehension, long-term retention, and mastery of the academic material.

3. To meet the challenges of the 21st century, students need, SMARTGRADES Processing Tools, to "learn and process" academic material for long-term retention, and for instant recognition and recall on tests.

4. Students will earn a diploma and an education.

The new learning technology, SMARTGRADES Processing Tools, are the fourth stepping stone of academic success that will reenvision, reinvent, and rebuild the American education system to meet the challenges of the 21st century, and bring us all four steps closer to a peaceful world.

Education Is the Only Path to a Peaceful World

Education Is Measured by Three Criteria:

1. In-Depth Comprehension (Critical Thinking Tools)

2. Long-Term Retention (SMARTGRADES Processing Tools)

3. Mastery of the Academic Material (Continuous Feedback of Strengths and Weaknesses)

Sharon Rose Sugar
Paladin of Education for the 21st Century
www.smartgrades.com

Every Student Is a Success Story!

PHOTON
SUPERHERO OF EDUCATION
www.BooksNotBombs.com

You Can Do More Than Survive You Can Succeed!

Every student is born with a powerful brain, that is capable of mastering the facts and earning an A grade.

Students who graduate with C grades suffer the "Pain of Inadequacy" and bear the "Scars of Incompetence." These students earn a diploma, but not an education.

Let's Recap: How Does Learning Take Place?

Reenvision, Reinvent, and Rebuild

The Fifth Stepping Stone of Academic Success

NEW GRADING SYSTEM
Mastery: Every Student Is a Success Story

The fifth stepping stone for academic success is the "New Grading System." In the Quality Over Quantity Learning-Processing Education System, there are only two grades: Grade A or REDO. Teachers will have time for continuous feedback of strengths and weaknesses until students achieve mastery of academic material: "Every Student Is a Success Story."

According to Stephen R. Covey, "To focus on technique is like cramming your way through school. You sometimes get by, perhaps even get good grades, but if you don't pay the price day in and day out, you'll never achieve true mastery of the subjects you study or develop an educated mind" (Stephen R. Covey, *Principle-centered Leadership*, Free Press, 1992, p. 58).

Let's examine this astute insight by breaking the quote down into two disparate messages. The first message is that "cramming your way through school," "getting by," and "good grades" earns you a diploma, but not an education. The second message of "achieve mastery" and "develop an educated mind" are what is required to obtain a diploma and an education.

For students to meet the challenges of the 21st century, mastery of academic material will be required. There is really no point in handing out the grades of B, C, D, and F. These grades are signs that students have not mastered the academic material and that students need to reread, rethink, reprocess, rewrite, and REDO the school assignment until mastery of academic material is achieved and an A grade is earned.

When a student enters my office, one of the first conversations we have is about the grades A, B, C, D, and F. I explain that grades are the percentage of facts that a student returns to the teacher on a homework assignment, research report, and test:

Grade A = 100% of the facts are returned to a teacher.
Grade B = 80% of the facts are returned to a teacher.
Grade C = 70% of the facts are returned to a teacher.

Let's Recap: The Grade A Facts
Grades are not about a student. Grades are all about the facts. A student's job is to retrieve the facts and return the facts. A student retrieves the facts from the blackboard, textbook, and handouts. A student then returns the facts to the teacher on a homework assignment, research report, and test.

Let's Recap: The Superhighway of Academic Success
Academic facts move along the continuum called "The Superhighway of Academic Success." The facts move from the blackboard into a homework assignment, into a research paper, and through the student's brain and onto a test. The facts are like multicolored jellybeans. The facts are voluminous and they come in six different varieties:
1. There are WHO facts
2. There are WHERE facts
3. There are WHEN facts
4. There are WHY facts
5. There are WHAT facts
6. There are HOW facts

In some cases, I like to use the worst-case scenario to describe the obstacle course of academic achievement to my students:

Here is the worst-case scenario:
1. Pretend that your parents are lunatics. They can't agree on anything. Your father tells you to go the right, and your mother tells you to go to the left.

2. Pretend that your home is a war zone: Divorce

3. Pretend that you are in the worst school in the city: Metal detectors

4. Pretend that your teacher hates you: You like to tell jokes in class because you have a captive audience

5. Pretend that you have no friends in school: You have big ears

6. Pretend that a psychiatrist misdiagnosed you with A.D.H.D., an "incurable brain disorder: You are disconnected, depressed, distracted, disgruntled, and disobedient.

7. Pretend that every week you have to take a "hotdog" test

Now all of your excuses for academic failure have been exhausted. It doesn't matter if all of these real-life obstacles are in your life. You can still become an excellent student. A basketball player runs the ball up the court, gets in position, shoots and scores. The player sees only two things, the ball, and the basket. The opposing five players are obstacles to his success. In a perfect world, teammates work together, but in the worst-case scenario, your teammates are all vying for the ball and each one wants to be the one who shoots and scores. My students know that school has little to do with them and everything to do with the facts. That is why the student is never the problem. Students learn to "retrieve the facts" and "return the facts" and score an A grade.

Education Is the Only Path to a Peaceful World

When a failing student starts working with me, I first have to rebuild the student's self-confidence and make a student see that an A grade is a possibility, that is near at hand. I ask the student to write down his name on a piece of paper. I tell a student that his name is a "WHO" fact and give the student an A grade. I ask the student for his address. I tell the student that his address is a "WHERE" fact and I give the student an A grade. I ask the student for today's date. I tell the student that the date is a "WHEN" fact, and I give the student an A grade. We are moving very slowly in the right direction towards extracting the critical facts and earning A grades. This simple exercise begins the slow and steady climb to extracting the key facts from a sentence, and then from a paragraph, and before long, the student understands that doing well in school is all about the facts, and that earning A grades is within his reach, power, and control.

My students work on school assignments and earn a REDO until they have achieved mastery of academic material and earn an A grade. The grades of C and D make students feel inferior and destroy their self-confidence. There is no point to them. The grade of REDO tells students to fix their errors and learn from their mistakes. This is how learning takes place in the real world. Many times you have to get it all wrong, before you can get it all right. If you are afraid to fail, you will never be able to succeed because success is often a result of learning from mistakes and correcting the errors after you make them. Eventually, if you persist at the task of self correction, you will find the solution to the problem at hand. If you don't learn to correct your mistakes, you will continue to make the same mistakes over and over again. The learning curve is steep. It takes time to learn. Learning requires trial and error. Learning requires practice until an A grade is earned.

Teachers need to correct the essays, make a list of the strengths and weaknesses, and have students correct their errors until mastery is achieved and an A grade is earned.

It bears repeating as many times as is necessary throughout this book, ad nauseam, that:

The Second Universal Standard Gold Standard of Education

Children Cannot Raise Themselves. If a Child is Failing, It Is Never the Child's Fault.

It is irresponsible of educators to let children fall behind, flounder, fail, and fall through the cracks of the malfunctioning American education system. If a student spends eight hours a day in a school, then the school is responsible for teaching a student how to achieve academic success in school, and in life.

There is no point in letting students graduate with C and D grades and bear the "Scars of Incompetence." Students need to learn how to develop their strengths and iron out their weaknesses to overcome the obstacles to their success.

The two-tier grading system of Grade A or REDO allows teaching and learning to take place. Teachers are required to provide continuous feedback of strengths and weaknesses which is part and parcel of good teaching practices. If teachers have time to teach and students have time to learn, then mastery of academic material will be achieved: "Every Student Is a Success Story."

Sample School Assignment from New Grading System

Every Student in America Is a Success Story

Grade A: Strengths **REDO: Weaknesses**

1.   1.

2.   2.

3.   3.

　　　4.

　　　5.

　　　6.

　　　7.

　　　8.

　　　9.

　　　10.

　　　11.

Correct your weaknesses and resubmit your paper for an A Grade: "Every Student Is a Success Story"

SMARTGRADES: EVERY STUDENT IS A SUCCESS

Let's Recap: New Grading System of Grade A or REDO

1. New two-tier grading system of Grade A or REDO.

2. Teachers have time for continuous feedback of strengths and weaknesses.

3. Students correct their mistakes until mastery is achieved.

4. All students achieve mastery of academic material and earn an A grade: "Every Student Is a Success Story."

5. America will keep her promise to educate every student to meet the challenges of the 21st century: "Every Student Is a Success Story."

6. Students will earn a diploma and an education.

7. America will have the greatest education system in the world.

8. Students will be able to use their knowledge to further the progress of civilization.

The new two-tier grading system of Grade A or REDO and continuous feedback of strengths and weaknesses from teachers ensures mastery of academic material, and ensures that, "Every Student Is a Success Story." This is the fifth stepping stone of academic success that will reenvision, reinvent, and rebuild the American education system to meet the challenges of the 21st century, and bring us all five steps closer to a peaceful world.

Earn a Diploma, But Not an Education

- Teaching and learning sacrificed to push curriculum
- No time for in-depth comprehension
- No learning tools to process for long-term retention
- No continuous feedback of strengths and weaknesses to master the academic material
- Learn how to cut corners and cheat to survive
- "Read, Cram, Regurgitate, and Test"
- Suffer the "Pain of Inadequacy"
- Bear the "Scars of Incompetence"
- No practical business skills to earn a living
- Incur financial debt from school loans (40 years)
- Move back home with mom and dad and ask for help

I Have Never Let My Schooling Interfere with My Education.
Mark Twain

If a Child Can't Learn the Way We Teach,
Maybe We Should Teach the Way They Learn.
Ignacio Estrada

"The test of a good teacher is not how many questions he can ask his pupils that they will answer readily, but how many questions he inspires them to ask him which he finds it hard to answer."

Alice Wellington Rollins

Reenvision, Reinvent, and Rebuild

The Sixth Stepping Stone of Academic Success

Get a Clue: How Learning Takes Place

The sixth stepping stone for academic success is understanding the central question at the heart of education: How does learning take place? The next critical question that needs to be addressed is: Are educators running a school for academic success, or an education asylum riddled with academic insanity?

According to Lou Ann Walker, "Theories and goals of education don't matter a whit if you don't consider your students to be human beings." Ms. Walker's book, *A Loss for Words*, portrays her experience as one of three siblings growing up with two deaf parents (Lou Ann Walker, A Loss for Words, Harper Perennial, 1987).

This insightful remark reminds us that educators have to put the needs of the students first, not the bombastic curriculum. Students do not grow, develop, and mature at the same rate, and these innate and environmental differences have to be taken into account.

A simple plant has complex needs of soil, water, and sun. The soil must be full of nutrients, the water must be the right amount and the right temperature, and the sun must be direct or indirect sunlight. If any one of these variables is out of sync, the seeds will not be able to grow, develop, and mature properly.

I often tell parents that a child is a more complex life form than a plant and has more complex needs. If you stop watering your plant, your plant will start to die. Your child needs three daily meals for biological nourishment, and at least three daily doses of love for emotional nourishment. You don't find love, you create love. There is no such thing as too much love. Learning requires daily doses of emotional support and encouragement from parents, as well as from teachers.

Let's Recap: School is a brain gym. Students eat facts and build their brain muscles. School is a restaurant. Facts are on the menu and students eat facts and feed their brain. Like a sandwich, you cannot stuff a whole sandwich into your mouth, you have to take small bites, chew, chew, chew, and digest. Students need small amounts of digestible knowledge. Students need time to break down the facts into bite-size pieces to process the facts. To absorb knowledge, the mind needs just the right amount of facts, similar to a plant that needs to absorb just the right amount of water to grow. If a student is given too many facts, the mind will not absorb all of the facts and they will fall on deaf ears.

How Learning Takes Place

1. Brain Power: Learning requires nurturing and cultivating the awesome power of the human brain. The brain requires small amounts of digestible facts: Chew (in-depth comprehension), chew (long-term retention), chew (mastery of the academic material) and digest.

2. Time: The learning curve is steep. It takes time to learn.

3. Energy: Learning requires tremendous amounts of energy, namely, healthy eating habits and a regular bedtime.

4. Learning requires a peaceful environment that is conducive to the love of learning.

5. Learning requires breaking down big tasks into smaller tasks.

6. Learning requires in-depth comprehension.

7. Learning requires emotional support and encouragement.

8. Learning requires self-love, self-esteem, and self-reliance.

9. Learning requires realistic-time allotments for assignments

10. Learning requires detailed step-by-step instructions for assignments.

11. Learning requires, SMARTGRADES Processing Tools, for long-term retention.

12. Learning requires infinite patience.

13. Learning requires time for practice and repetition.

14. Learning requires time for trial and error.

15. Learning requires time to ask and answer questions.

16. Learning requires time for continuous feedback of strengths and weaknesses until mastery is achieved.

17. Education is measured by in-depth comprehension, long-term retention, and mastery of academic material.

Here is a typical school assignment from the, Quantity Over Quality, Curriculum-Driven American Education System. There are no realistic-time allotments and no detailed step-by step instructions:

Part 1.
Write a five-page research paper on "Education in America."
The paper is due April 10th.

Here is a sample school assignment from the, Quality Over Quantity Learning-Processing Education System, with realistic-time allotments and detailed step-by-step instructions:

Write a five-page research paper on "Education in America."
SMARTGRADES Research Skills: 20 hours
 1. Choose a researchable topic
 2. Use three primary sources
 3. Find the experts in the field
 4. Find interesting quotes from the experts
 5. Find pro and con arguments
 6. Paraphrase research material

SMARTGRADES Writing Skills: 20 hours
 1. Write an outline: Main ideas and supporting details
 2. Write a rough draft: Introduction, body, and conclusion
 3. Use transition words to build bridges between ideas
 4. SMARTGRADES Critical Thinking Skills: Analyze, synthesize, and evaluate arguments
 5. Add footnotes or endnotes
 6. Add a bibliography

SMARTGRADES Proofreading Skills: 20 hours
 1. Reread, revise, and rewrite as many times as is necessary
 2. Use a computer spellchecker

SMARTGRADES: EVERY STUDENT IS A SUCCESS

3. Use computer speech software to hear your paper read aloud (the ears can hear what the eyes cannot see)

4. Visit your school's writing center for a final proofreading

The estimated time required: 80 hours
The actual time required: _____
Due date: April 10th
Hand in your paper and a time log

Part 2.
Correct your errors and resubmit an error-free paper for an A Grade: "Every Student Is a Success Story"

Let's Recap: How Learning Takes Place?
1. To meet the challenges of the 21st century, educators need to get a clue: How Does Learning Take Place? Education is measured by in-depth comprehension, long-term retention, and mastery of academic material. Students earn a diploma and an education.

2. Education is not measured by "Read, Cram, Regurgitate, and Test" and abusive (tricky) "Hotdog" exams that are taken under psychological duress and given with a stopwatch. Two weeks after a test, the facts disappear into a black hole in the mind. Students are uneducated. Students suffer the "Pain of Inadequacy" and graduate bearing the "Scars of Incompetence." Students have become anxious, stressed, disconnected, distracted, depressed, disgruntled, and suicidal. Students earn a diploma, but not an education.

Understanding "How Learning Takes Place," is the sixth stepping stone of academic success that will reenvision, reinvent, and rebuild the American education system to meet the challenges of the 21st century, and bring us all six steps closer to a peaceful world.

The New York Times Newspaper
Comprehensive, up-do-date, and global,
the best education in the world is easily
accessible and entirely affordable because it is
attained by reading The New York Times newspaper.

Sharon Rose Sugar
The Paladin of Education for the 21st Century

Libraries Raised Me

I don't believe in colleges and universities.
I believe in libraries because most students
don't have any money. When I graduated from
high school, it was during the Depression and we
had no money. I couldn't go to college, so I went to
the library three days a week for ten years.

Ray Bradbury

Teacher Empowerment Book for Academic Success
The Universal Gold Standard of Education

1. Nurture and Cultivate the Awesome Power of the Human Brain
2. Feed the Whole Student: Mind, Body, and Spirit
3. Students Mature at Different Rates and Have Unique Minds
4. Academic Planner Tools
5. New Learning Technology: SMARTGRADES Processing Tools
6. Realistic Time Allotments for School Assignments
7. Step-by-Step Instructions for Essays and Research Reports
8. School Assignments Come with a Student Checklist (easier to grade)
9. The Craft of Writing is an Art Form: Growth, Development & Maturation
10. The Continuous Feedback of Strengths and Weaknesses
11. New Grading System: Grade A or REDO
12. Every Student Is a Success Story

Reenvision, Reinvent, and Rebuild

The Seventh Stepping Stone of Academic Success

THE UNIVERSAL GOLD STANDARD OF EDUCATION

The seventh stepping stone for academic success is "The Universal Gold Standard of Education." These are the blueprints that will lay the foundation for a "Quality Over Quantity Learning-Processing Education System." This blueprint will ensure that all students receive an education that nurtures and develops their brain power to unlock its potential, cultivate its power, and set free its promise: "Every Student Is a Success Story."

According to Albert Einstein, "It is, in fact, nothing short of a miracle that the modern methods of instruction have not entirely strangled the holy curiosity of inquiry." Albert Einstein is the greatest scientist of the 20th century. Einstein is also the world's most famous high school dropout. Although he received exceptional marks in mathematics and physics, Einstein failed one of those "Hotdog" entrance exams and this academic failure has never been understood, until now. To pass the entrance exam, Einstein had to "Read, Cram, Regurgitate, and Test" voluminous academic facts under psychological duress and a stopwatch. Einstein's family life had destabilized. Einstein's family moved from Germany to Italy, and it is within reason to assume that he was distracted by family problems. In Switzerland, he enrolled in school and earned his high school diploma. He had "time to learn" the academic material and pass his college entrance exam.

Notwithstanding his academic setbacks, Albert Einstein, resumed his studies and made his mark on the world. Einstein is best known for his Theory of Relativity and the equation, mass–energy equivalence, $E = mc^2$. Einstein received the Nobel Prize in 1921 for his work on the Law of the Photoelectric Effect (1905) (Einstein, Wikipedia).

Here is the short list from "The Universal Gold Standard of Education" that lays the groundwork for the, "Quality Over Quantity Learning-Processing Education System." These education principles ensure that teaching and learning are not compromised, so that students earn an education and a diploma (*The Universal Gold Standard of Education*, Appendix G).

The 1st Universal Gold Standard of Education
The human brain is the most powerful biological machine in the world. The human brain needs to be nurtured and cultivated to fulfill its potential.

The 2nd Universal Gold Standard
Children Cannot Raise Themselves
If a Child Is Failing, It Is Never the Child's Fault

The 3rd Universal Gold Standard
All Children Want To Do Well, They Just Don't Know How

The 4th Universal Gold Standard
If You Want Something to Come Out of a Child,
You Have to Put Something into the Child.
If You Want Students to Earn Good Grades,
You Have to Give Students Learning Tools,
SMARTGRADES Processing Tools.

The 5th Universal Gold Standard
Students Have Unique Minds that Require Early Intervention

The 6th Universal Gold Standard
Educate the Whole Student: Mind, Body, and Spirit

The 7th Universal Gold Standard
Get a Clue: How Does Learning Take Place?

The 8th Universal Gold Standard
Learning Requires a Peaceful Environment that is Conducive to the Love of Learning

The 9th Universal Gold Standard
Learning Requires an Environment that is Free of Anxiety, Stress, Depression, and Suicidal Thoughts

The 10th Universal Gold Standard
Learning Requires Constant Support and Encouragement

The 11th Universal Gold Standard
If You Want to Do Something Right You Have to Put Time into it

The 12th Universal Gold Standard
The Learning Curve is Steep. It Takes Time to Learn.

The 13th Universal Gold Standard
Teaching and Learning Are Time-Intensive Activities

The 14th Universal Gold Standard
Learning Requires In-Depth Comprehension

The 15th Universal Gold Standard
Learning Requires School Assignments
with Realistic-Time Allotments

The 16th Universal Gold Standard
Learning Requires School Assignments with
Detailed Step-By-Step Instructions

The 17th Universal Gold Standard
Learning Requires Infinite Patience

The 18th Universal Gold Standard
Learning Requires Time to Practice

The 19th Universal Gold Standard
Learning Requires Time for Trial and Error

The 20th Universal Gold Standard
Learning Requires Time for Continuous Feedback
of Strengths and Weaknesses

The 21st Universal Gold Standard
Learning Requires Time to Ask Questions and
Explore Answers

The 22nd Universal Gold Standard
Learning Requires Mastery
Learning requires continuous feedback of strengths and
weaknesses until mastery is achieved

The 23rd Universal Gold Standard
Learning Requires Daily Rewards
Punishment humiliates a child
Learning requires a bulletin board
showcasing excellent schoolwork

The 24th Universal Gold Standard
Learning Requires Energy to Learn
Students are required to eat a healthy
breakfast and have a regular bedtime
Q: Did you eat a healthy breakfast today?
Q: What time did you go to sleep?

The 25th Universal Gold Standard
Learning Requires Taking Small Steps
Learning requires breaking down big tasks into smaller steps
Q: Did you break the problem down into smaller steps?

The 26th Universal Gold Standard
Learning Requires Love
1. You have to put love into everything that you do
2. You don't find love, you create love
3. There is no such thing as too much love

Q: Did you put some love into it?

The 27th Universal Gold Standard
Learning Requires that Students Hand in
Time Logs with School Assignments:
Estimated Time: 5 hours
Actual Time: 7 hours

Education Is the Only Path to a Peaceful World

The 28th Universal Gold Standard
The lateral right-brain development of students, namely, intuition, insight, imagination, and creativity are the life blood of the movers and shakers of the world who are able to think "outside the box"

The 29th Universal Gold Standard
Education is not measured by abusive (tricky) "Hotdog" exams. Students cram voluminous academic with meager comprehension no learning tools, and for short-term retention, to regurgitate the facts onto a stressful, time-sensitive exam. Two weeks after the test, the academic facts disappear into a black hole in the mind an vanish into thin air. Students earn a diploma, but not an education. The students are uneducated. Students cannot use the academic material to enhance their own lives, or further the progress of civilization.

The 30th Universal Gold Standard

Education is Measured by Three Criteria:

1. In-Depth Comprehension: SMARTGRADES Critical Thinking Skills

2. Long-Term Retention: SMARTGRADES Processing Skills

3. Mastery of Academic Material: Continuous Feedback of Strengths and Weaknesses Until an A Grade is Earned

---

SMARTGRADES: EVERY STUDENT IS A SUCCESS

The 31st Universal Gold Standard
Prepare Students to Become Thinkers, Problem Solvers, and Leaders Who Contribute and Further the Progress of Civilization

The 32nd Universal Gold Standard
Prepare Students to Meet the Challenges of the Real World

The 33rd Universal Gold Standard
The Education Goalpost Is Students Who Are Self-Reliant and Life-Long Learners

The 34th Universal Gold Standard
Every Student Is a Success Story

The 35th Universal Gold Standard
Education Is the Only Path to a Peaceful World

(Book: The Universal Gold Standard of Education)

You are welcome to send in your suggestions for Universal Gold Standards of Education.
E-Mail: educate@smartgrades.com

The Universal Gold Standard of Education is the seventh stepping stone of academic success that will reenvision, reinvent, and rebuild the American education system to meet the challenges of the 21st century, and bring us all seven steps closer to a peaceful world.

Education Is the Only Path to a Peaceful World

Albert Einstein's Report Card
Board of Education of the Canton Aargau
School: Aargau Kantonsschule
Einstein Only Earned Top Grades for Math and Science

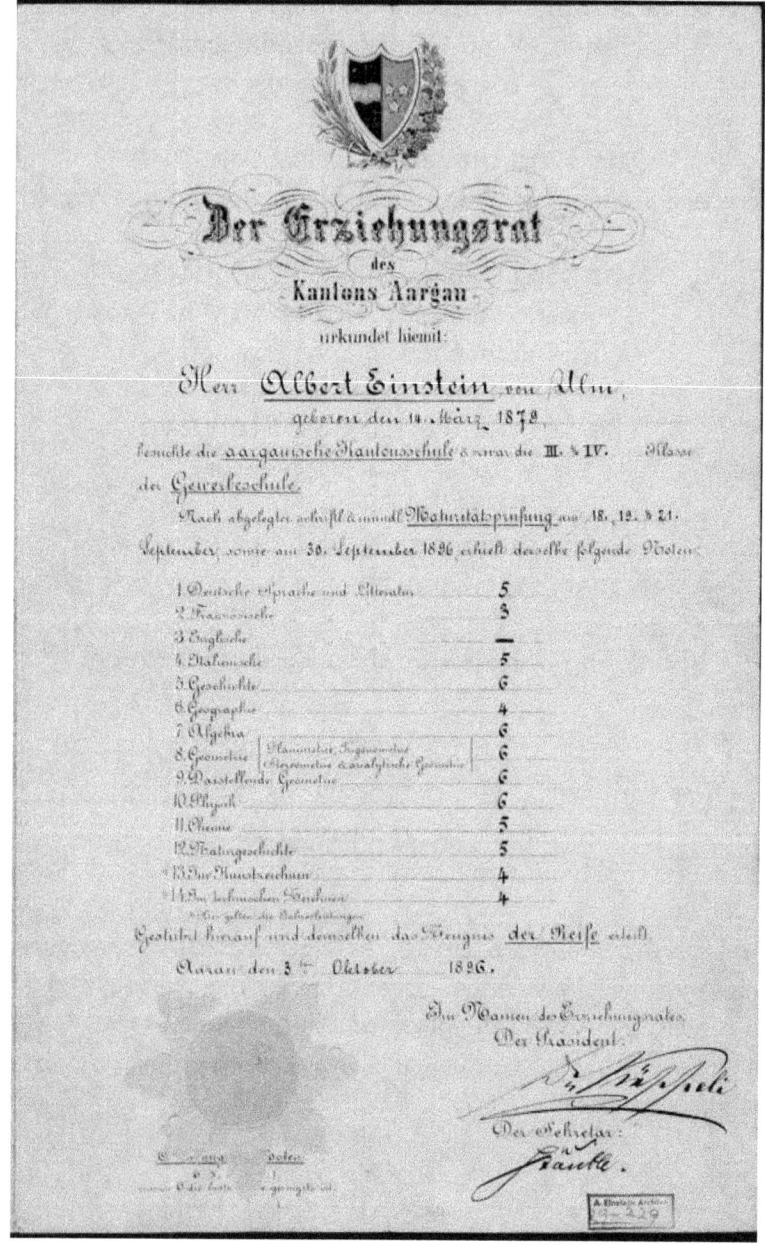

(© "Einstein," Wikipedia)

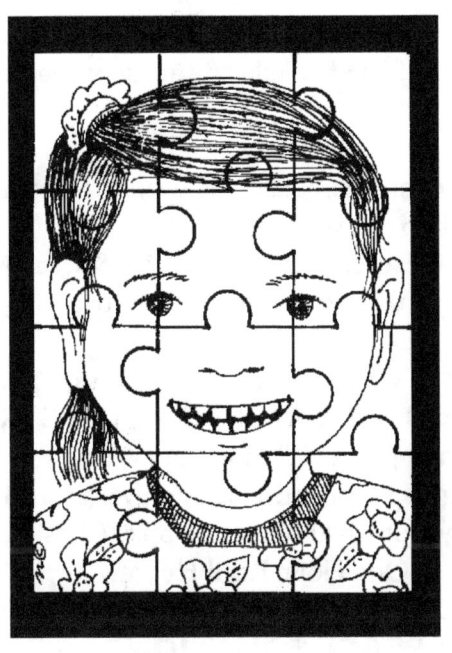

No [Wo]Man Is Born into the World
Whose Work Is not Born with [Her]Him.
James Russell Lowell

A Note for the Reader

Mrs. Eve Lampert was the only person to recognize the unique mind and special gifts embodied in her beautiful and brilliant daughter Sharon Esther Lampert, at the tender age of nine.

There are no special schools, teachers, or psychiatrists who can develop the innate gifts of this kind of creative genius.

Sharon's left eye is a human telescope and her right eye is a human microscope. Her brain processes the big picture and the small details. Sharon Esther is able to see all of the dots, and connect all the dots.

In the blink of an eye, automatic writing, Sharon brings new knowledge into the world:
- Prodigy: 10 Esoteric Laws of Genius & Creativity
- Philosophy: 10 Esoteric Laws of Inextricability
- Theology: GOD IS GO! DO!
- Theology: 22 Commandments, Universal Moral Compass
- Education: **SMARTGRADES SUCCESS STRATEGY**
- Poetry: Poetry World Record and World Famous Poems
- Psychology: 13 Steps to True and Everlasting Happiness and the 3 Stages of Child Abuse: Cripple, Parasite, and Predator
- Language: In One Hour, Read Hebrew
- C.A.P.S. Children's Science Curriculum, Grades 1-4
- **WORLD PEACE EQUATION**

Sharon exhibits extreme levels of emotional intensity and sensitivity. Neighbors often say, "That child is so intense. What is wrong with that child?" Religious people often say, namely rabbis, reverends, and Buddhists that, "The holy spirit is inside of her." These fan letters are published in her poetry book, "IMMORTALITY IS MINE."

If you want to see life through the eyes of a creative genius, visit Sharon Esther Lampert's websites:
- www.sharonestherlampert.com
- www.poetryjewels.com
- www.worldfamouspoems.com
- Thousands of websites around the world

Age 9
Letter from Mommy, Mrs. Eve Lampert to her daughter Sharon Esther:

"Dear Darling Sharon,
My Daughter is a Poet, Philosopher, and Teacher.
 Beauty and Brains!
I Love You, XXX"
— MOMMY

Mommy Update: Happy Birthday Mommy
The first printed copy of this book arrived on Mommy's birthday, June 3, 2009. This book of poetry, philosophy, and education is the best ever birthday present.

Age 9
Oral message from Daddy, Mr. Abraham Lampert to his daughter Sharon Esther:

"My Daughter Is Fabrent."*
— DADDY

* Fabrent is a yiddish word that means, "born with a fire burning under her tushee."

Learning **Differences** Not Labels

"No child needs to fail. Every child craves mastery and recognition. Every child can succeed-in his or her own way. The root system of a mind is getting established during childhood and adolescence. We must ensure that its branches will grow and bear fruit.

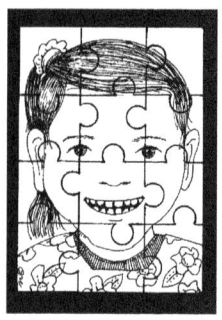

When a student experiences undue frustration in school, it is up to us to pinpoint precisely where a learning breakdown is occurring. We now possess the scientific know-how to identify even the most subtle problems with memory or language or attention or some other brain process that stands in the way of achievement in a promising yet faltering child or adolescent. We can then provide the right kind of help at the right time. We can and should accomplish this without having to resort to labels that oversimplify a person and have little therapeutic value. We can be far more specific and helpful than that. Most importantly, we can diagnose a child's strengths and affinities, making very sure that those aptitudes and interests are getting strengthened throughout her or his young life. After all, when you grow up, what really counts is how strong your strengths are! It is your strengths that will enable you to succeed in a career and contribute meaningfully as an adult. All children possess them. Let's not extinguish, undervalue, or ignore these assets.

No one should have to grow up with a misinterpreted mind, falsely accused or educationally mishandled. Success is like a vitamin—so essential if a child is to thrive and sustain motivation. Kids must feel a sense of optimism and excitement as they ponder their possibilities.

We will need new kinds of teachers, new kinds of schools that can understand and educate every kind of mind. To do so, we have to enlighten those who do the educating, along with policy makers, clinicians and parents. Our children themselves ought to be learning about learning while they are learning, and, in particular, they should never cease to acquire insights into the unique "wiring" of their own minds. We must help all of them discover who they are and where they need to head. Society can either benefit from their differences or else pay a heavy price for neglecting them."

Dr. Melvin Levine

Reenvision, Reinvent, and Rebuild

The Eighth Stepping Stone of Academic Success

Children Have Unique Minds that Require Early Intervention

The eighth stepping stone for academic success is that students are not blank slates, but come to school bearing the seeds of natural affinities, talents, and gifts. These seeds must be respected, nurtured, and cultivated as early as possible to ensure that students find their passion and purpose, fulfill their potential, and achieve peace and prosperity.

According to Professor Howard Gardner "We are not all the same; we do not all have the same kinds of minds… and education works more effectively if these differences are taken into account." His theory of multiple intelligence helps educators become aware of their students natural affinities (Howard Gardner, *Intelligence Reframed: Multiple Intelligences for the 21st Century*, Basic Books, 2000, p. 91).

The American school system is not designed to pay attention to individual students, but to treat them as fairly as possible within a group dynamic.

On the whole, students pursue their own interests during after-school hours and on weekends. Students struggle to juggle their schoolwork and extracurricular activities.

First, teachers should be encouraged to make an effort to discover the natural affinities of their seed-bearing students.

Second, teachers should be encouraged to help guide students in the direction that nurtures and cultivates a unique mind and natural affinity. Most schools have science fairs to showcase science experiments. Perhaps this idea can be expanded and students can have their own exhibition space within the school, to showcase their own special interests. Students have personal lockers, but need personal exhibition spaces to showcase their heros, heroines, and dreams for the future.

Teachers can recognize the unique minds of students by having a monthly student showcase called, "Follow Your Bliss." Set aside a special area in the school to showcase students' unique interests. Students are encouraged to contribute something that showcases their own interests, and is not graded. The following examples showcase students' unique minds:

Find Your Passion & Fulfill Your Potential

September: Student Reinventions of Inventions

October: Writing Exhibition of Poems, Essays, and Scribbles

November: Photography Exhibition of City Landscapes

December: Fashion Exhibition of Clothing Design Ideas

January: Exhibition of Drawings of Daydreams and Doodles

February: A Exhibition of Student Heros and Heroines

March: A Photography Exhibition of Country Landscapes

April: The Funnies: The Jokes that Make Us All Laugh and Smile

In some cases, your passion and purpose in life are deep within you and they come pouring out of you. My innate gift for poetry pours out of my soul effortlessly. My poems are written in minutes and there are no drafts. In this case, you don't find art; art finds you.

In other cases, you have to go in search of a passion and purpose and you may find them before they find you. For example, I initiated and pursued my passion of transforming F students into A students with the new learning technology, SMARTGRADES Processing Tools. I am on a mission to place the new learning technology, SMARTGRADES Processing Tools, directly into the hands of all students.

Every student doodles from time to time. When I catch a student drawing a cartoon in my office, I hang the drawing up in my office and celebrate the artistic achievement. In most cases, a student drawing a cartoon is enjoying a pleasurable escape from the "Academic Pressure Cooker." It is usually a sign of a break in concentration and that a student needs an impromptu respite. In some cases, it is a sign that a student is an artist and inspiration can strike without warning and interfere with studies. In some cases, it is both a sign that a student is stressed and needs a break and is an artist. The answer to the conundrum is found by examining the student's artwork for interpretation and meaning.

Early intervention in the natural affinities of seed-bearing students make up the eighth stepping stone of academic success that will reenvision, reinvent, and rebuild the American education system to meet the challenges of the 21st century, and bring us all eight steps closer to a peaceful world.

Education Is the Only Path to a Peaceful World

Intelligence Plus Character —
That Is the Goal of True Education.

Martin Luther King, Jr.

If You Want to Accomplish
the Goals of Your Life,
You Have to Begin with the Spirit.

Ms. Oprah Gayle Winfrey

Some of the most important things — patience, kindness, loyalty, curiosity, dependability, steadfastness, grit, wonder — cannot be measured on an exam."

Beverly Beckham

Kindness:
Kindness is a language which the deaf can hear and the blind can see.

Mark Twain

Courage:
Courage is the most important of all the virtues, because without courage you can't practice any other virtue consistently. You can practice any virtue erratically, but nothing consistently without courage.

Maya Angelou

Love:
Love recognizes no barriers. It jumps hurdles, leaps fences, penetrates walls to arrive at it destination full of hope.

Maya Angelou

Circle of Responsibility:

My Problems Have Solutions...
when I take responsibility for my problems have solutions
when I take responsibility for my problems have solutions
when I take responsibility for my problems have solutions
...When I Take Responsibility.

PHOTON SUPERHERO OF EDUCATION
EVERYBODY IS SOMEBODY SPECIAL
WORLD PEACE IS COMING TO PLANET EARTH
www.BooksNotBombs.com

Reenvision, Reinvent, and Rebuild

The Ninth Stepping Stone of Academic Success

Educate the Whole Student: Mind, Body, and Spirit

The ninth stepping stone for academic success is the spiritual development of students. The mind and the body follow the dictates of the spirit or the "Light from Within." In the, Quality Over Quantity Learning-Processing Education System, the spirit of a student is developed for the mind to be receptive to learning. Students learn that the 24-hour life cycle requires biological sustenance of food, sleep, and exercise and the spiritual sustenance of self-esteem, self-love, and self-actualization: "Every Student Is a Success Story."

According to Dr. Elizabeth Kubler-Ross, "People are like stained glass windows. They sparkle and shine when the sun is out, but when the darkness sets in, their true beauty is revealed only if there is a light from within" (Dr. Elizabeth Kubler-Ross, *On Death and Dying*, Scribner, 1969).

Spiritual education develops the "Light from Within." That "Light" is the inner voice in good times and bad times. Journal writing is an excellent way for students to simultaneously develop their English language writing skills and build the internal spiritual resources that are necessary to survive in a difficult, demanding, and dangerous world. The "human being" is a man-made artificial construct. Spiritual education socializes the nasty human animal into a loving human being. Students learn how to choose cooperation over competition, sharing over selfishness, love over hatred, and truth over lies.

Ms. Oprah Winfrey's ever popular "Gratitude Journal" is a great idea that needs to be implemented as early as possible to begin the spiritual development of students. Learning how to show appreciation and gratitude for what is good is perhaps the most important daily spiritual exercise of the day. The journey through life is a very bumpy road filled with obstacles, setbacks, delays, distractions and detours. It is important to learn how to take it all in stride and ride out the rough patches and get back on the track to take advantage of life's rich and infinite possibilities.

Journal Writing: The Integration of Mind, Body, and Spirit
The integration of the desires of the heart and ideas within the mind is an important goal of spiritual development.

Q: How do you get your heart and your head to work together and move in the same direction?

Journal Writing: Develop the Inner Voice of Students
Journal writing helps develop a student's inner voice and strengthens it in the face of competing voices of parents, school, society, and friends that can undermine a student's real needs and personal desires.

Q: How do you live your own life and fulfill your own dreams?

Journal Writing: The Daily Connection to Feelings and Thoughts
Journal writing helps students stay connected on a daily basis to their own feelings and thoughts and this inner connection is vital for maturation from childhood to adulthood.

Q: How do you stay connected to your own spirit and hear the quiet voice, the soft gentle whisper that emanates from one's own soul?

Journal Writing: The Processing of Life Experience

A journal acts as a reminder of past events, as well as casting a spotlight on the present moment, and on tracking future goals. It allows students to process their experiences. Students learn how to make more informed decisions Students learn how to develop their strengths and overcome their weaknesses.

Spiritual Education: My "Light From Within"

I begin all lessons with the spiritual development of my students. I ask my students the following two questions:

Q: Write down five things you are grateful for?

Q: What is your level of self-esteem on a scale of 1-10?

In other words, "What is your confidence level today? Are you feeling up to the challenge of reading, researching, writing, rewriting, and proofreading?" My students hardly ever say that they feel greater than an eight on a scale of one to ten. Eight is usually the best that my students feel on any given day.

My students need to rebuild their self-esteem and repair their broken wings. My students begin their lessons by reciting three spiritual affirmations:

1. **PHOTON SUPERHERO** Self-Esteem Affirmation

2. **PHOTON SUPERHERO** Circle of Responsibility Affirmation

3. **PHOTON SUPERHERO** Personal Empowerment Affirmation

PHOTON SUPERHERO* Self-Esteem
Self-Love Affirmation for Students:

I love you (insert student's name).
I will do everything in my power to help you achieve your dream.
My dream is to become a ....
Everything else that I say to myself is just NOISE.

Photon's* Circle of Responsibility
Affirmation for Students:

My Problems Have Solutions...
when I take responsibility for my problems have solutions
when I take responsibility for my problems have solutions
when I take responsibility for my problems have solutions
...When I Take Responsibility

*PHOTON SUPERHERO OF EDUCATION
www.BooksNotBombs.com

Students' Personal Problems
Every student has a personal problem that needs resolution. It is important for students to become good problem solvers. I teach my students that life is all about solving problems. Problems are composed of compound and complex variables. There are only imperfect solutions to imperfect problems.

Q: What personal problems do you want to tackle today?

Q: What personal problems do you have that have solutions?

Q: What personal problems do you have that are unsolvable?

Solve and Resolve: Action Plan, Detailed Steps, Analysis
Q: What is your plan of action? Take out your academic planner and we will map out detailed steps to solve and resolve the problem, as follows:

Plan A, Plan B, Plan C, Plan D, Plan E, Plan F . . . Plan Z

Students take out their "Academic Planner" and map out the day with a realistic game plan that takes into account their personal and academic lives. I teach my students to be grateful, if their list of personal problems have real solutions. Life is so outrageously unfair and too many people have chronic problems that are unmanageable, e.g., incurable diseases. My students learn how to make a list of the problems that need to be solved and resolved. Students learn how to tackle their personal problems by making an action plan of detailed baby steps that will resolve the problem. For example, almost all students have to learn how to make better food choices and manage their weight:

Breakfast: Large Meal
- Fiber and Fruits, e.g., Oatmeal Pie with Fresh Berries
- Hydrate (sugar-free)

Lunch: Large or Medium Meal
- Lean Protein, Fresh Vegetables, Carbohydrate
- Hydrate (sugar-free)

Dinner: Small Meal
- Soups and Salads (no bread or pasta)
- No Big Meals after 7:30 p.m.
- Hydrate (sugar-free)

Let's Recap: Q: What Did You Eat Today?

I always ask my students: "What did you eat today?" I will not teach students who are running on empty. When students run out of the house on an empty stomach, they know that I will send them into the kitchen to prepare a slice of oatmeal pie. I will not prepare food for students. They have to learn how to prepare their own nutritious breakfast and feed themselves before we start a lesson. Too often students are dependent on their parents for healthy food and when a parent is not at home, students only know how to order in greasy fast food, or pick-up junk food.

Let's Recap: Q: What Time Did You Go To Bed?

I always ask my students: "What time did you go to bed?" Students don't know how to connect the dots between food, sleep, and the incredible amount of energy that is required to learn: Read, research, write, proofread, memorize, and test. Students have to learn to think like academic athletes, because every day is a mini marathon, jam packed with fearless academic feats that require tremendous output of energy.

Let's Recap: Q: Did You Put Some Love Into It?

I always ask my students: "Did you put some love into it today?" You don't find love, you create love. To do something well, you have to put love into it. You have to care. You have to open your heart and put your heart on the line. There is no such thing as too much love. First, you have to develop self-love and take good care of yourself. Second, you have to treat yourself the way you deserve to be treated and that is usually better than the way that other people will treat you. Third, you have to treat the people around you with respect, tolerance, and patience. When you look at people, you will see that most people do not have enough love inside of themselves to do what they need to do for themselves, let alone to love you. Keep in mind my initial premise: You don't find love, you create love, and love needs to be recreated each and every day.

Students' lives are composed of personal conflicts as well as parental conflicts in the home and these internal and external conflicts create emotional, spiritual, and intellectual turmoil. These conflicts need to be solved and resolved before students can focus their wholehearted energy on academic achievement.

Spiritual Education: My "Light From Within"
Step One: My Spiritual Affirmations:
a. My Daily Affirmation of Self-Love
b. My Daily Affirmation of Personal Responsibility
c. My Daily Affirmation of Personal Empowerment

Step Two: My Gratitude Journal
a. I am thankful for the following:
b. The good deeds I did today are as follows:

Step Three: How to Solve a Personal Problem
a. Brainstorm for solutions to my personal problems
b. Detailed step-by-step solutions
c. Execution of action plan
d. Analysis of action plan

Educating the whole student: Mind, Body, and Spirit "The Light from Within" of students make up the ninth stepping stone of academic success that will reenvision, reinvent, and rebuild the American education system to meet the challenges of the 21st century, and bring us all nine steps closer to a peaceful world.

Education Is the Only Path to a Peaceful World

"You Can Get All A's and Still Flunk Life."
Walker Percy

Human History Becomes More and More a Race Between Education and Catastrophe.

H. G. Wells

More Dirty Secrets of Education in America

"The dirty secret of higher education is that without underpaid graduate students to help in laboratories and with teaching, universities couldn't conduct research or even instruct their growing undergraduate populations. That's one of the main reasons we still encourage people to enroll in doctoral programs. It is simply cheaper to provide graduate students with modest stipends and adjuncts with as little as $5,000 a course — with no benefits — than it is to hire full-time professors.

In other words, young people enroll in graduate programs, work hard for subsistence pay and assume huge debt burdens, all because of the illusory promise of faculty appointments."

(Professor Mark C. Taylor, Columbia University, *New York Times*, April 24, 2009)

Enlightenment: AHA!
Empowerment: YES I CAN!

Brand Name Business Or Brand Name School?
80% of all businesses in America are small businesses. High schools and colleges have to step up to the plate and offer required business skills. There are far too many college graduates wandering aimlessly, not knowing what to do with their lives, who are in serious financial debt and do not have the required business skills to build their own businesses. And there are many parents who are working more than one job to pay the astronomical cost of private school tuition. Send your child to a free public school and a state university, and give the private school tuition money ($30-$50,000 a year) to the child as a graduation present to start a business. Invest your money in your brand name child and a brand name business instead of in a brand name school (and incur hefty school loans and 40 year repayment plans, especially when your child is clueless as to what he/she wants to do in life).

Reenvision, Reinvent, and Rebuild

The Tenth Stepping Stone of Academic Success

Prepare Students to Meet the Challenges of the Real World

The tenth stepping stone for academic success is preparing students to meet the challenges faced in the real world. In the, Quality Over Quantity Learning-Processing Education System, students have basic business skills that are required to achieve academic success in school and professional success in the real world: Academic Planner Skills, Time Management Skills, Planning Management Skills, Decision Making Skills, Team Player Skills, Typing Skills, Money Management Skills, and Entrepreneurship Skills: "Every Student Is a Success Story."

According to George Santayana, "A child educated only at school is an uneducated child" ("Santayana," Wikipedia). Students do not even have the learning tools required to achieve academic success in school, let alone, the rudimentary business skills to achieve professional success in the real world.

Every living creature on the planet makes sure that their offspring can survive in the real world. It is immoral to let high school students graduate without a rudimentary set of business skills, knowing full well, that many of them may drop out, or don't have money to go to college and will need to find a decent job. If 80% of all businesses in America are small businesses, then business skills are required courses that need to be taught along with reading, writing, and arithmetic, in elementary school, high school, and college.

In addition, it is immoral to let students graduate from college with hefty school loan payments, e.g., $160,000, without a rudimentary set of required business courses under their belt.

To solve this dilemma, I propose teaching the same skill sets that are required for academic success in school and are required for professional success in the real world:

"The Academic Planner" is critical for academic success in school and for professional success in the real world.

"Time Management Tools" are critical for academic success in school and for professional success in the real world.

"Planning Management Skills" are critical for academic success in school and for professional success in the real world.

"Decision Making Skills" are critical for academic success in school and for professional success in the real world.

"Setting Priorities" are critical for academic success in school and for professional success in the real world.

"Money Management Skills" are critical for academic success in school and for professional success in the real world.

"People Skills and Team Player Skills" are critical for academic success in school and for professional success in the real world.

"Professional Typing Skills" are critical for academic success in school and for professional success in the real world.

My students don't do anything that is first not written down on paper and mapped out with detailed step-by-step instructions and realistic time allotments. School assignments are composed of many time-consuming steps. It takes professional planning and management skills to connect all the dots ... and earn an A grade. In every action plan, students have to make time for delays, detours, distractions, and setbacks. That's how life is lived in the real world. Real life is a never-ending obstacle course.

Q: Take out your academic planner and let's see your daily plan, weekly plan, monthly plan, and yearly plan?

SMARTGRADES Academic Planner Skills
Breakfast: Oatmeal Pie (fiber, fruit, hydration)
School: 8 a. m. to 3 p. m.
Homework: 4 p. m. to 8 p. m. = 4 hours including dinner time
My Academic Planner:

Step 1.	Prepare for test	4-6 p.m.
Step 2.	Do the research for the paper	6-7 p.m.
Step 3.	Complete the homework assignment	7-7:30 p.m.
Step 4.	Practice my piano lesson	7:30-8 p.m.
Step 5.	Ask mom to proofread my written work	8-9 p.m.
Step 6.	Regular Bedtime	10 p. m.

Record: Estimated time and actual time
Record: The strengths and weaknesses of today's action plan
Record: Delays, detours, distractions, and setbacks.

Preparing students to meet the challenges of academic success in school and professional success in the real world make up the tenth stepping stone of academic success that will reenvision, reinvent, and rebuild the American education system to meet the challenges of the 21st century, and bring us all ten steps closer to a peaceful world.

Education Is the Only Path to a Peaceful World

A Healthy Heart Brings Forth
True Love, Real Friends, and Long Life.
Sharon Esther Lampert

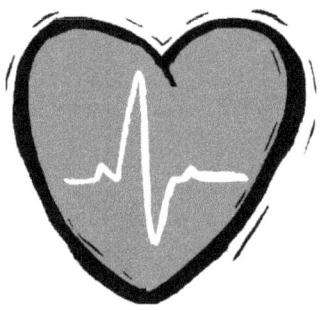

The Children We Teach Will Not Care How Much
We Know Until They Know How Much We Care.
Thomas Sergiovanni

Change the daily question from,
"Do you want something to eat?" to:
"Do you want some energy?"

A Daily Food Journal Will Solve the Problem of Obesity
1. Write down what you will be eating before you eat
2. Meals: Fiber enriched meals with whole grains, fresh fruits, and vegetables
3. No added sugar, salt or butter, no fried foods
4. Use spices to enhance flavor, e.g., basil, cinnamon
5. No caffiene after 5 p.m.
6. No meals after 7:30 p.m. (plan a healthy snack)

I Am Always Ready to Learn Although I Do Not Always Like Being Taught.
Winston Churchill

"There is, in world affairs, a steady course to be followed between an assertion of strength that is truculent and a confession of helplessness that is cowardly."

President Dwight David Eisenhower

Reenvision, Reinvent, and Rebuild

The Eleventh Stepping Stone of Academic Success

Prepare Students to Become Thinkers, Problem Solvers, and Leaders Who Contribute and Further the Progress of Civilization

The eleventh stepping stone for academic success is teaching students how to brainstorm, plan, execute, solve, and resolve a problem. Students have the academic facts at their fingertips and the cognitive skills to solve problems: Critical Thinking Skills, Creative Thinking Skills, Scientific Thinking Skills and Mathematical Thinking Skills. Students can solve a real-world problem in their own lives or solve a real-world problem in the world at large. Students are not victims, but victors.

According to James Baldwin, "Children have never been very good at listening to their elders, but they have never failed to imitate them" (James Baldwin, Wikipedia). This brilliant observation addresses the problem of how do we get our students to break free of our past mistakes and take this sad and broken world that they inherit from us, in new directions.

I think students can do more than sit in a classroom and discuss what is right or wrong with the world and write an essay about it. Students can learn how to make an action plan, implement a plan, and solve a real-world problem in their own lives.

There are so many problems in the world-at-large. Every student has a set of personal problems that need an action plan, execution, follow through, reward system, and resolution:
- Famiy problems
- Health problems
- Social problems
- Political problems
- Religious problems
- Economic problems

Many of my students have weight-management problems and this is the first real-world problem that students need to learn how to solve. Before the age of puberty, many students leave for school without a nutritious breakfast, and later in the day, grab greasy fast food for lunch and dinner. For dessert, students binge on cakes and cookies loaded with white flour, butter, and processed sugar. They drink caffeinated soft drinks at dinner and then have trouble falling asleep at a decent hour.

Monday: Fast Food Hamburger, Frankfurter, and Fries

Tuesday: Fast Food Pizza

Wednesday: Fast Food Tacos

Thursday: Fast Food Fried Chicken Wings

Friday: Fast Food Deli Sandwich Drowning in Mayonnaise

The first real-world problem most students have in common is how to develop healthy eating habits, how to eat for the energy to learn, how to manage their weight, and how to deal with stress and anxiety from the "Academic Pressure Cooker."

Most students are anxious, stressed, and depressed from the unremitting bombardment of the "Academic Pressure Cooker," and seek relief from the "Pain of Inadequacy" and the 'Scars of Incompetence." Some students visit the mental health clinic and are given psychotropic drugs, e.g., anti-anxiety pills, anti-depressants, and sleeping aids. Some students seek relief by bingeing on comfort foods. Junk food makes students fat and does not supply the vitamins, nutrients, and energy that students need to learn. Many American students have become overweight or obese, as these gross statistics reveal:

"Approximately 30.3 percent of American children (ages 6 to 11) are overweight and 15.3 percent are obese. For adolescents (ages 12 to 19), 30.4 percent are overweight and 15.5 percent are obese. Many adverse health effects associated with overweight are observed in children and adolescents. Overweight during childhood and particularly adolescence is related to increased morbidity and mortality in later life: Asthma, Diabetes (Type 2), Hypertension Psychosocial Effects & Stigma, and Sleep Apnea" (American Obesity Association, 2002).

This very serious real-world problem of childhood obesity can be solved by early intervention in an elementary school class by a science teacher who make this real-world problem a part of science instruction:

Q1: Do you eat to live or live to eat?

Q2: What is the relationship between food and energy?

Q3: What kinds of food will give you the energy to learn?

Q4: What kinds of food make you tired and sleepy?

Q5: What is processed food?

Q6: How much water do you need to drink during the day?

Q7: How does greasy fast food affect your heart?

Q8: How many fresh fruits did you eat today?

Q9: How many fresh vegetables did you eat today?

Q10: How much junk food did you eat today?

Change the Question: Do You Want Some Energy?
I tell parents that if they change the question that they ask their kids each day, then the answer will change?

Q: Do you want some energy?

Q: What kind of energy would you like for dinner?

Food Journals Will Solve the Problem of Childhood Obesity
Students need to learn how to become conscious eaters. All students should be required to keep a food journal and keep track of every morsel of food that enters their mouth. I ask my students to record what they are eating, when they are eating it, and why they are eating it.

Q: What did you eat today?

Q: When did you eat it?

Q: Why did you eat it?

Q: Did you get any energy from the food?

Q: Did you get bad or good fats from the food?

Q: Did the food make you sleepy or keep you up?

Q: Did the food make you thirsty?

Q: Did the food fill you up or are you still hungry?

Q: Did you eat slowly or gobble it up quickly and forget to taste it?

Let's Recap: Solve and Resolve the Problem of Childhood Obesity
- This real-world problem of childhood obesity can be solved in elementary school by a science teacher.

- Students need classes on energy and nutrition.

- Students should be required to to keep a daily food journal.

- The goalpost is students who are conscious eaters.

Preparing students to become thinkers, problem solvers, and leaders make up the eleventh stepping stone of academic success that will reenvision, reinvent, and rebuild the American education system to meet the challenges of the 21st century, and bring us all eleven steps closer to a peaceful world.

A university professor set an examination question in which he asked what is the difference between ignorance and apathy. The professor had to give an A+ to a student who answered:
I don't know and I don't care.

Richard Pratt

People don't realize how much
suicidal people hurt, how long they hurt,
and how hopelessly they hurt.

Psychiatrist Kay Redfield Jamison

New York University

"At 5:07 a.m., Hunter simultaneously sent his father, mother, and brother a text message that said simply,

"I love you."

Mr. Hunter said he believes that his son jumped just six minutes later."

(Sarah Portlock, *"NYU Freshman's Suicide Raises Adjustment Issues"* N.Y. Sun, September 24, 2007).

When You Reach the End of Your Rope,
Tie a Knot In It and Hang On.
President Thomas Jefferson

Reenvision, Reinvent, and Rebuild

The Twelfth Stepping Stone of Academic Success

Remove Stress, Anxiety, Depression and Suicidal Thoughts from the Learning Environment

The twelfth stepping stone for academic success is creating a school environment that is conducive to the love of learning. Anxiety and stress inhibit learning and higher-order thinking because they force the brain to switch to survival mode. Depression (internalization of disappointment, pain, and rage) leads to psychological paralysis (students can't function), suicidal thinking, attempted suicide, and suicide. It is time for educators to take responsibility for the academic games riddled with "Academic Insanity" that they ask students to play that make a sizeable contribution to their mental-health problems. Implementing minor and major systemic repairs can minimize academic stress.

According to Albert Einstein, "I never teach my pupils; I only attempt to provide the conditions in which they can learn" ("Einstein," Wikipedia).

Young children enter a first grade classroom filled with intense curiosity, overwhelming enthusiasm, and irresistible excitement. Of course, this is only the case if nursery and kindergarten students have resolved their bonding, separation, anxiety, and control issues with their parents.

By the fifth grade, most of these initial feelings for the love of learning have been replaced by stress, anxiety, and depression.

Q: Why Did this Brilliant M.I.T. Student Jump?

Philip Gale, Age 19
pioneering internet software developer and computer prodigy, and avid musician

The Red Flag
"For weeks, Gale had been asking classmates how to access the roof of M.I.T.'s tallest structure, the Green Building."

The Suicide: March 13, 1998
"Philip wrote out Isaac Newton's equation for how an object accelerates as it falls, along with a sketch of a stick figure of someone tossing a chair. He signed the message, "Phil was here," picked up a chair, hurled it and then himself through a window on the fifteenth floor."

Philip's Suicide Note
"Presumably I have jumped from a tall building... I am not crazy, albeit driven to suicide. It is not about any single event, or person. It is about stubborn sadness, and a detached view of the world. I see my life -- so much dreary, mundane, wasted time wishing upon unattainable goals -- and I feel little attachment to the future. But it is not so bad, relatively. I exaggerate. In the end, it is that I am unwilling (sick of living) to live in mediocrity. And this is what I have chosen to do about it... take care world, Philip." Gale closed his handwritten suicide note, found at his apartment, with a smiley face and the words "And stay happy!" ("Philip Gale," Wikipedia).

Philip Gale was one of America's Brightest Minds. What really happened to the brilliant M.I.T. student, Philip Gale, who jumped from the fifteenth floor? He used a physic's equation to explain his gravitational descent into suicide. He was so academically accomplished, but his spirit was encased in a debilitating clinical depression that he was unable to shake. In his own suicide note, he says:

> "It is about stubborn sadness, and a detached view of the world."

A student commits suicide. Parents are clueless. Educators are clueless. The clueless psychiatrist has a clue: The student had a "undiagnosed preexisting mental disorder."

Students are stuck in a deepening depression and educators are stuck in a deepening denial.

The educators have to start connecting the dots ... between the unremitting stress of the "Academic Pressure Cooker" and the anxiety, stress, "bouts of depression," clinical depression, and suicidal thoughts (the ticking-time bomb) of their students.

Here are the critical questions that need analysis:

Q: Why is the entire student body anxious, stressed, and suffering from "bouts of depression"?

Q: Why is every day of class a competition for academic survival?

Q: Why do all students fall behind, flounder, and play catch-up.

Q: Why are most students surviving, but not thriving?

As a result of the "Academic Pressure Cooker," most elementary high school, and college students suffer from anxiety, stress, and "bouts of depression." Educators are clueless. Get a clue: Regurgitating voluminous facts with meager comprehension, no learning tools, and for short-term retention is stressful. Faulty regurgitation of academic facts under pressure is a demoralizing and painful experience especially when American dreams are hanging in the balance. Students have become disconnected, depressed, distracted, disgruntled, and disobedient Some disgruntled students threaten bogus bomb scares. Some students have become suicidal.

Q: Why are all students anxious and stressed?

Q: Why are many students disconnected, depressed, and distracted?

Q: Why did that student shutdown?

Q: Why is that student blocked?

Q: "Why is that student raging and acting out?"

Q: "Why does that student have suicidal thoughts?"

Q: "Why did that student attempt suicide?"

Q: "Why did that student commit suicide?"

Soldiers are asked to put their lives on the line. It is an accepted medical fact that soldiers will bear the burden of life-long psychological scars such as, "Post-Traumatic Stress Syndrome." Depression varies from "bouts of depression" to clinical depression to suicidal thinking. No one dares to say:
Q: What is wrong with those soldiers?

Quality Over Quantity Learning-Processing Education System

Q: Why are soldiers anxious, stressed, and depressed?

Q: Why do soldiers have psychological disorders?

When students enter a private or public school, they are asked to play four academic games that erode their emotional well-being:

- Academic Game One: Catch Up
Q: Why am I falling behind after a week and floundering after a month?

- Academic Game Two: "Read, Cram, Regurgitate, and Test"
Q: Why can't I cram one-thousand facts into my mind and regurgitate the facts onto a test in an hour?

- Academic Game Three: Abusive (tricky) "Hotdog" exams
Q: Why did I perform poorly on the test and lose my American dream?

- Academic Game Four: Students learn how to cut corners and cheat to pass, survive, and graduate
Q: Why don't I have time to read my textbooks, write my papers, and prepare to take my tests?

The students are like soldiers who are fighting for their American dream. They will take unfair hits of tricky test questions, and some students will be shot down and their American dream will be destroyed by the "Academic Insanity" of the malfunctioning "Curriculm-Driven" American education system. Over time, like soldiers, the constant stress from the "Academic Pressure Cooker" takes its toll.

Education Is the Only Path to a Peaceful World

Learn to Think Like the Enemy

When I prepare students for tests, I teach them to "think like the enemy." I teach students how to pay attention for those itsy-bitsy, teeny-tiny insignificant details, because they will see them on the abusive(tricky) "Hotdog" exam. I treat my student-soldiers like warriors who are fighting on the battlefield for their American dream on American soil.

Like any other illness, anxiety, stress, and depression are debilitating, deteriorating, and destructive, as follows:

Stage One: Stressors
A confluence of overwhelming internal and external stressors

Stage Two: Anxiety
Zaps energy, inability to focus and concentrate

Stage Three: "Bouts of Depression"
Weighted down with feeling of sadness, numbness sets in, the inability to feel

Stage Four: Depression
Internalization of disappointment, pain, and rage

Stage Five: Clinical Depression
Psychological paralysis, Inability to function

Stage Six: Suicidal Thinking
Hopelessness, No light at the end of the tunnel

Stage Seven: Attempted Suicide
Stage Eight: Suicide
"I can't take it anymore"

There are many disappointments in life and the pain builds up. Students seeks relief from three painful wounds, as follows:

a. Painful wounds of the heart

b. Painful wounds of the mind

c. Painful wounds of the body

a. Wounds of the Heart: Rejection, abandonment, separation anxiety, or death of a loved one

b. Wounds of the Mind:
Pain of Inadequacy, "I am not as smart as I thought I was"

c. Wounds of the Body: Internalization of disappointment, pain, and rage. "bouts of depression" escalate into depression and clinical depression (debilitating psychological paralysis)

Parents and educators set up unrealistic expectations and inevitably students will fail to meet them, as follows:

a. There is too much sugarcoating of a fantasy, and when the harsh realities set in, students are caught unprepared:

The fantasy: College is the greatest time of your life
The reality: College is a very stressful experience

b. Students are legal adults, but not psychological adults

c. Fragile identity formation: Who am I? There is an ongoing conflict with oneself and parents, "I don't want to be a

(Let's Recap) Major Repair: One Test Per Day Reduces Stress
There is little coordination among teachers when it comes to test dates. One time-sensitive "Hotdog" exam is stressful, but three time-sensitive abusive (tricky) "Hotdog" exams on the same day is another example of "Academic Insanity." A simple minor repair that would put an end to students taking three exams on one day is assigning one day of the week to a subject area:

Monday is for Math Tests

Tuesday is for Science Tests

Wednesday is for English Tests

Thursday is for History Tests

Friday is for Language Tests

Major Repair: Morning Exams Reduce Stress
Students should be required to take exams in the morning. Like athletes, students need to warm-up their brain muscle, and get the facts ready to regurgitate onto a time-sensitive abusive (tricky) "Hotdog" exam. It is stressful to make students sit through other classes and try to focus on learning new academic material, when they have to take a test during the latter half of the school day.

(Let's Recap) Major Repair: Limits on Research Papers Reduce Stress
There is a tendency among teachers to give out research paper assignments as if they are the only teacher in your life. On any given day, a student can receive three research report assignments from three different teachers. Research papers should be limited to no more than five pages, and three primary sources.

Major Repair: Realistic-Time Allotments Reduce Stress

It is time to do more than schedule classes and exams, it is time to assign realistic-time allotments for school assignments:

Part 1. Read chapter 1: 4 hours

Write a 3-page essay: 25 hours

Prepare to take a test: 20 hours

Major Repair: Detailed Step-By-Step Instructions Reduce Stress

Write a five-page essay: 51 hours

1. Go to library and return home (travel time): 2 hours
2. Read library books: 10 hours
3. Research topic for experts in field and memorable quotes: 5 hours
4. Research topic for pro and con arguments: 3 hours
5. Write an outline of main ideas and supporting examples: 5 hours
6. Write a rough draft: introduction, body, and conclusion: 10 hours
7. Add citations: 3 hours
8. Add footnotes: 3 hours
9. Add a bibliography: 2 hours
10. Proofread essay (reread, revise, and rewrite): 5 hours
11. For final edit, read essay aloud using computer software: 3 hours
12. Hand in your essay with a time log
13. Part 2. Correct all errors and resubmit your research paper for an A Grade: "Every Student Is a Success Story": 5 hours

Major Repair: Teaching is a Time-Intensive Activity

- Teaching requires time for in-depth comprehension

- Teaching requires time for continuous feedback of strengths and weaknesses for mastery of the academic material

- Teaching requires time to teach the craft of writing (ten to twenty rough drafts) and proofreading skills

A Major Repair: Learning is a Time-Intensive Activity

- Learning requires "time to learn" and learning tools to "learn and process" academic material

- Educators can place the new learning technology, SMARTGRADES Processing Tools, directly into the hands of their students. Every student will have organization skills, time management skills, and academic planner skills. Every student will have detailed step-by-step instructions on how to write English essays and research papers.

Major Repair: Abolish Hotdog Examinations
Q: How many hotdogs can you stuff into your mouth in one hour to win the Coney Island Hotdog Contest in Brooklyn?

Q: How many academic facts do students have to cram and regurgitate with meager comprehension, no learning tools, for short-term retention, under psychological duress and a stopwatch to earn a diploma?

- Under stress, every student draws at least one blank
- Under stress, most students will draw more than one blank
- Two weeks after a test, academic facts vanish into the thin air
- Pain of Inadequacy: "I am not as smart as I thought I was!"

SMARTGRADES: EVERY STUDENT IS A SUCCESS

Major Repair: Grades Need Regulation "Grading Expectations"
Teachers need to hand out a grading sheet of "Grading Expectations," as follows:

Grade A =

Grade B =

Grade C =

At the end of a term, students should be able to grade themselves based on the "Grading Expectations."

Major Repair: Tests Need Regulation (25% of Grade)
1. Students need, SMARTGRADES Processing Tools, for instant recall on tests: Extraction, condensation, association, and visualization.

2. Tests should only account for 25% of a grade, as follows:
   Daily School Assignments   50%
   Research Paper/Project   25%
   Quizzes/Tests   25%

- Test questions should be written clearly and concisely

- Tests should have no more that 25 questions

- Tests should last at least three hours. Students need time to think. Thinking takes time. Students should have time to read a question five times, if necessary. Students need time to read the question and the answers. Students need time to write legibly. Students need time to reread what they wrote and proofread their essays.

Let's Recap: Anxiety, Stress, Depression, and Suicide

Like any other illness, anxiety, stress, and depression are debilitating, deteriorating, and destructive, as follows:

1. Parents and educators set up unrealistic expectations for students who will inevitably fail to meet those expectations

2. Disappointments build up and does the emotional pain

3. "Bouts of depression" escalate into clinical depression.

4. Clinical depression escalates into suicidal thoughts, attempted suicide, and suicide.

5. Students do not have any lifelines:

    a. Self: No internal self-empathy, self-compassion, and self-love

    b. Competitive isolation. Students have become fierce competitors

    c. Inadequate/Abusive parenting

    d. Broken American psychiatric system: The vacuous pills

Q: What happens to students when clinical depression escalates into suicidal thoughts, attempted suicide, and suicide?

   a. Inability to break through the cement casing of clinical depression

   b. Hopelessness: No light at the end of the dark tunnel

c. The student's inner voice mimics the critical voice of the parent as the "punisher"

d. The student's inner voice is self-critical

PAIN: Q: "What is wrong with me?"

PAIN: Q: "I am not as smart as I thought I was!"

f. The student can no longer tolerate the pain, self-punishes, and commits suicide

"I can't take it anymore!"

Creating a school environment that is conducive to the love of learning and free of anxiety, stress, and depression make up the twelfth stepping stone of academic success that will reenvision, reinvent, and rebuild the American education system to meet the challenges of the 21st century, and bring us all twelve steps closer to a peaceful world.

I Touch the Future. I Teach.
Christa McAuliffe

I like a teacher who gives you something to take home to think about besides homework.
Edith Ann, [Lily Tomlin]

He Can Never Tell Where His Influence Stops.

Henry Brooks Adams

I've come to the frightening conclusion that I am the decisive element in the classroom.

It's my daily mood that makes the weather.

As a teacher, I possess a tremendous power to make a child's life miserable or joyous.

I can be a tool of torture or an instrument of inspiration.

I can humiliate or humor, hurt or heal.

In all situations, it is my response that decides whether a crisis will be escalated or de-escalated and a child humanized or de-humanized.

Dr. Haim Ginott

The mediocre teacher tells.
The good teacher explains.
The superior teacher demonstrates.
The great teacher inspires.

William Arthur Ward

Reenvision, Reinvent, and Rebuild

The Thirteenth Stepping Stone of Academic Success

Stop the Education Blame Game There Are No Beneficiaries

The thirteenth stepping stone for academic success is ending the blame game. In the malfunctioning Quantity Over Quality Curriculum-Driven American Education System, teachers don't have time to teach for in-depth comprehension and are scapegoated as poor teachers and blamed for poor test scores. Students don't have "time to learn" and learning tools to "learn and process" voluminous academic material and are blamed for poor study habits and poor test scores. Parents are asked to teach their children what teachers don't have time to teach, and incur the financial costs associated with private tutoring or face ridicule for non-involvement in their children's education.

According to Robert G. Ingersoll, "It is a thousand times better to have common sense without education than to have education without common sense" ("Robert G. Ingersoll," Wikipedia). Once a little common sense is sprinkled on the problem of who is at fault for the malfunctioning education system, it will become crystal clear that teachers, students, and parents are all blameless. It is as if they are seated together in the back seat of an old rusty jalopy and the brakes malfunctioned and landed them into a deep ditch. They all have bumps and bruises from the unfortunate accident, however, they are innocent victims of an out-of-condition, rusty beat-up car, that should have been junked a long time ago and recycled into scraps of reusable metal.

Academic Insanity: Teachers Don't Benefit
Teachers are blamed for being poor teachers and for bad test scores. If the truth be told, teachers do not have time to teach for in-depth comprehension because their primary objective is to keep moving the massive curriculum forward to stay on schedule. It is not uncommon for teachers to run out of time; sometimes they don't even have time to give a brief overview of the academic material. Educators cut corners and cheat students out of an education: No in-depth comprehension, no time to teach the craft of writing, and no mastery of academic material.

Academic Insanity: Students Don't Benefit
Students are blamed for bad study habits and for poor test scores. Students study for hours, but do not have "time to learn," and learning tools to "learn and process," the academic material for long-term retention. They cram and regurgitate voluminous academic facts with meager comprehension for short-term retention. Two weeks after the test, the academic facts disappear into a black hole in the mind and vanish into thin air. Students learn how to cut corners and cheat to pass, survive, and graduate. Students earn a diploma, but not an education.

Academic Insanity: Parents Don't Benefit
a. Parents are asked to foot the bill for after-school tutoring, because teaching and learning are compromised to meet the goals dictated by the "Higher Standards."

b. Parents are asked to foot the astronomical bill for psychiatrists to heal the wounded spirits of their children. Students study for hours, but get sabotaged by abusive (tricky) test questions. Students have become anxious, stressed, disconnected, depressed, distracted, disgruntled, disobedient, and suicidal.

c. In some cases, psychiatrists add insult to injury, and put students on psychotropic drugs, a crutch with dangerous side effects. The student in pain keeps popping the vacuous pills, overdoses, and dies. Or a disgruntled student goes to school to shoot or massacre fellow students. Or a student uses the pills to commit suicide. The vacuous pills do not heal emotional problems.

d. In some cases, psychiatrists add insult to injury, and misdiagnose students with A.D.H.D., and put their powerful brains into virtual wheelchairs for life.

e. Parents are asked to foot the astronomical bill for preparatory classes for abusive (tricky) standardized "Hotdog" exams.

f. Parents pay all the bills and most of them see their hard-earned money, the academic material, their child's psychological health, and American dream vanish into thin air. To add insult to injury, parents are blamed for non-involvement in their children's education.

Academic Insanity: No Beneficiaries
- Teachers don't benefit

- Students don't benefit

- Parents don't benefit

Stopping the education blame game is the thirteenth stepping stone of academic success that will reenvision, reinvent, and rebuild the American education system to meet the challenges of the 21st century, and bring us all thirteen steps closer to a peaceful world.

Solve "Problem of Education" Save Entire World

"The human brain is the most powerful biological machine in the world, and the educational challenge before us, is to unlock its potential, cultivate its power, and set free its promise.

What if you could solve just one problem in the world, and by solving that one problem, you could solve every other problem in the world.

If we just solve the "Problem of Education," then we will be able to solve every other problem in the world: Famine, poverty, crime, disease, domestic violence, religious strife, and war.

I am on a mission to place, **SMARTGRADES SUCCESS STRATEGY STUDY SKILLS** directly into the hands of students, parenting tools into the hands of parents, and teaching tools into the hands of teachers.

Education is the only path to a peaceful world.

Feed the whole student: Mind, body, and spirit.

Teachers not politicians are the true peacemakers in the world.

Solve the problem of education and save the world.

Sharon Rose Sugar
The Paladin of Education for the 21st Century

August 12, 2005

"If we can just bring our education system into the 21st century, not only will our children be able to fulfill their God-given potential, and our families be able to live out their dreams; not only will our schools out-educate the world and our workers outcompete the world; not only will our companies innovate more and our economy grow more, but at this defining moment, we will do what previous generations of Americans have done - and unleash the promise of our people, unlock the promise of our country, and make sure that America remains a beacon of opportunity and prosperity for all the world."

War Update: July 23, 2009
"Biden Warns of More 'Sacrifice' in Afghanistan"
The vice president said Thursday that more British and U.S. troops will die but the war was "worth the effort."
(Alan Cowell, New York Times, July 23, 2009)

WORLD EDUCATION RANKINGS

UNICEF rankings of educational systems in the world's richest countries, indicating the percentage of 14 and 15 year olds scoring below a minimum level in literacy, math and science.

1. South Korea 1.4 percent
2. Japan 2.2
3. Finland 4.4
4. Canada 5
5. Australia 6.2
6. Austria 8.2
7. Britain 9.4
8. Ireland 10.2
9. Sweden 10.8
10. Czech Republic 12.2
- (tie) New Zealand 12.2
12. France 12.6
13. Switzerland 13
14. Belgium 14
- (tie) Iceland 14
16. Hungary 14.2
- (tie) Norway 14.2
18. United States 16.2
19. Germany 17
- (tie) Denmark 17
21. Spain 18.6
22. Italy 20.2
23. Greece 23.2
24. Portugal 23.6

Reenvision, Reinvent, and Rebuild

The Fourteenth Stepping Stone of Academic Success

Take Responsibility for the Failure to Educate Students: "Great Teachers, Great Students, Malfunctioning Education System"

The fourteenth stepping stone for academic success is for educators to wake up, become conscious, and take responsibility for their failure to educate students. The unsolved mystery of why the American Education System is failing has been solved. It is up to each and every school, on a grass roots level, to begin to implement the monumental changes that will transform the American education system into one of the greatest education systems in the world, and prepare students to meet the challenges of the 21st century: "Every Student Is a Success Story."

According to Alvin Toffler, "The illiterate of the 21st century will not be those who cannot read and write, but those who cannot learn, unlearn, and relearn." ("Alvin Toffler," Wikipedia.com). Educators have to reenvision, reinvent, and rebuild the American education system. Educators have to learn, unlearn, and relearn a new education operating system, so that students will earn a diploma and an education.

According to a recent study conducted by UNICEF, America's education system was ranked #18 in the world.

Here is a news bulletin that sums up the results of a UNICEF study.

"The United States is falling when it comes to international education rankings, as recent studies show that other nations in the developed world have more effective education systems. The researchers ranked the United States No. 18 out of 24 nations in terms of the relative effectiveness of its educational system.

In fourth grade, American kids do above average internationally. By eighth grade, they slip a bit, and by 12th-grade, they've slipped a lot," Marsh said. "We're the only country that slides down that much from fourth to 12th grade."

The UNICEF report finds that educational success or failure is not directly linked to funding, and that there is no clear link between student-to-teacher ratios and test results. By international standards, the United States spends a lot of money on education, and in terms of class sizes, a lot of countries that do well have larger class sizes than the United States, Marsh said.

Marsh said that he attributes U.S. rankings to a different set of reasons —**namely, the way material is being taught in classrooms. The United States focuses more on procedure, and we try to teach many topics fast. Other countries tend to break topics up and go much more in-depth"** (Elaine Wu, *"U.S. Falls in Education Rank Compared to Other Countries"* U-Wire, October, 2005).

In sum, Professor Marsh was hot on the trail and got very close to cracking the code and solving the mystery of why the American education system malfunctions.

Quality Over Quantity Learning-Processing Education System

If Steve Jobs (or Bill Gates) were in charge of the American education system, in less than one year a brand new education operating system would be in place, and every month, he would design an upgrade that would improve the education operating system.

When Steve Paul Jobs, invented the APPLE computer, he shifted the creativity paradigm, and put the power to create back into the hands of the artists. Artists can use a personal home computer to create and sell artistic works:

- Writers can write, edit, and publish their own books
- Filmmakers can write and edit their own movies
- Musicians can write and produce their own music
- Web designers can build their own websites

Apple's system engineers are also excellent teachers and customers are treated like students. All of Apple's computer software packages come with learning videos with realistic-time allotments and detailed step-by-step instructions. Every month, Apple sends me a software upgrade with a better computer tool, tip, or technique. Every week, I have to learn, unlearn, or relearn new software applications.

In addition, Steve Job's system engineers would make sure that parents have up-do-date parenting skills to nurture and nourish their children.

Finally, the awesome power of the human brain would be nurtured and cultivated for life-sustaining initiatives that bring the light of knowledge to all of the dark corners of human ignorance and suffering. In time, there would be less need for mental institutions, prisons, and armies.

Education Is the Only Path to a Peaceful World

The Malfunctioning Quality Over Quantity Curriculum-Driven American Education System

Educators are clueless as to, "How Does Leaning Take Place?"
1. Educators cut corners and cheat students out of an education
2. Teaching and learning are sacrificed to push curriculum forward
3. No realistic-time allotments for school assignments
4. No detailed step-by-step instructions for school assignments
5. No time for in-depth comprehension
6. No learning tools for long-term retention
7. No time for feedback of strengths and weaknesses for mastery
8. No time to teach the craft of writing: 10-25 rough drafts
9. Students earn a diploma, but not an education

Students
1. All students are anxious, stressed, and suffer "bouts of depression"
2. No time to learn
3. No learning tools to process voluminous academic material
4. Game 1. First week, fall behind and start playing "catch up"
5. Game 2. Read, Cram, Regurgitate, and Test
6. Game 3. Abusive (tricky) Hotdog Exams
7. Game 4. Students cut corners and cheat to pass, survive, and graduate
8. Students suffer the "Pain of Inadequacy"
9. Some students are disconnected, depressed, distracted, disgruntled, and disobedient
10. Some students are misdiagnosed with A.D.H.D., an "incurable brain disorder"
11. Students graduate bearing the "Scars of Incompetence"
12. Students are surviving, but not thriving

Schools (Public and Private Schools)
1. School resembles a war zone: Few heroes, heavy casualties, and senseless fatalities
2. America's education system is #18 in the world (UNICEF)

The New Education Operating System

The Quality Over Quantity Learning Processing American Education System

1. Nurture and cultivate the awesome power of the human brain

2. Feed the whole student: Mind, body, and spirit (the "Light From Within")

3. Realistic-time allotments and detailed step-by-step instructions for school assignments

4. Time for in-depth comprehension: SMARTGRADES Critical Thinking Tools

5. Long-term retention: SMARTGRADES Processing Tools

6. Time to teach the craft of writing: SMARTGRADES Writing Tools

7. Time for continuous feedback of strengths and weaknesses for mastery of the academic material

8. New grading system: Grade A or REDO

9. "Every Student Is a Success Story"

10. America has the greatest education system in the world

Educators taking responsibility for the failure to educate students enrolled in the malfunctioning, Quantity Over Quality Curriculm-Driven American Education System, make-up the fourteenth stepping stone of academic success that will reenvision, reinvent, and rebuild the American education system to meet the challenges of the 21st century, and bring us all fourteen steps closer to a peaceful world.

Education Is the Only Path to a Peaceful World

If We Wish to Create a Lasting Peace
We Must Begin with the Children.
Mahatma Gandhi

Education Is the Most Powerful Weapon Which You Can Use to Change the World.
Nelson Mandela

War Leaves No Victors,
Only Victims.

Elie Wiesel

The library is the temple of learning, and learning has liberated more people than all the wars in history.

Carl Thomas Rowan

The deliberate and deadly attacks which were carried out
yesterday against our country were more than acts of terror.
They were acts of war.
President George W. Bush
(True)

America must not ignore the threat gathering against us.
Facing clear evidence of peril, we cannot wait for the final proof,
the smoking gun that could come in the form of a mushroom cloud.
President George W. Bush
(True)

When we look around the world today, when we see in Afghanistan
that 10 million people have registered to vote in their upcoming
elections, including 40 percent of those people are women,
that's just unbelievable.
Laura Bush
(True)

The true history of my administration will be written 50 years
from now, and you and I will not be around to see it.
President George W. Bush
(False)
(George and Laura Bush Quotes, thinkexist.com)

Connecting the Dots: In-Depth Comprehension of the Problem:
1. The enemy is not a nation, but a diffuse group of "Evil Ones."
2. The enemy uses clandestine terror tactics, not big splashy parades.
3. Democracy can only exist when there is a separation between church and state. The people are voting, but the candidates are deter mined by religious leaders who curtail the individual freedom of men and women. These people are not free because they can cast a vote.
4. There are an inexhaustible supply of Islamic terrorists because of the earliest indoctrination of 2-year toddlers for martydom and murder, who will seek revenge for injuries sustained.
5. America has depleted her economic surplus, is in debt to China, has tripled her losses and pain and has more enemies than ever befor
6. The "tit for tat" violence continues into the 21st century.
7. In sum: The earliest reeducation is the only path to a peaceful world.

Sandstorm in Baghdad

Dust is Blowing.
Blood is Flowing.
Dead are Worming.
U.N. are Groaning.
French are Moaning.
Bush Gets Going.
Protestors are Crowing.
Osama bin Laden is Unknowing.
Saddam is Forgoing.
Muslims are Cheering and Jeering.
Weapons of Mass Destruction are not Unfolding.
Insurgents are Slowing.
U. S. Soldiers Keep Going.
Democracy is Growing.
Women are Showing.
Elections are Easygoing.
Freedom is Holding.
Peace is Plateauing.
U.S. Deficit is Owing.
Oil is Glowing.
U.S. Memorials are Knowing:
4, 221 Fatalities, 30, 920 Casualties (as of 12/2008).
When the Dust Settles Down Upon the Blood-Soaked
Earth Where Sacred American Lives were Sacrificed and
Slaughtered for Security: Freedom from Terrorism.
Was the Iraq War Fought for Naught?

Sharon Esther Lampert
Creative Genius

The Greatest Poems Ever Written on Extraordinary Events
www.WorldFamousPoems.com
#1 Website for School Students for School Assignments

It'll be a great day when education gets all the money it wants and the Air Force has to hold a bake sale to buy bombers.

— Unknown

Nations have recently been led to borrow billions for war; no nation has ever borrowed largely for education. Probably, no nation is rich enough to pay for both war and civilization. We must make our choice; we cannot have both.

— Abraham Flexner

"Thou shalt not be a victim,
thou shalt not be a perpetrator,
but above all,
thou shalt not be a bystander."

— Yehuda Bauer

FOR OUR WORLD

We need to stop.
Just stop.
Stop for a moment.
Before anybody
Says or does anything
That may hurt anyone else.
We need to be silent.
Just silent.
Silent for a moment.
Before we forever lose
The blessing of songs
That grow in our hearts.
We need to notice.
Just notice.
Notice for a moment.
Before the future slips away
Into ashes and dust of humility.
Stop, be silent, and notice.
In so many ways, we are the same.
Our differences are unique treasures.
We have, we are, a mosaic of gifts
To nurture, to offer, to accept.
We need to be.
Just be.
Be for a moment.
Kind and gentle, innocent and trusting,
Like children and lambs,
Never judging or vengeful
Like the judging and vengeful.
And now, let us pray,
Differently, yet together,
Before there is no earth, no life,
No chance for peace.

September 11, 2001
Matthew Joseph Thaddeus Stepanek
Book: Hope Through Heartsongs, Hyperion, 2002

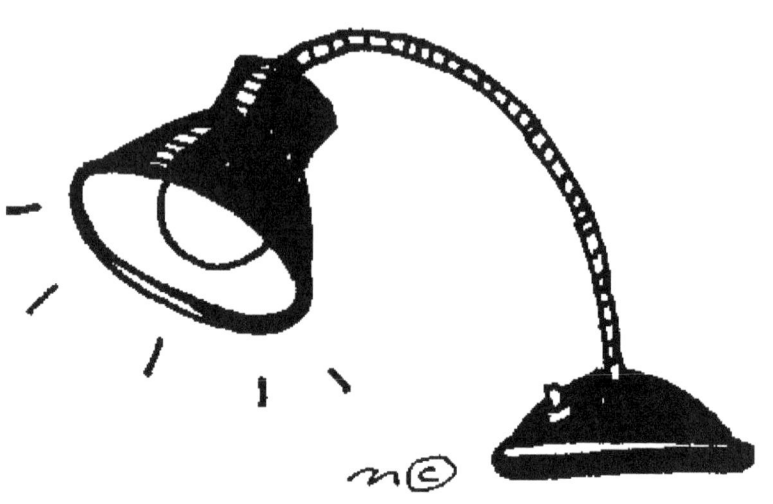

Peace is a daily, a weekly, a monthly process, gradually changing opinions, slowly eroding old barriers, and quietly building new structures.

Reenvision, Reinvent, and Rebuild

The Fifteenth Stepping Stone of Academic Success

Education Is the Only Path to a Peaceful World. Solve the "Problem of Education" and Save the World.

The fifteenth stepping stone for academic success is focusing on solving just one problem in the world. What if you could solve just one problem in the world, and by solving that one problem, you could solve every other problem in the world? If we just solve the "Problem of Education," then we will be able to solve every other problem in the world: Famine, poverty, illiteracy, crime, disease, domestic violence, religious strife, and war.

According to Maria Montessori, "Establishing lasting peace is the work of education; all politics can do is keep us out of war." Every nation in the world has people whose lives have been shattered and destroyed by the brutality of war ("Montessori" Wikipedia).

In America, as a result of the invasion of Iraq and Afghanistan, there are more than 7,800 American fatalities and 30,000 American casualties of war. The 20th century was the most violent century in history. The 21st century has already witnessed its first genocide in Sudan, Africa.

According to Sidone Gruenberg, "Home is the place where boys and girls first learn how to limit their wishes, abide by rules, and consider the rights and needs of others." Every nation of the world has mental institutions and prisons that are filled beyond capacity with people whose lives were destroyed before the age of puberty. According to Dr. Phil Mcgraw, "You got to rise above your raisin."

The education system is failing to meet the social, economic, science, and technological challenges of the 21st century. If we can fly like birds in airplanes that soar through the sky and defy gravity in rocket ships that travel to the moon, we can reenvision, reinvent, and rebuild the American education system.

There are laymen and scholars who will argue that you can't change human nature. Technological innovations are easier problems to solve than trying to transform a "human animal" into a "human being" through the process of socialization.

History will bear witness to the fact that the human animal is the nastiest animal on the face of the planet, and that other species don't engage in acts of genocide that continue to persist in every generation and in all four corners of the globe:

Genocide in the 20th Century
1915-1918	Turkey: Armenians	1.5 Million
1932-1933	Ukraine	7 Million
1937-1938	Rape of Nanking: Chinese	300,000
1938-1945	Europe: Jewish Holocaust	6 Million
1975-1979	Cambodia	500,000
1980	Iraq: Kurds	50,000-100,000
1990	Yugoslavia: Bosnia Muslims	200,000
1994	Rwanda: Tutsi	800,000

Genocide in the 21st Century
2003   Sudan: Darfur   In Progress
(www.TheHistoryPlace.com)

World War III: Worldwide Terrorism
2001- In Progress

History will also show that "Planet Hell" is a far better fitting name for "Planet Earth," because it deftly portrays the pain and suffering of every living creature that inhabits this planet.

Genocide: The Theory of the Double Whammy
Human animals have to fight for biological survival like any other animal, and grow into nasty predators, like alligators. And human animals are also nurtured to be nasty, e.g., Nazism. According to the poet, philosopher, and educator, Sharon Esther Lampert, genocide happens because it is a "Double Whammy."

Nature is Nasty and Nurture is Nasty = Double Whammy

The Double Whammy = Genocide

(Sharon Esther Lampert, *"The Science of Evil: The Double Whammy,"* Kadimah Press).

The Inhumanity of Men
The most devastating problem in the world is how men treat other men. Our sweet and adorable male children will inevitably grow into full-grown predators and fight for acquisition of biological resources. During war, the barbaric way that men treat other men supports the argument that our animal nature cannot be reconfigured through the process of socialization. Nature is a greater force than nurture, and our male children are destined to grow into vicious predators who will never learn how to share their childhood toys, or biological resources with each other.

Education Is the Only Path to a Peaceful World

There Is No Flower in Darfur

The first genocide of the 21st century began in Sudan.
Slavery is cursed: Black-African Muslims strike first.
Arab Muslims strike back with a whack.
Running barefoot, Black-African Muslims flee the attack.
Political opposition descends into ethnic cleansing.
War descends into war crimes.
Rape descends into orphans.
Refugees descend into Chad.
Drought descends into starvation.
The rainy season descends into disease.
There are no villages.
There are no mosques.
There are no cattle.
There are no fields.
There are no crops.
There is no food.
There is no faith.
There is no Koran.
There are no lessons learned:
There is no GENOCIDE(?)
There is no cemetery:
The remains of mothers and fathers, sisters and brothers
Lie scattered among the lies of the Janjaweed militias.
From pools of blood, flowers cannot grow.
There is no flower in Darfur.

Sharon Esther Lampert
Creative Genius

The Greatest Poems Ever Written on Extraordinary Events
www.WorldFamousPoems.com

Without question, we are still living in the dark ages of civilization. Across the globe, there are millions of people who are starving. There are millions of refugees living in outdoor tents. There are millions of people who don't have access to the seven basic necessities of life that make it bearable: Food, clothing, shelter, medicine, education, work, and world peace.

According to the poet, philosopher, and educator, Sharon Esther Lampert, the "Dark Ages" and the "Age of Enlightenment" are defined as follows:

The Definition of the Dark Ages
The dark ages is when you talk like a human being, but behave like a human animal.

The Definition of Enlightenment
Enlightenment is when you talk like a human being and behave like a human being.

(Sharon Esther Lampert, *"The Science of Truth: The Study of Natural Philosophy,"* Kadimah Press).

Socialization, Chocolate, and World Peace
Before the age of puberty, the process of socialization, whereby we instill love, education, and law into the human animal and transform the human animal into a human being is the only hope for mankind. Similarly, when we add milk, butter, and sugar to a tasteless cocoa bean, we transform it into a delicious chocolate bar.

Nasty Human Animal + Education, Love, Law = Human Being

Tasteless Cocoa Bean + Milk, Sugar, Butter = Chocolate Bar

Education Is the Only Path to a Peaceful World

An Artificial Construction
The "human being" is an artificial construction. When you meet a loving, kind, and generous human being, that person is a man-made artificial construction, like a delicious man-made chocolate bar. Before the age of puberty, a parent has to put love into the child, just like a chef adds sugar to a cookie (Sharon Esther Lampert, *The Theory of Reality: 40 Absolute Truths*, Kadimah Press).

The New World Order
We need more than change. We need a "New World Order" for all people around the world: Food, clothing, shelter, medicine, "earliest reeducation" work, and world peace.

According to television ads, it takes just one dollar a day to save the life of a child living in Africa. According to Secretary Arne Duncan, he has 100 billion dollars in his education budget to save the lives of children living in America. It is time to move the front lines of the battlefield from Iraq, Afghanistan, and Pakistan to the anxious, stressed, depressed, distracted, disgruntled, disobedient, blocked, and suicidal students in classrooms across America--to begin the fight on behalf of our children to stop the destruction of America's Brightest Minds. There are American children dying on American soil.

Q: When will America's children become America's first priority?

When we shift the education paradigm to the, Quality Over Quantity Learning-Processing Education System, all students will be able to nurture and cultivate their brain power, develop their natural affinities, and use their unique potential to make a significant contribution to further the progress of civilization. As a result, America will have the greatest education system in the world: "Every Student Is a Success Story."

New Learning Technology: SMARTGRADES Processing Tools

Like any scientist worth her salt, I want to duplicate the results that I achieved by transforming borderline students of a malfunctioning American education system into A grade students. I want to extrapolate my methods and techniques to help all students in America by placing learning tools, SMARTGRADES Processing Tools, directly into the hands of all students.

The Fifteen Stepping Stones for Academic Success

Fortunately, we are only fifteen stepping stones away from transforming the American education system into one of the greatest education systems in the world. The fifteenth stepping stone of academic success is to solve the, "Problem of Education," by transforming "The Fifteen Stumbling Blocks of Academic Failure" into "The Fifteen Stepping Stones of Academic Success."

Let's Recap: Education Is the Only Path to a Peaceful World

I believe that by solving just one problem, "The Problem of Education," we will be able to solve every other problem in the world: Famine, illiteracy, poverty, crime, disease, domestic violence, religious strife, and world peace. Teachers--not politicians--are the true peacemakers in the world. Education is the only path to a peaceful world.

Solving the "Problem of Education" is the fifteenth stepping stone of academic success that will reenvision, reinvent, and rebuild the American education system to meet the challenges of the 21st century, and bring us all fifteen steps closer to a peaceful world.

TSUNAMI

How many tears can the ocean hold?
What the history books don't tell you
Is that the Indian Ocean was formed
By thousands of years of tears
That flowed from the fishermen of Sumatra.
Their pain was unbearable.
Their poverty was immeasurable.
Little to eat, little to wear,
Little to learn, too little work.
They were abandoned and forsaken.
Deep within their broken silent hearts,
An echo was heard.
The little earth quaked -
As it could no longer hold their tears.

Tens of thousands of tears overflowed
Deadly waves, crashing ashore
Sweeping their pain out from under
Their tattered rugs of impoverishment -
Out onto the front pages of newspapers worldwide.

Finally, the world took notice of their tears:
They sent care packages of food, clothing, shelter, schools, and cash.

They sent care packages of compassion, mercy, tolerance, and love.

The tears of the fisherman brought new life to tens of thousands in pain.

Salty, salty, sea water, tears of the fallen.
Salty, salty, sea water, heals the wounds of grief.
What the history books don't tell you is
How many tears can a human heart hold
Before it cracks beneath the surface
From the strain and pain and swells open
And learns how to love.

Sharon Esther Lamp
Creative Genius

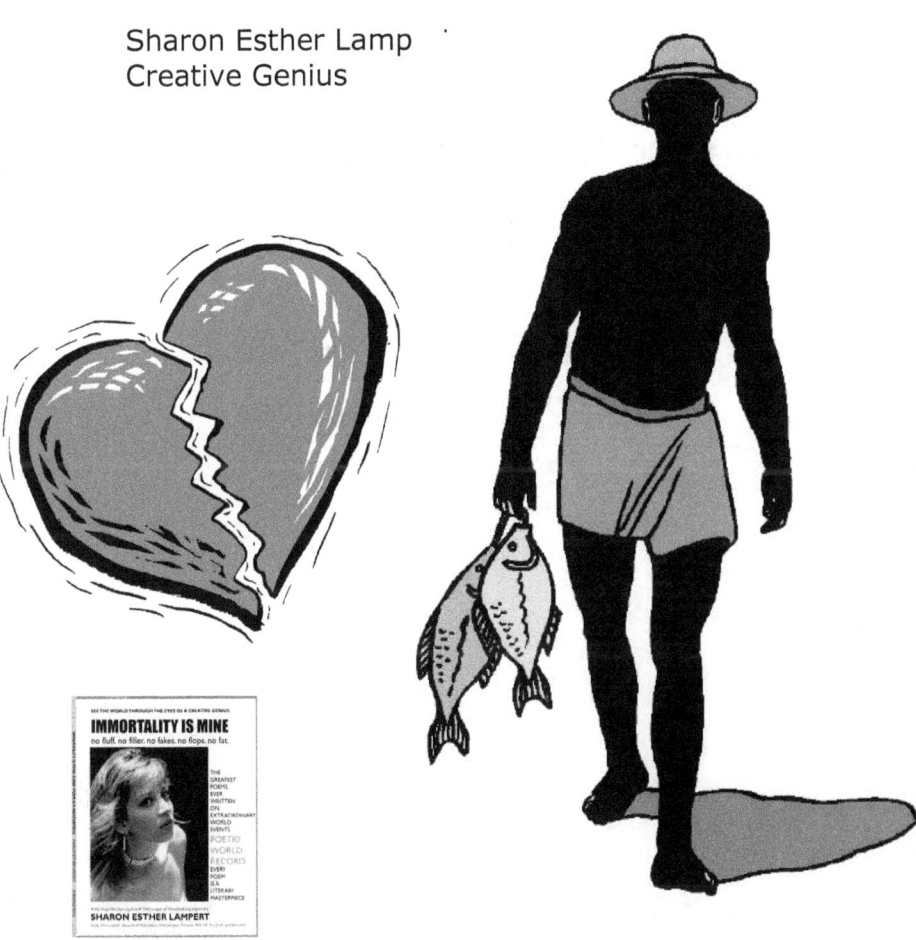

The Greatest Poems Ever Written on Extraordinary Events
www.WorldFamousPoems.com
#1 Website for School Students for School Assignments

"In War, Truth Is the First Casualty."

Aeschylus
Greek Tragic Dramatist
(525 BC - 456 BC)

THERE IS ONLY ONE
TRUTH
NO ONE HAS THE TRUTH

Sharon Esther Lampert
SEE THE WORLD THROUGH THE WORLD THE EYES OF A CREATIVE GENIUS
www.sharonestherlampert.com

Only The
[Earliest Re-educated]
Are Free.

Epictetus

It is Impossible for a Man To Learn What He Thinks He Already Knows.
Epictetus

Everyone Is On The Same Page

Q: When will America's children become America's first priority?

This book was also written to put students, parents, teachers, psychiatrists, and politicians on the same page to break the vicious cycle of unintentional child abuse (blind leading the blind). Let's connect most if not all of the dots …

Bullet 1. Inadequate/Abusive Parenting
Bullet 2. Malfunctioning American Education System
Bullet 3. Broken American Psychiatric System
Bullet 4. Broken World: Nasty Nature and Nasty Nurture

Bullet 1. Inadequate/Abusive Parenting
Parents put the first bullet into the child because they have inadequate/abusive parenting practices that they justify with the callous remark, "I hit him for his own good." The inability to show love is the first wounded arrow that is plunged deep into the sensitive soul of a powerless child. Most children will pay for the sins of their clueless parents, and children who survive, thrive, and flourish are entitled to be called creative geniuses.

Bullet 2. The Malfunctioning American Education System
(The Fifteen Stumbling Blocks of Academic Failure)

Bullet 3. The Broken American Psychiatric System
Psychotropic drugs do not resolve the underlying emotional problems and heal depression. This is why it is not uncommon to hear about a patient who overdoses and dies from taking these drugs. When patients are in emotional pain, they keep popping the pills, thinking that more pills will stop their pain. But the emotional pain keeps bubbling up to the surface and the patients keep popping the pills, overdose, and die. Abusing prescription drugs leads to devastating consequences to oneself: Addiction, accidental death (an overdose), or a planned suicide.

A recently reported death from an overdose of prescription drugs was the tragic loss of the gifted and talented actor, Heath Ledger:

"Heath Ledger's Tragic Overdose Death And What Can Be Done To Prevent Others--While tens of millions now have heard of Heath's tragic death, far fewer are aware of America's overdose epidemic. Accidental deaths from illegal and increasingly from legal drugs have doubled in the last decade. An estimated 22,000 Americans died last year alone from accidental overdoses, second only to motor vehicle accidents. More people died of accidental overdoses in New York last year than from murder. Yet our government spends not a single federal penny on overdose prevention!" (Tony Newman, "Heath Ledger's Tragic Overdose Death and What Can Be Done to Prevent Others," *The Huffington Post,* July 18, 2008).

For the most part, American psychiatrists do not teach emotional empowerment that is at the heart of emotional healing, "Mrs. Cohen, I am sorry to hear that your husband passed away--you appear to be depressed--would you like some Prozac, Luvox, Zoloft, or Paxil? Mrs. Cohen replied: "Can these pills help me grieve the loss of a twenty-year marriage, mend a broken heart, and prevent loneliness in my old age? If not, then no, I don't want any anti-depressants."

The question that needs to be examined is:

Q: Do you want to take a psychotropic drug (a dangerous crutch with serious side effects) for depression, or do you want to confront your emotional problem and heal the underlying disappointment, pain, and rage that cause depression?

Like cigarettes, a warning label should be placed on psychotropic drugs:

WARNING
These drugs are mood stabilizers.
These drugs will not heal the underlying emotional problem of disappointment, pain, and rage that cause depression. When you feel pain, do not keep popping these vacuous pills.

FEEL TO HEAL

If you drink five cups of coffee, you may be able to stay awake and complete a long overdue school assignment, but in the long run, it is better to learn how to set priorities, manage your time, and master the, SMARTGRADES Processing Tools, to work smarter.

It is a better choice to eat an orange than take a vitamin C tablet. If you walk into a vegetable market, you will bring home fresh fruits and vegetables filled with vitamins and minerals.

If you walk into a vitamin shop, you will bring home bottles of vitamin supplements that are helpful, but are not as nutritious as the fresh fruits and vegetables from the market.

If you visit a psychiatrist's office, to treat your emotional problems, you will return home with a psychotropic drug (a dangerous crutch with serious side effects) to prop you up and allow you to function with your depression.

It is better to walk into the office of an enlightened spiritual healer who will help you to confront the underlying emotional issues and heal the disappointment, pain, and rage, because then your depression will lift. You may cry your eyes out for weeks, month, or years, and feel completely drained from dealing with your emotional pain, but after, your depression will lift and you will heal.

Disappointments build up and so does emotional pain:

1. Paying for Sins of Clueless Parents Is Painful
   a. Poor parenting skills. Most parents are winging it, hit or miss
   b. Inability to love themselves and teach you to love yourself
   c. Use verbal abuse to teach you right from wrong
   d. Use physical abuse to teach you a lesson, e.g., hit or spank
   e. Identity issues: They want you to become like them or to fulfill their dreams, not yours

2. Paying for Sins of Toxic Relationships Is Painful
   a. Rejection is painful
   b. Abandonment is painful
   c. Separation anxiety is painful
   d. Toxic relationships are painful
   e. A broken heart is painful
   f. Unrequited love is painful

3. Loss of "True Love" Is Even More Painful
   a. Loss of a loved one is painful
   b. Loss of a beloved pet is excruciating (unconditional love)

4. Paying for Sins of Clueless Educators Is Painful
   a. Earn a diploma, but not an education
   b. No time to teach for in-depth comprehension
   c. No learning tools: Why can't I cram 1000-academic facts into my mind and regurgitate them onto a test in an hour?
   d. Hotdog exams: How many academic facts do students have to cram into their mind with meager comprehension?
   e. Vacuous test scores: Cram facts for short-term retention
   f. Pain of Inadequacy: "I am not as smart as I thought I was"
   g. Scars of Incompetence: No mastery of academic material
   h. Emotional problems: Stress, anxiety, depression, and suicide
   i. School loans, financial debt, 50-year repayment plans, and no required basic business or entrepreneurial skills
   j. Destroy "America's Brightest Minds"
   k. Contribute to building America's rising prison population

5. Paying for Sins of Clueless Psychiatrists Is Painful
   a. **The Vacuous Pills**
      Hand out dangerous psychotropic drugs with serious side effects to depressed, disconnected, distracted, disgruntled, and disobedient children

   b. **Psychiatrists Put the Third Bullet into the Child**
      Misdiagnose healthy children with incurable brain disorders who have parents with inadequate parenting tools (bullet one) and are enrolled in a malfunctioning American education system (bullet two)

   c. **Psychiatrists Increase the Suffering of the Patient**
      The patient is in emotional pain and suffering from the dangerous side effects of the medication. The patient has to FEEL to HEAL, and grieve their losses, and the vacuous pills mask the bad feelings that need to come to the surface and be released in tears, like rain.

   d. **Failure to Comprehend 3 Realities: Nature, Nurture, and Nature** - Nurture The human animal is the nastiest predator on the face of the planet. The human being is an artificial construction: Love, law, and education. Fusion: The nasty nature and nasty nurture results in evil, e.g., genocide.

11. Paying for Sins of Clueless Politicians Is Painful

a. Clueless: The "earliest" education is the only path to a peaceful world. Feed the whole child: Mind, body, and spirit. Without love, education, law, and a job, the human animal is a savage, the nastiest animal on the face of the planet.

b. Ironically, the "earliest" education is a top priority for terrorists. There is an inexhaustible supply of suicide bombers; the indoctrination of 2-year-old toddlers for martyrdom and murder

c. Democracy cannot exist if there is no separation between church(mosque) and state, e.g., Iran.

d. The vicious cycle of "tit for tat" violence continues into the 21st century (the 20th century was the most brutal in history). Survivors war transmit their war torn horror stories to the next generation, f centuries to come and will exact revenge and justice.

e. Drop vacuous billion-dollar bombs on the "evil ones" who are gu by association and simultaneously destroy thousands of innocent live

f. Borrow money from China to fund war in Iraq: $10 billion a mont or $120 billion a year (rough estimate)

---

g. Use the NCLB Education Policy indirectly to find soldiers for the war, as follows:
No Child Left Behind Act of 2001 (Public Law 107-110)
"The Act also requires that the schools distribute the name, home phone number and address of every student enrolled to **military recruiters** and institutions of higher education, unless the student (or the student's parent) specifically opts out" ("No Child Left Behin Act" Wikipedia, 2008).

---

h. Tell soldiers, young men who are in the prime of life, that they are dying for a just and right cause, when in fact, they have been dying in vain, for centuries, for the sins of clueless politicians.

Here is what you need to do to heal from depression:

Step 1. Confront your disappointment, pain, and rage

Step 2. Feel to heal: Communicate your pain and cry your eyes out for days, weeks, months, or even years

Step 3. Rebuild your shattered self-esteem with self-love

Step 4. Self-love: Nurse your wounds and nurture your soul

Step 5. Change the tune of the autopilot tape in your mind

Step 6. Every 5 minutes, you will have to climb over something

Step 7. For unconditional love, adopt a furry best friend from an animal shelter

Step 8. Don't believe everything you hear. The ratio is 75% lies: 25% truth

Step 9. Rewrite the map: Change the direction of your life

Step 10. Set realistic expectations: Plan A, Plan B, Plan C... Plan Z

Step 11. Get a lifeline: Find a spiritual healer, not a prescription-pushing drug dealer

Step 12. Read this book, "*Integration Therapy*"

Step 13. Survive, Thrive, and Flourish

Step 14. New disappointment: Repeat steps 1-13

Let's Recap: The Vacuous Test Scores
Educators are preoccupied with their vacuous test scores.
• Test scores have no value if students can't remember the academic facts two weeks after a test.

• Students will not be able to use the academic knowledge in their own lives, or to further the progress of civilization.

• Students don't learn how to succeed in school or in life, they only learn how to survive the malfunctioning education system.

• It is immoral to let students incur thousands of dollars in debt and graduate without any practical business skills to earn a living or entrepreneurial skills to start their own businesses.

Johns Hopkins: A Student Survey on Stress Levels
The Student Government Association of Johns Hopkins surveyed the entire student body and the results are as follows:

1. "Of those who admitted to being unhappy at Hopkins, the vast majority attribute their unhappiness to academic, rather than social, factors."

2. "They had come to Hopkins primarily for the academics, and that they are often too stressed out by their schoolwork to socialize."

3. "Over 60 percent of students surveyed said they feel that the administration "rarely" or "never" shows that they care about its undergraduates."

(Stephanie Delman, "SGA Surveys Students' Happiness, Stress Levels," *Johns Hopkins Newsletter,* December 4, 2008).

Let's Recap: The Vacuous Pills

The psychiatrists are preoccupied with their vacuous pills. The psychotropic drugs (antianxiety, antidepressants, and antipsychotics) prop students up, but do not solve emotional problems and heal the students emotional pain, or empower students with survival tactics to overcome the inevitable internalization of disappointment, pain, and rage that cause depression. More often than not, students use these drugs to overdose and commit suicide, as this example deftly illustrates:

University of California-Davis

A recent suicide was the junior, Jennifer Tse, who died on January 22, 2007. "As 20-year-old Jennifer Tse was dying in January, she typed a message on her laptop to the coroner's investigators she expected would examine her body. The lonely UC Davis sophomore, depressed and struggling with her studies, had swallowed cold pills, antidepressants, dishwashing liquid, and insect poison.

'It's kind of rather sad, it's no way out,' she wrote as she described her blurred vision, shaking muscles and a sense that her head was detached from her body. 'Hopefully my IQ will stay at the same level. If I end up dead, then oh well.'

For five days, no one seemed to notice her absence until her roommate realized something was amiss, used a screwdriver to open the locked door to Tse's room and found her body on the floor.

Tse's death is another grim statistic in what university administrators say is an escalating mental health crisis on campuses across the nation" (Richard C. Paddock, "Suicides a Symptom of Larger UC Crisis," *The Los Angeles Times,* May 23, 2007).

Let's Recap: The Vacuous Bombs

The politicians are preoccupied with their vacuous bombs. America has been at war for more than eight years and there is no end in sight. There is an inexhaustible supply of suicide bombers. Thousands of "guilty by association" and innocent lives were sacrificed here and abroad to attain a flawed, fickle, and fragile peace--real peace can only be attained through the "earliest" education. The future looks grim: Every war leaves battlefield scars of hatred and calls for revenge and justice that live on in the broken hearts of the survivors. Books will be written--not about how to attain a real and everlasting peace--but filled with war memories that are transmitted from one generation to the next. Here is a joke that has been passed down for generations and will continue to be passed down for generation to come:

> A Christian walks over to a Jew and hits him.
>
> The Jew says: "Why did you hit me?"
>
> The Christian says: "Because you killed Christ, Our Lord and Savior."
>
> The Jew says:
> "Jesus was a Jew, and that happened 2000 years ago."
>
> The Christian says: "But I just found out yesterday."

First, politicians have to get a clue? Early education is the only path to a peaceful world. Books--not--bombs are the long-term solution to the problem. There are no quick fixes. Children, the world over, receive an education by the age of seven that clearly delineates their friends from their foes. They know what religion to love and which people to hate, infidels and apostates. By age five, the vicious cycle of religious, ethnic, and racial intolerance has been transmitted from one generation to another.

For more than two thousand years, deicide was the excuse for dehumanizing and humiliating Jewish people, e.g., expulsions, pogroms; and genocide of six million Jewish people. Moreover, it is completely irrational for Christians and Muslims who are the majority of the human population to be so preoccupied with the Jews, who are less than .5% of the human population. -- Twelve of the most famous Christmas songs were written by Jews.

Here is the religious conundrum that needs resurrection:

Q: Why is the death of Jesus good for Christians and bad for Jews?

For Christians:
"Jesus Died For You, So You Can Live"

Through the death of Jesus, Christians are absolved of their earthly sins and given "Eternal Life." The death of Jesus is good.

For Jews:
"Jesus Died, the Jews Killed Him and Deserve to Die"
As far as the Jews go, the death of Jesus is bad.

This Is the Greatest Lie Ever Told in the Name of God.

Get a clue: You have to fight early miseducation with the "earliest" reeducation. The hand that rocks the cradle, has the power to start and stop wars, and this is why parenting initiatives, as discussed in this book, are where the taxpayers dollars have to be invested. Early miseducation is the problem, and vacuous billion-dollar bombs will not be able to resolve the problem of early miseducation. World-wide terrorism cannot be snuffed out by fighting "tit for tat" across the Arabian deserts. "World Peace" can only be attained by the "earliest" reeducation.

Here are three political conundrums that need analysis:
Q: Why were all of the 9/11 hijackers (except for Fayez Banihammad) from Saudi Arabia?

Q: How did America get way off course and end up in Iraq?

Q: Are we in Iraq because of President G.W. Bush's lingering painful memory of his father, who was targeted for assassination by Saddam Hussein?

"Bush said: 'After all, this is the guy who tried to kill my dad.'--The alleged assassination attempt came when former President Bush visited Kuwait during the Clinton administration. The former president had orchestrated the U.S.-led coalition that pushed the Iraq army from Kuwait in the Persian Gulf War" (John King, "Bush Calls Saddam 'The Guy Who Tried to Kill My Dad'" CNN, September 27, 2002).

If the truth be told, the real reason America invaded Iraq is because of Saddam Hussein's assassination attempt on the senior President George H.W. Bush. The political had become deeply personal. President George W. Bush's bad memory lingered on, and took America way off course. If President George H. Bush did not have this painful memory, then we would probably not be in Iraq. Bush's lingering bad memory was the inciting incident. He was not the only son who suffered many sleepless nights tossing and turning in his bed worrying about his father. As a matter of historical fact, there are many brutal memories shared by countless victims who have indirectly suffered at the hands of Saddam Hussein. Saddam will not be missed. Saddam Hussein was a menace to his own people and to his neighbors. President Bush will also not be missed, because he left America more vulnerable than ever before by depleting America's Democratic economic surplus, doubling her losses and quadrupling her pain: 7,800 fatalities and 30,000 casualties (2009). Moreover, America has more enemies than ever before, who will seek justified revenge for injuries sustained. From the start, this was a lose-lose scenario with no end in sight ...

The former, President H. W. Bush, also had a lingering bad memory of broccoli, and stated the following:

"I do not like broccoli. And I haven't liked it since I was a little kid and my mother made me eat it. And I'm President of the United States and I'm not going to eat any more broccoli" ("Bush" Wikipedia).

On March 22, 1990, the former President George H.W. Bush banned broccoli from being served at the White House and on Airforce One menus. This is how one man's personal history seeps into a political decision that affects the lives of others, with little regard for the needs of others. Broccoli is good for you. War is bad for you. Big boys have to learn to eat their broccoli like men, and "Beat their swords into plow-shares. Nation will not take up sword against nation, nor will they train for war anymore" (Isaiah 2:4 & Micah 4:3.).

Here are more political conundrums that need analysis:

It is far to easy to engage in the vicious cycle of violence and react with military firepower to combat sustained injuries, as in, "He hit me first."

Q: Has America lost her moral authority to tell other countries to stop the "tit for tat" incessant bloodshed?

Q: How many more vacuous billion-dollars bombs are we going to drop to attain a fragile, fickle, and flawed peace? (democracy cannot exist if there is no separation of church(mosque) and state)

Q: Has America lost her moral authority to tell other countries to stop diverting foreign aid for food, housing, and education to military arms?

Q: Isn't it time for America to stop the vicious cycle of "tit for tat" violence by the "earliest reeducation" of children.

Q: How can the American government tell its citizens to stop living on credit and start living within their means when they borrow money from China to drop vacuous bombs?

Q: Isn't it time for America to send foreign aid to countries for building schools that hand out school books, such as, "World Peace for Dummies."

Q: Isn't it time for America to divert her own resources from the wasteland of war-torn battlefields in the burning sands of the Arabian deserts to overhauling her own malfunctioning education system that is destroying "America's Brightest Minds?"

The Cemetery: Real and Everlasting Peace
There is only one place on Planet Earth where you can find a real and everlasting peace--the cemetery. Dropping vacuous billion-dollar bombs and building cemeteries can bring about a real and everlasting peace--but the real challenge before us is to cultivate the awesome power of the human brain--by building billion-dollar schools--and harnessing brain power to bring about a real and everlasting peace on Planet Earth, not by destroying its inhabitants to have peace.

For centuries, men (semi-socialized human animals) have always been far too preoccupied with war games and building vacuous billion-dollar bombs rather than with using the millions, billions, or trillions of tax payers dollars to nurture and cultivate the awesome power of the human brain.

Let's Recap: Long-Term Returns on Financial Investments
The hand that rocks the cradle has the power to start and stop wars. Reeducation is the only path to a peaceful world.

Every problem under the sun is a problem of nature. Before the age of puberty, the infusion of love, respect, tolerance, compassion, and truth is the only hope for the "human animal--who like a caterpillar wants to become a butterfly--the "human animal" yearns for metamorphosis into a "human being."

America would have had a better return on her investment, if she built schools in Afghanistan, Iraq, and Pakistan rather than by spending millions, billions or trillions of dollars on dropping vacuous billion-dollar bombs for the past five years and destroying thousands of lives that are guilty by association, as well as innocent lives, here and abroad.

After 9/11, America had an easy way out, such as racial profiling, beef-up intelligence, tighten immigration, and secure borders. America complains that she gives foreign aid to countries that hate America, and then pisses away billions of dollars on small dicks who want to destroy America.

America has embassies in many countries. What about libraries?

Q: Why not build libraries that contain FREE books on democracy?

FREE BOOKS
LIBRARY OF DEMOCRACY
Civil Rights, Free Speech, and Unlimited Personal Potential

Caveat: Democracy cannot exist if there is no separation between church/mosque/temple and state. The religious leader decide who the male candidates are and whether women can wear lipstick... etc... (I hate to be a party pooper...but NO real democracy.

Here are the political conundrums that need analysis:
Q: Why do our enemies engage in nickel and dime covert operations to achieve martyrdom and murder?

Q: Why can't America engage in small scale covert operations that target the handful of "Evil Ones" who masterminded 9/11? For example, like Simon Wiesenthal. Get a clue: Read the poem: --->

Q: Why is there an inexhaustible supply of suicide bombers?

Q: Why does America have more adversaries (playmates) willing to engage in martyrdom and murder after 9/11 than before 9/11?

Let's Compare America's Fighting Tactics to the Enemy
America's Tactics
1. Loud and noisy
2. Spend billions of dollars: trillion dollar deficit, bankrupt's country
3. Doubles her losses: > 7,800 fatalities
4. Quadruples her pain: > 30,000 casalties (cripples)
5. Triples the number of terrorist playmates, here and abroad
6. Ten years later, completely clueless as to where her enemy is hiding
7. Clueless: No in-depth comprehension of her enemy or problem

The Enemy's Tactics
1. Quiet and sneaky
2. Doesn't spend any money
3. Sends one person to blow something up
4. Always hits its target, waits patiently for years, if necessary
5. Earliest education of 2-year old toddlers for JIHAD
6. An inexhaustible supply of suicide bombers
7. Will continue this murderous game for centuries to come

The facts are fickle and education can make people even more ignorant, because the knowledge acquired and the theories promulgated are deeply flawed:
1. Broken American Education System: Vacuous Test Scores
2. Broken American Psychiatric System: Vacuous Pills
3. Broken American Political System: Vacuous Bombs
4. Broken World: Nature is Nasty and Nurture is Nasty

World's Greatest Nazi Hunter
Simon Wiesenthal: A Survivor's Burden

After six million Jews were silenced:
Simon speaks above a hush.
Simon speaks above a whisper.
Simon speaks above an earshot.
Simon speaks out loud above the deafening scream of EVIL.

After six million Jews were silenced:
Simon's voice shatters the ghetto walls of anti-Semitism.
Simon's voice bellows in the streets of Argentina.
Simon's voice hallows in the halls of JUSTICE.
Simon's voice harkens in the International Arena of INJUSTICE.

After six million Jews were silenced:
Simon Wiesenthal WALKS his TALK and JUSTICE is done:
Adolf Eichman is brought to JUSTICE.
Franz Stangl is brought to JUSTICE.
Franz Murer is brought to JUSTICE.
Erich Rajakowitsch is brought to JUSTICE.
Hermine Braunsteiner is brought to JUSTICE.
Karl Silberbauer is brought to JUSTICE.
Josef Schwammberger is brought to JUSTICE.
1,100 Nazi War Criminals are brought to JUSTICE.

After six million Jews were silenced:
Simon Says: "This man is on my list as a suspected war criminal."
Simon Says: "When history looks back I want people to know the Nazis weren't able to kill millions of people and get away with it."
Simon Says: "If we don't do anything about evil, that will encourage future perpetrators."
Simon Says: "My work is a warning for the murderers of tomorrow."
Simon Says: "Survival is a privilege which entails obligations. I am forever asking myself what I can do for those who have not survived."
Simon Says: "I have received many honors in my lifetime; when I die, these honors will die with me, but the Simon Wiesenthal Center will live on as my legacy."
Simon Says: "My epitaph should read simply "SURVIVOR."
Simon Says (in the afterlife... to the six million Jews murdered in the Holocaust): "I didn't forget you."

Sharon Esther Lampert
Creative Genius

We Will Have Peace with the Arabs When They Love Their Children More Than They Hate Us
Golda Meir

What Is the Greater Evil? Who Is the Greater Enemy?

Is it: The Israeli army who vanquishes the enemy from their teeny-tiny home of desert, OR their own family members of Arab brothers who don't make them feel at home and treat their own kin like refugees in their 22-Arab nation and oil-rich oasis, for 60 years?
Sharon Esther Lampert
8Th Prophetess of Israel

Let me tell you something that we Israelis have against Moses. He took us 40 years through the desert in order to bring us to the one spot in the Middle East that has no oil!
Golda Meir

www.WorldFamousPoems.com
The Greatest Poems Ever Written on Extraordinary World Events

The Militant Palestinian Toddler Terrorist

At my mother's breast
I learned how to thirst for the blood of Jews

Other toddlers learn how to live and love
I will learn how to hate Jews and die as a martyr

Other toddlers have parents that love them
My parents love to hate Jews

Other toddlers wear blue and pink
I wear a belt packed with explosives to kill Jews

Other toddlers love to cuddle adorable stuffed animals
I love to clench rocks to throw at Israeli soldiers

Other toddlers have a favorite blanket
I love to stomp on and burn American and Israeli flags

Other toddlers love to play games and laugh out loud
I have a toy chest filled with loud katyusha rockets that make Jews cry

Today, I plan to kill Jewish mothers and fathers, and
Tonight we will all be together in heaven

In heaven, I will know the love of a Jewish mother and father
And I will rest in peace

Sharon Esther Lampert

> "America is a great power possessed of tremendous military might and a wide-ranging economy, but all this is built on an unstable foundation which can be targeted, with special attention to its obvious weak spots. If America is hit in one hundredth of these weak spots, God willing, it will stumble, wither away and relinquish world leadership."

Usamah Bin Mohammed Bin Laden

1. Al Qaeda was founded in 1988; Sudan (1991-1996), Afghanistan
The Agenda: Advancement of Islamic revolutions throughout the Muslim world and repelling foreign intervention in the Middle East.

2. First Gulf War: (August 2, 1990 – February 28 1991)
Al Qaeda is disgruntled over the growing U.S. presence in the Middle East, particularly in Saudi Arabia, home to Islam's most sacred shrines. Al Qaeda vociferously opposed the stationing of U.S. troops on what it considered the holiest of Islamic lands.

3. Saudi regime subsequently deported bin Laden in 1992 and revoked his citizenship in 1994.

4. February 6, 1993: First World Trade Center bombing

5. February 1998: Formed a coalition called the International Islamic Front for Jihad Against the Jews and Crusaders to fight the U.S. The militants signed a fatwa (religious opinion) outlining the Front's ideology and goals. The fatwa was published in a London-based Arabic paper, Al Quds Al Arabi; it called on all Muslims to "kill the Americans and their allies - civilians and military," wherever they may be.

6. August 1998: Al Qaeda bombed two U.S. embassies in East Africa (Nairobi, Kenya, and Dar es Salaam, Tanzania) killing more than 200 people, including 12 Americans. In retaliation, the U.S. attacked targets in Sudan and Afghanistan.

7. October 2000: U.S.S. Cole, an American guided-missile destroyer at Aden, Yemen, killing 17 American servicemen.

8. September 11, 2001: World Trade Center Attack
(ADL.org, 2009)

Final Note to the Reader

The pain and suffering from the terrorist attack on September 11, 2001, is bleeding us dry emotionally and economically. It is time to look beyond our pain of innocent lives lost and our fear of terrorism. Our enemy uses clandestine operations and we need to do the same, instead of a big splashy American parade. There is no end in sight because we have tripled our playmates.

It is time to get a clue and connect all the dots ... and see the problem clearly for what it really is: Osama bin Laden had only one agenda, and that was to destroy the economic power of the United States of America. American fatalities are mere collateral damage. His modus operandi is to use our own power against us: He used our own airplanes to destroy the World Trade Center. When we drain our economic resources in Afghanistan and Iraq, we are helping Osama bin Laden to achieve his primary objective, the destruction of America's economic power. To quote President Mahmoud Ahmadinejad of Iran, "The American empire in the world is reaching the end of its road (Ahmadinejad: 'American empire' nearing its end. CNN, September 24, 2008).

We have spent more than eight years helping Osama bin Laden achieve his primary objective, the destruction of America's economic power. Osama bin Laden only counts American dollars lost--one trillion, two trillion, three-trillion dollars lost--eleven-trillion dollars and the eventual fall of the American empire.

It is time to reinvest our economic resources in America, namely, our education system, which is the heart and soul of every great nation, so that American ingenuity and free enterprise can flourish. This is the only worthwhile "WIN" worthy of the attention of the free and democratic world.

Sharon Esther Lampert
Poet, Philosopher, Paladin of Education, Peacemaker, Pioneer, and Prophet

#1 Poetry Website for School Projects

The Greatest Poems Ever Written on Extraordinary Events
www.WorldFamousPoems.com

Annual Reading of Poem
In September, there is an annual reading of this poem
in New York City with audience participation.
Sharon reads the verse and the audience reads the refrain
For date and time, visit website, www.poetryjewels.com

Live Podcast Reading of Poem
There are live recordings of this poem on u-tube.

A Literary Note About the Poem
There are seven verses.
The first part of every stanza is "spiraling downward"
and the last part of every stanza is "spiraling upward."

Spiraling Downward, Upward We Stand United
The World Trade Center Tragedy in 7 Powerful Poetic Verses

By Sharon Esther Lampert

Verse 1

(1) Maniacal terrorists strike at the big apple of America's eye. Famed majestic landmarks, the Twin Towers crumble, imploding into billions of bits of molten steel, jagged glass, seared human flesh, and flailing broken bones. Escaping spiked and surging fire balls, staff vaulted through windows. A canine-toothed wing of the Pentagon is broken in the aftermath of the devastation: a massive death toll of innocents remains lodged, buried alive, fifty feet under, feeling the cold-bloodied hard rubble, a steely glint of hope, five warm-blooded survivors are unearthed. Every save a divine miracle. Subways evacuate. First-aid crews take to the streets and man the flaming towers.

Spiraling Downward, Upward We Stand United

Verse 2

(2) Flattened, the first company of New York City's finest fire fighters, police, and first-aid crews CRASH and BURN inside the cascading avalanche of steel daggers. The 110-story Twin Towers are brought to their saber knees and then to their foiled ankles. Grieving, a 47-story sister building 7, collapses in distress into ragged ruins. Billowing, nearby brother buildings in the zone remain ablaze. WTC mass exodus: pyre and plumes of smoke hover, flying concrete shards and soot, repugnant jet fuel, raining dust and debris, thousands of frightful fleeing bystanders are entombed. Fatalities, makeshift morgues ferry the sacrificial corpses to New Jersey. The Pile, 1.2 billion tons of scorched scraps are hauled to The Hill of Fresh Kills Landfill. DNA matches:a gruesome, grueling, and grisly task, steam still rising, pickaxes poke for parts. Dogs sniff and succor. Ground Zero: dug-up remains are draped with the U.S.A. flag, saluted, and reburied. Every find a divine miracle. FDNY Firefighters, Jack Tipping finds his fallen son, John Jr. Tipping. A carnivorous crater, vestiges of an office complex, in the dangerous pit of dignified souls, hard hat archaeologists dig among the ruins: 13 bodies, 10 fearless firemen and 3 fearful civilians are found 30 feet below ground. High-flying stars and stripes fly low at half staff. Busy bees swarming, scalpeled surgeons, bedpan nurses, and selfless volunteers man the hospitals. Boiling vigorously, New Yorkers from every mosaic melting hot-pot take to the streets and wait for hours to donate their warm vital blood.

Spiraling Downward, Upward We Stand United

Verse 3

(3) Slamming, ramming into Grade A U.S. Steel,
four American jumbo jets are commandeered:
flight crews are maced; by razor blade box cutters,
pilots are knifed, passengers use their cell phones:
"I Love You" are their final words. Diabolical,
suicide bombers -- American men, women, and
children transfigured into four human missiles:
8:45 a.m.:Flight 11, Boeing 767, Boston to L.A.,
81 Americans, eleven crew members, CRASH
and BURN, into the north tower, N.Y.C.
9:03 a.m.:Flight 175, Boeing 767, Boston to L.A.,
56 Americans, nine crew members, CRASH
and BURN, into the south tower, N.Y.C.
9:45 a.m.:Flight 77, Boeing 757, Washington to L.A.,
58 Americans, six crew members, CRASH
and BURN, into the Pentagon, in D.C.
10:00 a.m.:Flight 93, Boeing 757, N.J. to San Francisco,
38 Americans, seven crew members, CRASH
and BURN, into an empty field, in PA, by unsung
heroes:"Let's Roll!" Federal aviation officials ground
flights: 4000 planes take a nose-dive at the nearest airport.
Soaring sky high, safe and sound, squawking seagulls with
whimpering wings remain in flight and brave the fight.
Zippered up, bridges, tunnels, and highways lock gates.
Fiercely, five warships, frigate ships, and aiming bull's-eye,
guided missile destroyers man the N.Y. coast: Two aircraft
carriers: USS George Washington and USS John F. Kennedy
man the N.Y. skies. Operation Noble Eagle: combat air
patrol to shoot-em-up and shoot-em-down. In steely
determination, it is business, but not business as usual.

Spiraling Downward, Upward We Stand United

474

Verse 4

(4) It is more than a terrorist attack -
It is an act of war! It is a national tragedy!
The free and democratic world is attacked:
White House evacuates.
United Nations evacuates.
Treasury evacuates.
State Department evacuates.
Justice Department evacuates.
World Bank evacuates.
All Federal office buildings evacuate.
Israel evacuates all diplomatic missions - 12 months of merciless jihad: soulless suicide bombers maim, mutilate, and murder Jews. All N.Y. State government offices evacuate. New York's primary elections are postponed. Trading is suspended: The American Stock Exchange, Nasdaq, and New York Stock Exchange. 110 stories, Chicago's Sears Tower evacuates. Homeless, a frozen zone, 20,000 N.Y.C. residents are displaced. Chartering a Saudi jet, on a one way ticket to Mecca, 11 Bostonian bin Ladens evacuate. Slumbering, F.B.I., C.I.A., I.N.S., and N.S.A. agents rouse. It is the first war of the 21st century! No-man's land, hermetically sealed, the President of the U.S.A. is whisked away. Blinding black smoke and clouds raining ash, heroic, Lady Liberty stands tall in the New York Harbor.

Spiraling Downward, Upward We Stand United

Verse 5

5) Mayor Rudolph W. Giuliani addresses New York:
"Deaths are more than any of us can bear."
Senator Hillary D. Rodham Clinton addresses New York:
"We will not be cowed by evil, despicable acts of terror."
President George W. Bush addresses the nation:
"These acts shattered steel but they
cannot dent the steel of American resolve."
"We will make no distinction between the terrorists
who committed these acts and those who harbored them."
"Whether we bring our enemies to justice, or bring
justice to our enemies, justice will be done."
Nefarious doings, suspect numero uno is "The Evil One,"
cannibal Saudi militant Osama bin Laden and his vile circus
of vicious cavemen. Virulent videos made visible, rallying all
Muslims with venom and vitriol: "God Willing, America's
end is near..." UPWARD UNITED WE STAND: OPERATION
INFINITE JUSTICE: SEEK AND DESTROY AL QAEDA.
OPERATION ENDURING FREEDOM: target cells, villainous
metastasizing cancers. Flight 93 terrorist manhunt: Who is the
20th hijacker? Ramzi Omar or Moussaoui (?) Americans man
their maps and ask: Where the HELL (?) is Afghanistan(?)
WW III: Worldwide Coalition Bombers vs. Terror-Bender
Troglodytes. Oct 7th: Billion dollar bombs drop. Tora Bora
caves are wiped off the map: "Osama, Peek-a-Boo, Where
Are You?" Taliban women see the light of day, Taliban men
will never again see the light of day. Anthrax: Biological,
nuclear, and radiological weapons. Inhalation. Evacuation.
Annihilation. "Our nation, in our fight against terrorism,
will uphold the doctrine of either you're with us or against
us." "And the rockets' red glare, the bombs bursting in air"
"America was targeted for attack because we're the brightest
beacon for freedom and opportunity in the world. And no
one will keep that light from shining." "God Bless America,
land that I love. Stand beside her, and guide her..."

Spiraling Downward, Upward We Stand United

Verse 6

(6) Heaven sent, where 70 virgins await each Islamic martyr on a homicidal-suicidal mission, 19 corrosive terrorists pulverize into an Arabian desert sand storm: desolate and deserted; no bad guys; no car chase; no planes; no black boxes, no survivors, no witnesses, no testimonies, no revenge to seek; no justice to exact; no war to win; and no Hollywood movie. Arise: Awake. New world order and Office of Homeland Security: cockpit dead bolts, armed pilots and martial art stewardesses, no curb side check-in and Arab profiling strip searches. An inferno, charred bodies incinerate into ashes, few funerals, many memorial tributes, urns of WTC dirt comfort. Cremated. Sobbing. Closure. Weeping widows, wailing orphans, donations flood the Red Cross. International terrorism: a worldwide menace. Terrorists: a worldwide monstrosity. Arise: Reborn. One true empyrean: a phoenix, names of loved ones are inscribed on the walls of the observation deck, sacred ground, a shrine, the hatched angels hover, protecting the Twin Towers rebuilt. Lighting a blowtorch, ironworkers, engineers, teamsters, laborers, and dock builders take turns... Last steel column of 2WTC, 58 tons, no. 1,001B, is cut down at 8:17 p.m. Heartbroken, resting in peace, archangel-chief architect Minoru Yamasaki said, "A beautiful solution of form and silhouette. "WorldWISE: democracy, liberty, freedom, love, prosperity, goodness, security, and peace. We Shall Overcome.

Spiraling Downward, Upward We Stand United

Verse 7

(7) A cataclysmic collision course between good and evil; angels aflight and devils afoot. "Thou Shalt Not Murder," the first set of twin tablet's of the Ten Commandments crumble into rubble, and are reengraved: Operation Infinite Circle. Singed aftershocks: fear, disbelief, terror, rage, grief, depression, revenge, numbness, and nightmares... and 2,990 children are without parents. Twin Tower totals: 90,000 tourists a day, 50,000 employed; 25,000 rescued; 35,000 in subway evacuated; and two-thirds empty airplanes. 8,700 casualties, each story a miracle: a raging fire ball, 82% of her body burned, Lauren Manning lives. Innocents: Fatalities from 92 nations, 343 firefighters, 265 airplane passengers, 184 at the Pentagon, and 25, 0000 people work at the Pentagon. Mournfully, 2,749 people are consumed. Outstretched, GOD's hand of mercy, love, compassion, and nerves of steel, vanquished the evil incarnate, God willing.

Spiraling Downward, Upward We Stand United

By Sharon Esther Lampert
Poet, Philosopher, and
Paladin of Education
Book: IMMORTALITY IS MINE

#1 Poetry Website for School Projects
www.WorldFamousPoems.com
The Greatest Poems Ever Written on Extraordinary World Events

9/11 Al-Qaeda Terrorist Update

Terrorism is a Double Whammy: Nasty Nature and Nasty Nurture

At Large
- Osama Bin Laden
- Ayman al-Zawahiri
- Abu Hamza al-Muhajir
- Abu Ayyub al-Masri
- Sheikh Said
- Saif al-Adel
- Abu Mohammed al-Masri
- Sulaiman Abu Ghaith
- Thirwat Salah Shirhata

In Custody
- Abu Faraj al-Libbi
- Khalid Sheikh Mohammed
- Abu Zubaydah
- Zubaydah
- Ramzi Binalshibh
- Abd al-Hadi al-Iraqi
- Mohammed Haydar Zammar
- Haydar Zammar
- Ali Abdul Rahman al-Ghamdi
- Mohamedou Ould Slahi
- Mohsen F

Jailed
- Zacarias Moussaoui
- Mounir al-Motassadek
- Richard Reid
- Abd al-Rahim al-Nashiri

Dead or Believed Dead
- Abu Musab al-Zarqawi
- Amjad Farooqi
- Mohammed Atef
- Ali Qaed Senyan al-Harthi
- Abu Hazim al-Shair
- Omar al-Farouq

New Problem: American Muslim Jihad
It is interesting to note that many of the recent attempts to attack America on American soil were executed by fell Americans who are Muslim, but not Ar Some were Christian converts to Islam

The Eternal Paradox of the Penis

Why is it that the men with no dicks, the cowards, become the dicks, the bullies?

Sharon Esther Lampert

There Are Only Two Kinds of Men in This World: The big dicks who like to build things and the small dicks who like to destroy everything.

Sharon Esther Lampert

There Are No Believers.
There Are Only Make-Believers & Non-Believers

Sharon Esther Lampert

GOD IS GO DO!
God Can Only Do for You What God Can Do Through You!
GodIsGoDo.com

BOOKS

WHO KNEW GOD WAS SUCH A CHATTERBOX
GOD TALKS TO ME: A WORKING DEFINITION OF GOD
www.GodIsGoDo.com

Q: Is Life a Gift or a Punishment?

God of What? 11 Esoteric Laws of Inextricability
www.PhilosopherQueen.com

DEADICATION

Every single second of the day,
A suffering is taking place:
Shake-Me. Wake-Me. Save Me.

Every single second of the day,
My belief in a God is shaken:
Shake-Me. Wake-Me. Save Me.

GOD IS DEAD.

Sharon Esther Lampert

Be patient toward all that is unsolved in your heart and try to love the questions themselves.

Rainer Maria Rilke

Take a "Hotdog" Exam

Cram voluminous academic facts into your mind and regurgitate them onto a test in two hours to earn a diploma.

Save America's Children of Privilege
1. Do you agree or disagree with the author's opinion that this book can save the lives of millions of American children?

World Peace
2. Do you agree or disagree with the author's opinion that "Education Is the Only Path to a Peaceful World?"

3. Do you agree or disagree with the author's opinion that, "If we solve the "Problem of Education," we can solve every other problem in the world: Famine, illiteracy, poverty, crime, disease, domestic violence, religious strife, and war."

Education
4. Do you agree or disagree with the author's opinion that educators are clueless as to "How Does Learning Take Place?"

5. Do you agree or disagree with the author's opinion that, educators cut corners and cheat students out of an education: No in-depth comprehension, no long-term retention, and no mastery of the academic material?

6. What are "The Fifteen Stumbling Blocks of Academic Failure"?

7. What are "The Fifteen Stepping Stones for Academic Success"?

8a. What is a "Hotdog" exam? How did it get its name?

8b. Do you agree or disagree with the author's opinion that, education is not measured by cramming voluminous facts into your mind, and regurgitating the facts under psychological duress and a stopwatch onto abusive (tricky) "hotdog" exams?

9a. What is the "Quantity Over Quality Curriculum-Driven American Education System"?

9b. Why is this education paradigm failing to educate students to meet the challenges of the 21st century?

9c. Why do students earn a diploma, but not an education?

10a. What is "The Quality Over Quantity Learning-Processing Education System?"

10b. Why is this education paradigm the solution to the "National Crisis of Education in America"?

10c. Why will students earn a diploma and an education?

11. What is the "New Grading System," and how does it ensure that, "Every Student Is a Success Story"?

12. What is "The Universal Gold Standard of Education"?

13. What is "The Silent Crisis Destroying America's Brightest Minds?"

14. Do you agree or disagree with the author's opinion that, education is measured by in-depth comprehension, long-term retention, and mastery of the academic material?

New Learning Technology
15. List ten "SMARTGRADES Processing Tools" that help students "learn and process" voluminous academic material and achieve academic success?

16. Do you agree or disagree with the author's opinion that, placing "SMARTGRADES Processing Tools" directly into the hands of students will empower all students for academic success?

Academic Intervention
17. List five academic interventions that transform borderline students into Grade A students?

A.D.H.D.
18. Why do doctors misdiagnose students with A. D. H. D.?

19. This book courageously tackles many hot-button issues in education. Pick one issue. Do you agree or disagree with the author's analysis and resolution to the following problems?

a. The Silent Crisis Destroying America's Brightest Minds
b. The Rising A. D. H. D. Epidemic
c. The Rising Rate of High School Dropouts
d. The Rising Rate of America's Prison Population
e. The Rising Rate of America's School Shootings
f. The Amethyst Initiative and College Binge-Drinking
g. The Rising Rate of College Depression and Suicide
h. The Rising Rate of Childhood Obesity
i. The Destruction of Lateral Right-Brain Students
j. The Genius, Albert Einstein, Fails a "Hotdog" Exam
k. American Stop-Loss Soldiers Fighting on Foreign Soil
l. One in Six Children Live in Poverty in America

The Philosopher and Poet, Sharon Esther Lampert

20a. What is Lampert's definition of the "Dark Ages?"

20b. What is Lampert's definition of "Enlightenment?"

21a. What is Lampert's definition of Genocide?

21b. Does her theory of "The Double Whammy" explain genocide?

PHOTON SUPERHERO OF EDUCATION ON PLANET EARTH

22. Do you think the superhero, Photon, will fulfill her mission to save clueless Earthlings and bring "World Peace to Planet Earth?" (see page 538)

23. What are Photon's two extra-sensory superpowers?

24. What is the name of Photon's spaceship?

25. Where was Photon born (planet and galaxy)?

26. What is Photon's's Self-Esteem Affirmation?

27. What is Photon's Circle of Responsibility Affirmation?

28. What is Photon's Empowerment Affirmation?

29. What is Photon's math equation for world peace?

30. What is the special relationship between Sharon Rose Sugar and Photon, The Superhero of Education on Planet Earth?

Education Update: April 16, 2009

Secretary Arne Duncan's "Race to the Bottom"

This book is the wake-up call that Secretary Arne Duncan needs to dig deeper into the core issues of why the American education system is malfunctioning, namely, the "Fifteen Stumbling Blocks of Academic Failure" that are destroying America's Brightest Minds.

Here is America's education agenda according to Secretary Arne Duncan: "Under the economic stimulus package—more than $100 billion in new funding for education over the next two years -- the primary goal of the stimulus is to save jobs—but the larger goal is to drive a set of reforms that we believe will transform public education in America. --The four issues are: higher standards, data systems, turning around underperforming schools, and teacher quality." In addition, there is a 5-billion dollar, "Race to the Top Fund," to reward states that make good on their pledges" (National Science Teachers Association Conference, Ed.gov.com, March 20, 2009).

There are no new ideas set forth in Secretary Arne Duncan's education agenda for American children. He is still on the same path and will get the same results, a race to the bottom.

1. Get a Clue: The Fifteen Stumbling Blocks of Academic Failure

2. Get a Clue: The Fifteen Stepping Stones to Academic Success

3. Get a Clue: The Universal Gold Standard of Education

4. Get a Clue: How Does Learning Take Place? How Do You Nurture and Cultivate the Awesome Power of the Human Brain?

Education Is the Only Path to a Peaceful World

5. New Education Paradigm
   The Learning-Processing American Education System
   1. Realistic-Time Allotments and Detailed Step-By Step Instructions
   2. In-Depth Comprehension: SMARTGRADES Critical Thinking Skills
   3. Long-Term Retention: SMARTGRADES Processing Tools
   4. Mastery of Academic Material: Strengths and Weaknesses
   5. Every Student Is a Success Story: Grade A or REDO
   6. Education is Measured by In-Depth Comprehension, Long- Term Retention, and Mastery of Academic Material
   7. Students Earn an Education and a Diploma
   8. The Education Goalpost: Self-Reliant and Life-Long Learners

6. 8 GOALPOSTS OF EDUCATION By PHOTON SUPERHERO
   1. EDUCATION: KNOWLEDGE!
   2. ENLIGHTENMENT: AHA!
   3. EMPOWERMENT: YES I CAN!
   4. EXCELLENCE: MASTERY!
   5. EMANCIPATION: ALL CAN DO!
   6. EGALITERIANISM: EQUAL RIGHTS!
   7. EQUALITY: NEW WORLD ORDER!
   8. ECONOMIC STABILITY: WORLD PEACE!

This book deftly explains that the national crisis of education in America is much larger than, Secretary Arne Duncan, acknowledges. Without question, he has underestimated the gravity of the problem of education in America. Similar to the war in Iraq, when President Bush underestimated the social, political, and religious realities on the ground and made promises to Americans and Iraqis, and was unable to extricat himself from Iraq, or make America safer. President Bush made America more vulnerable than ever before. He depleted the Democratic budget surplus and quadrupled her losses and her pain. Get a Clue: There is an inexhaustible supply of suicide bombers, because of the "earliest education" and indoctrination of 2-year-old toddlers for martyrdom an murder. The "earliest re-education" is the only path to a peaceful worlc

To Reiterate Ad Nauseam: World Peace For Dummies

Democracy cannot exist if there is no separation between church (mosque) and state. As of today, April 15, 2009, Osama bin Laden has won his war on America, because he wanted to destroy America's economic power in the world (Americans fatalities are mere collateral damage). He used our own airplanes to destroy the World Trade Center, (the symbolic fulcrum of America's economic power), and he used our fear, pain, and rage to get us to drain and deplete our economic resources and destroy innocent lives, here and abroad, that are guilty by association.

Let's crunch some numbers (rough estimates):

9/11/01 3,000 American fatalities
         Democratic economic surplus
4/15/09 > 7,800 American fatalities
         > 30,000 American casualties (cripples)
         > Republican eleven trillion-dollar deficit (bankrupt)
         > 100,000 Iraqi fatalities and casualties
         Afghani fatalities and casualties (?)
         Pakistani fatalities and casualties (?)

Tragically, there is no end in sight because America has new playmates: Taliban militants, Iraqi Insurgents, Al-Qaeda, and HAMAS suicide bombers. President Obama needs 84 billion dollars, for more vacuous bombs, and 25,000 American soldiers, for his war in Afghanistan. Get a clue: This war was won by Osama bin Laden when America had a one-trillion-dollar deficit.

Democracy or Democrisy?

In sum: America is fighting for her soul. America's real fight is to transform her "Democrisy," that is laden with hypocrisy, into a true red, white, and blue "Democracy." The real war front is in Chicago: 508 school students shot and 36 students murdered.

Education Is the Only Path to a Peaceful World

Appendix

Appendix A
Definitions: The Fifteen Stumbling Blocks of Academic Failure
495

Appendix B
Definitions: The Fifteen Stepping Stones to Academic Success
503

Appendix C
The Silent Crisis Destroying America's Brightest Minds
513

Appendix D
The Downward Spiral of Academic Failure
517

Appendix E
Academic Insanity
521

Appendix F
Thinkers in Education
Sharon Rose Sugar - Sharon Esther Lampert
525

Appendix G
SMARTGRADES SUCCESS STRATEGY STUDY SKIILLS
www.smartgrades.com
56

EDUCATION UPDATES

- **Charter School Update**
"The problem is underscored in an eye-opening study by Stanford University's Center for Research on Education Outcomes. -- The study, which looked at schools in 15 states and the District of Columbia, showed that 17 percent of charter schools provided a better education than traditional public schools in the same states. But charter backers and state officials were startled to learn that 37 percent of charters offered a worse education than children would have received had they remained in traditional schools ("Lessons for Failing Schools" New York Times, July 6, 2009).

- **Positive College Update**
"THOMAS COLLEGE, a liberal arts school in Maine, advertises itself as Home of the Guaranteed Job! Students who can't find work in their fields within six months of graduation can come back to take classes free, or have the college pay their student loans for a year" (Kate Zernike, New York Times, January 2, 2010).

- **School Shootings Update:**
2023: There have been 27 school shootings this year that resulted in injuries or deaths, according to an Education Week analysis. There have been 171 such shootings since 2018. There were 51 school shootings with injuries or deaths last year, the most in a single year since Education Week began tracking such incidents in 2018. There were 35 in 2021, 10 in 2020, and 24 each in 2019 and 2018 (Education Week, August 29, 2003).

- **College Student Suicide Update:**
2023: After 14 student deaths, North Carolina State confronts a national crisis. NC State convened a mental health task force in November to examine the problem. Seven students died by suicide, and two fatally overdosed (ABC News, Peter Charalambous, May 13, 2023).

Appendix A

Definitions
The Fifteen Stumbling Blocks of Academic Failure
The Malfunctioning American Education System

Appendix A

Definitions: The Fifteen Stumbling Blocks of Academic Failure

First Stumbling Block of Academic Failure
The Quantity Over Quality Curriculum-Driven Education System
The first stumbling block students encounter is how to keep up with the voluminous academic facts in a "Quantity Over Quality, Curriculum-Driven American Education System." It only takes the first week of school for most students to fall behind and start playing catch up. Some students are not able to catch up and fall behind, flounder, fail, and fall through the cracks of the malfunctioning American education system. Some students fail and go to summer school. Some students fail and change schools. Some students fail and choose homeschooling. Some students fail and dropout. The majority of students are surviving, but not thriving.

Second Stumbling Block of Academic Failure
Poor Learning Tools to Process Academic Facts
The second stumbling block students encounter is that they do not have "time to learn" or learning tools to "learn and process" voluminous academic facts to achieve academic success: Organization Skills, Time Management Skills, Academic Planner Skills, Critical Thinking Skills, English Essay Skills, Research Paper Skills, Proofreading Skills, and Test Preparation Skills.

Third Stumbling Block of Academic Failure
The Fast Food Restaurant: Cursory Comprehension
The third stumbling block students encounter is that teachers don't have time to teach for in-depth comprehension of the academic material. Teachers only have time to teach a brief overview of the academic material. The teacher's first priority is to stay on schedule and cover the curriculum on time. Sometimes, teachers don't even have time for a brief overview. Parents are asked to fill in the gaps (gigantic potholes) where the teacher left off.

Fourth Stumbling Block of Academic Failure
In One Ear and Out the Other Ear: Short-Term Retention
The fourth stumbling block students encounter is that they do not absorb academic material into their minds for long-term retention. Students cram voluminous academic facts with meager comprehension into their short-term memory and regurgitate facts onto a stressful, time-sensitive "hotdog exam." Students spend hours performing the academic exercise of "read, cram, regurgitate, and test." It is an exercise in futility. Two weeks after the test, the facts disappear into a black hole in the mind and vanish into thin air. Students go into education, but education does not go into students. Students will not be able to use the academic material to further their own goals, or to make a contribution to mankind, and further the progress of civilization. American students are uneducated.

Fifth Stumbling Block of Academic Failure
The Pressure Cooker: Cram Voluminous Academic Facts with Meager Comprehension, No Learning Tools, and Faulty Regurgitation onto a Stressful, Time-Sensitive Abusive Hotdog Exam
The fifth stumbling block students encounter is that education is measured by "hotdog exams." How many hotdogs can you stuff into your mouth in an hour to win the Coney Island Hotdog Contest in Brooklyn? How many academic facts do students have to cram with meager comprehension into their mind and regurgitate onto a stressful, time-sensitive test to earn a diploma? Students do not have the required association skills to memorize voluminous academic facts. Stressed-out students draw blanks, perform poorly, and see the academic facts, their self-esteem, and American dream vanish into thin air.

Sixth Stumbling Block of Academic Failure
The Darwinian Grind of Cutthroat Competition
The sixth stumbling block students encounter is the Darwinian grind, a contest of the survival of the fittest. Every student is an island unto himself or herself. It is difficult for students to work as a team, cooperate for the good of any individual member, or for the common good of the group. Students have become fierce competitors for admission into the malfunctioning American schools.

Seventh Stumbling Block of Academic Failure
Student Survival Strategies: Cutting Corners and Cheating
The seventh stumbling block students encounter is that students don't learn how to succeed; they only learn how to cut corners and cheat to pass, survive, and graduate. The learning curve is steep. Learning takes time. Students don't have "time to learn" or learning tools to read their textbooks, write and proofread their papers, and prepare for tests. The teachers also cut corners and cheat students out of an education: No in-depth comprehension, long-term retention, and mastery of academic material.

Eighth Stumbling Block of Academic Failure
Escapism: Seeking Refuge from the Pain of Inadequacy
The eighth stumbling block students encounter is the constant feeling of inadequacy that permeates their every academic endeavor. Students study for hours, but they can't read fast enough, write fast enough, or memorize fast enough. Students can't seem to catch up. The academic pressure is unremitting: Voluminous facts, papers, projects, and tests. Students find refuge from the "Academic Pressure Cooker" and the "Pain of Inadequacy" by escaping into mind-numbing activities: TV, movies, internet, mp3, video and computer game addictions, shopping addiction, chain smoking and caffeine addiction, overeating and obesity, dangerous drugs, gambling addiction, college binge-drinking, promiscuous sex, teenage pregnancy, and pornography.

Ninth Stumbling Block of Academic Failure
The Downward Spiral of Academic Failure
The ninth stumbling block students encounter is the "Downward Spiral of Academic Failure." Most students are surviving, but not thriving. A bad grade hurts. Failure is painful. Students have become disconnected, depressed, distracted, and disobedient. Some students have shut down. Some students have become angry and act out. Some students will change schools, choose home schooling, or drop out. In some cases, parents, teachers, and psychiatrists misdiagnose students with learning deficits, learning disabilities, and A. D. H. D. In these cases, born in perfect health, the brain, the most powerful biological machine, is placed into a virtual wheelchair for life. These students will not be able to grow, develop, and mature properly because they internalize the A. D. H. D. label and their self-talk is, "I can't do this, and I can't do that, because I have A.D.H.D."

Tenth Stumbling Block of Academic Failure
The War Zone: Few Heroes, Heavy Casualties, and Senseless Fatalities
The tenth stumbling block students encounter is that their school resembles a "War Zone" with a few heroes, heavy casualties, and senseless fatalities. Students have not learned how to achieve academic success in school, or in life. Students have only learned how to survive the malfunctioning American education system. Students will suffer from the "Pain of Inadequacy" and graduate bearing the "Scars of Incompetence." The students go into the education system, but education does not go into students. Every student has a horror story to tell about an injustice suffered.

Eleventh Stumbling Block of Academic Failure
The Desert: Wander Aimlessly with No Direction
The eleventh stumbling block students encounter is that most students do not have an opportunity to explore an area of study that is interesting, engaging, and meaningful to them. There is little time during their formative years to develop their natural affinities, talents, or gifts to find their purpose and passion to give meaning to their short-term existence.

Twelfth Stumbling Block of Academic Failure
The Wasteland: One Size Does Not Fit All or Any
The twelfth stumbling block students encounter is that the one size fits all education system does not serve the needs of teachers, students, or parents. Teachers don't benefit because there is no time to teach for in-depth comprehension. Teachers are then scapegoated for being poor teachers and blamed for poor test scores. Students don't benefit because they don't have "time to learn" or learning tools. Parents don't benefit because they are asked to fill in the gigantic potholes with tutors, learning specialists, and psychiatrists.

Thirteenth Stumbling Block of Academic Failure
American Dreams Deferred, Denied, and Destroyed
The thirteenth stumbling block that students encounter is that before the age of puberty, their childhood dreams have vanished into thin air. Students study for hours. They promise their parents and teachers that they will work hard. Students are unable to keep the promise to their parents, because meager comprehension, no learning tools, abusive hotdog exams, the "Pain of Inadequacy," and the "Scars of Incompetence" undermine their best effort and destroy all hope of a bright future filled with American dreams that come true.

Fourteenth Stumbling Block of Academic Failure
Get A Clue: How Does Learning Take Place
The fourteenth stumbling block that students encounter is that educators are clueless when it comes to understanding "How Does Learning Take Place?" School is a restaurant and facts are on the menu. Children eat facts and build their brain muscle. You cannot stuff a whole sandwich into your mouth. You have to take small bites, chew, chew, chew, and digest. You cannot stuff voluminous academic facts into your brain. The human brain is the most powerful biological machine in the world, and educators have not yet learned how to nurture, cultivate, and mine its extraordinary depths and infinite possibilities.

Fifteenth Stumbling Block of Academic Failure
Unintentional Institutionalized Child Abuse
The fifteenth stumbling block students encounter is unintentional child abuse from a parent, teacher, or psychiatrist. You used to be a brainy, creative, happy-go-lucky kid with a very bright future ahead of you. It is all your fault that you are falling behind, floundering, failing, and falling through the cracks of the Quantity Over Quality, Curriculum-Driven malfunctioning American education system.

2009 First Book Review

The same day that **EDNEWS.org** published a review of this book, a parent left this comment under the review.

Hi,

Just a small comment, about the above article. I agree totally with the article, because my daughter have been struggling since first grade, now she is in 7th, school don't agree. I feel like i'm up against a army, no one is listening, comprehension is her main challenge. the school curriculum that is given, she has a very hard time keeping up. and yes, she suffers from the pain of inadequacey, depression, because she tries hard and get overwhelmed, because so much information.

Connie King
8-4-09
8:23 p.m.

Appendix B

Definitions
The Fifteen Stepping Stones for Academic Success
Reinventing the American Education System

Appendix B
Definitions: The Fifteen Stepping Stones for Academic Success

First Stepping Stone of Academic Success
Cultivate Brain Power
The first stepping stone for academic success is understanding the human brain. The human brain is the most powerful biological machine in the world. The human brain must be nurtured and cultivated to fulfill its potential. The only thing that is wrong with students is that the brain does not come with an instruction manual and students do not know how to use it. Educators do not know how to nurture and cultivate the awesome power of the human brain: "Every Student is a Success Story."

Second Stepping Stone of Academic Success
New Education Paradigm: Shift Paradigm from Quantity over Quality Curriculum-Driven to a Quality over Quantity Learning-Processing Education System
The second stepping stone for academic success is to shift the education paradigm to a Quality Over Quantity Learning-Processing Education System. Teachers will have time to teach for in-depth comprehension. Students will have the "time to learn" and the learning tools to "learn and process" the academic material for in-depth comprehension, long-term retention, and mastery of academic material. The new grading system will ensure that "Every Student is a Success Story." Students will be able to use their education to enhance their own lives, further the progress of civilization, and meet the social, economic, science, and technological challenges of the 21st century.

Third Stepping Stone of Academic Success
In-Depth Comprehension: Give Teachers Time to Teach for In-Depth Comprehension

The third stepping stone for academic success is in-depth comprehension. In a Quality Over Quantity Learning-Processing Education system, teachers have time to teach the academic material for in-depth comprehension. Students will obtain the "**SMARTGRADES** Critical Thinking Skills" to analyze, synthesize, and evaluate academic material for in-depth comprehension. Students will have time to ask interesting questions, and teachers will have time to examine questions and explore answers: "Every Student Is a Success Story."

Fourth Stepping Stone of Academic Success
New Learning Technology: Give Students the SMARTGRADES Processing Skills to Process Academic Facts for Long-Term Retention

The fourth stepping stone for academic success is the new learning technology called **SMARTGRADES** Processing Tools. In a Quality Over Quantity Learning-Processing Education System, students will have "time to learn" and obtain learning tools to "learn and process" academic material for in-depth comprehension, long-term retention, and mastery of academic material. The education goalpost is self-reliant and life-long learners.

SMARTGRADES Learning Tools for Academic Success:
- **SMARTGRADES** Organization Tools
- **SMARTGRADES** Time Management Tools
- **SMARTGRADES** English Essay Tools
- **SMARTGRADES** Research Report Skills
- **SMARTGRADES** Test Preparation Tools

Fifth Stepping Stone of Academic Success
New Grading System: Mastery
The fifth stepping stone for academic success is the "New Grading System." There are only two grades in a Quality Over Quantity Learning-Processing education system: Grade A or REDO. Teachers will have time for continuous feedback of strengths and weaknesses until students achieve mastery of the academic material: "Every Student Is a Success Story."

Sixth Stepping Stone of Academic Success
Get a Clue: How Learning Takes Place
The sixth stepping stone for academic success is understanding the central question at the heart of education: Q: How Does Learning Take Place? The next critical question that needs to be addressed is: Q: Are Educators Running a School for Academic Success, or an Education Asylum Riddled with Academic Insanity?

Seventh Stepping Stone of Academic Success
The Universal Gold Standard of Education
The seventh stepping stone for academic success is "The Universal Gold Standard of Education." This is the blueprint that will lay the foundation for a Quality Over Quantity Learning-Processing Education System. This blueprint will ensure that all students receive an education that nurtures and develops their brain power to unlock its potential, cultivate its power, and set free its promise: "Every Student Is a Success Story."

Eighth Stepping Stone of Academic Success
Children Have Unique Minds that Require Early Intervention
The eighth stepping stone for academic success is that students are not blank slates, but come to school bearing the seeds of natural affinities, talents, and gifts. These natural affinities must be respected, nurtured, and cultivated as early as possible to ensure that students find their passion and purpose, and fulfill their potential: "Every Student Is a Success Story."

Ninth Stepping Stone of Academic Success
Educate the Whole Student: Mind, Body, and Spirit
The ninth stepping stone for academic success is the spiritual development of students. The mind and the body follow the dictates of the spirit or the "Light from Within." In a Quality Over Quantity Learning-Processing Education System, the spirit of a student is developed for the mind to be receptive to learning. Students learn that the 24-hour life cycle requires biological sustenance of food, sleep, and exercise and the spiritual sustenance of self-esteem, self-love, and self-actualization: "Every Student Is a Success Story."

Tenth Stepping Stone of Academic Success
Prepare Students to Meet the Challenges of the Real World

The tenth stepping stone for academic success is preparing students to meet the challenges faced in the real world. In a Quality Over Quantity Learning-Processing Education System, students graduate from elementary, high school, and college with basic business skills that are required to achieve academic success in school and for success in the real world: Academic Planner Skills, Time Management Skills, Planning Management Skills, Decision Making Skills, Team Player Skills, Typing Skills, Money Management Skills, and Entrepreneurship Skills: "Every Student Is a Success Story."

Eleventh Stepping Stone of Academic Success
Prepare Students to Become Thinkers, Problem Solvers, and Leaders Who Contribute to and Further the Progress of Civilization

The eleventh stepping stone for academic success is teaching students how to plan, execute, solve, and resolve problems. Students have the academic facts at their fingertips and the cognitive skills to solve problems: Critical Thinking Skills, Creative Thinking Skills, Scientific Thinking Skills, and Mathematical Thinking Skills. Students can solve a real-world problem in their own lives or solve a real-world problem in the world at large. Students are not victims, but victors.

Twelfth Stepping Stone of Academic Success
Remove Stress, Anxiety, Depression, and Suicidal Thoughts from Learning Environment

The twelfth stepping stone for academic success is creating a school environment that is conducive to the love of learning. Anxiety and stress inhibit learning and higher-order thinking because they force the brain to switch to survival mode. Depression (the internalization of disappointment, pain, and rage) leads to psychological paralysis (students can't function), suicidal thinking, attempted suicide, and suicide. It is time for educators to take responsibility for the academic games riddled with "Academic Insanity" that they ask students to play that make a sizeable contribution to their mental-health problems.

Thirteenth Stepping Stone of Academic Success
Stop the Education Blame Game: There Are No Beneficiaries: "Poor Teachers," "Lazy Students," and "Ineffectual Parents"

The thirteenth stepping stone for academic success is ending the blame game. In a malfunctioning Quantity Over Quality Curriculum-Driven American Education System, teachers don't have time to teach for in-depth comprehension and are scapegoated as poor teachers and blamed for poor test scores. Students don't have "time to learn" and learning tools to "learn and process" the voluminous academic material and are blamed for poor study habits and poor test scores. Parents are asked to teach their children what teachers don't have time to teach, and incur the financial costs associated with tutoring or face ridicule for non-involvement in their children's education.

Fourteenth Stepping Stone of Academic Success
Take Responsibility for the Failure to Educate Students: "Great Teachers, Great Students, Malfunctioning Education System"
The fourteenth stepping stone for academic success is for educators to wake up, become conscious, and take responsibility for their failure to educate students. The unsolved mystery of why the American Education System is failing has been solved.
It is up to each and every school, on a grass roots level, to begin to implement the monumental changes that will transform the American education system into one of the greatest education systems in the world, and prepare students to meet the challenges of the 21st century: "Every Student Is a Success Story."

Fifteenth Stepping Stone of Academic Success
Solve The Education Problem and Save The World
The fifteenth stepping stone for academic success is focusing on solving just one problem in the world. What if you could solve just one problem in the world, and by solving that one problem, you could solve every other problem in the world. If we just solve the "Problem of Education," then we will be able to solve every other problem in the world: Famine, poverty, crime, disease, domestic violence, religious strife, and war.

"I found myself struggling in my coursework. My papers, I was told, were verbose, poorly structured, and replete with rookie mistakes like the use of the passive voice. My teachers at Stuyvesant had never warned me my writing skills were weak... To the contrary, I'd always gotten excellent grades. This seemed terribly unfair. I was quite a diligent student and would have worked to improve my writing if I'd been warned it was lacking. Instead they'd sent me off to college unprepared. Luckily, Penn had a writing clinic and I visited it religiously."

Eva Sarah Moskowitz
Founder & CEO
Success Academy Charter Schools
Book: "The Education of Eva Moskowitz"
Chapter 18, page 117
Harper Collins Publishers, 2017

Appendix C
The Silent Crisis Destroying America's Brightest Minds

Appendix C
The Silent Crisis Destroying America's Brightest Minds

1. The human brain is the most powerful biological machine in the world. It does not come with an instruction manual and students do not know how to use it.

2. Children cannot raise themselves. If a child is failing, it is never the child's fault.

3. Educators are clueless as to "How Does Learning Take Place?" They do not know how to nurture and cultivate the awesome power of the human brain. You cannot stuff voluminous facts into the brain. Facts are food. Like a sandwich you have to take small amounts of information and process the academic facts with in-depth comprehension, long-term retention, and mastery of the academic material.

4. Students are enrolled in a "Quantity Over Quality Curriculum-Driven Malfunctioning American Education System."

5. Teaching and learning are compromised to push the curriculum forward to meet the goals dictated by the "Higher Standards."

6. After the first week of school, students fall behind and start playing catch up.

7. Students study for hours, but do not have "time to learn" and learning tools to "learn and process" voluminous academic material.

8. Students suffer from the "Pain of Inadequacy," and their self-talk is "What is wrong with me? Why don't I have time to read the textbooks, write the papers, and prepare to take the tests?"

9. Before the age of puberty, most students have become anxious and stressed. Some students have become disconnected, depressed, distracted, disgruntled, and disobedient. In some cases, "bouts of depression" escalate into clinical depression, suicidal thoughts (the ticking time-bomb), and suicide. Clinical depression causes psychological paralysis. The student has internalized the pain and rage from disappointments. In addition, the student has internalized a self-critical inner voice, and the external critical voice of the parent as "the punisher." A student seeks relief from the pain and commits suicide.

10. The Academic Pressure Cooker: Students cram voluminous facts with meager comprehension, no learning tools, and for short term retention into the mind, and then regurgitate academic facts, under psychological duress and a stopwatch onto abusive (tricky) hotdog exams to earn a diploma.

11. Educational outcomes are measured by abusive (tricky) hotdog exams. Faulty regurgitation of academic facts on an abusive (tricky) "hotdog exam" destroys a student's self-esteem and American dream.

12. Students learn how to cut corners and cheat to pass, survive, and graduate.

13. Escapism: Students seek relief from the "Pain of Inadequacy" and the "Academic Pressure Cooker," and escape into mind-numbing activities, e.g., drugs, alcohol, and gambling. Escapism and addictions can spiral out of control.

14. The school resembles a "War Zone": Few heroes, heavy casualties, and many fatalities.

a. The heroes master the academic game of "read, cram, regurgitate, and test." Two weeks after the test, even the heroes can't remember most of the academic facts.

b. The students who fall behind, flounder, fail, and fall through the cracks are as follows:
1. The sensitive, imaginative, and creative students are the first to fall
2. Students fall behind, flounder, fail, and go to summer school
3. Students fall behind, flounder, fail, and change schools
4. Students fall behind, flounder, fail, and choose homeschooling
5. Students fall behind, flounder, fail, and are misdiagnosed with A.D.H.D.
6. Students fall behind, flounder, fail, dropout and go to work
7. Students fall behind, flounder, fail, dropout, commit crimes, and go to prison

15. Most students will earn a diploma, but not an education. Graduates bear the "Scars of Incompetence" that are defined by the following criteria:
1. No in-depth comprehension
2. No long-term retention
3. No mastery of academic material
4. Students cannot use their education to further the progress of civilization

Appendix D
The Downward Spiral of Academic Failure

Evaluate, Analyze, and Synthesize:
Psychiatrists don't even have a medical test for it, but they label a child with, A. D. H. D., and then blurt out, "By the way, its an incurable brain disorder."

Q: Are You Inattentive?
Q: Are you hyperactive?
Q: Are you impusive?

For every other medical condition there is hope, except for this condition, that they don't even have a medical test to prove that it exists.

As a matter of fact, from time to time, every child is a bit inattentive, hyperactive, and impulsive. Most parents have inadequate parenting tools and are just winging it.

Years ago, psychiatrists performed lobotomies, and later, labeling patients and drugging them became the norm. Psychiatry is a science that is still in the dark ages. The central failure of psychiatry is its failure to understand the true nature of the human animal and how the process of socialization creates a human being, who is an artificial construct (Book: The Science of Neurosis, Sharon Esther Lampert). The only hope for patients is the development of their own inner voice and following their own bliss (Integration Therapy: 13 Steps to True and Everlasting Happiness, Let the Healing Begin and Make it Last Forever Appendix G).

Appendix D
The Downward Spiral of Academic Failure

1. Students are enrolled in a "Quantity Over Quality Curriculum-Driven American Education System." Teaching and learning are sacrificed to push the curriculum forward at a frenetic pace.

2. Students study for hours, but do not have "time to learn" or learning tools to "learn and process" voluminous academic facts.

3. It only takes the first week of school for a student to fall behind and start playing catch-up.

4. After the first month of school, students start to flounder and earn C grades.

5. A bad grade hurts and is painful. A student has become disconnected, depressed, distracted, disobedient, and blocked.

6. Some failing students will be misdiagnosed with learning disabilities, learning deficits, and A.D.H.D.

7. A student has become depressed and says, "Leave me alone."

8. A student has become apathetic and says, "I don't care."

9. A student suffers from the "Pain of Inadequacy" and says, "I am stupid."

10. A student's effort is unrewarded and says, "School is stupid."

11. A student has become blocked and says, "The teacher hates me."

12. A student shuts down and says, "School sucks."

13. Biology 101: Flight or Fight Response
A student is in a state of eternal "flight" because a student does not have learning tools to "fight."

14. Escapism: A student seeks relief from the "Pain of Inadequacy" and finds mind-numbing escapes: TV, movies, internet, mp3, video and computer game addictions, shopping addiction, chain smoking and caffeine addiction, overeating and obesity, dangerous drugs and alcohol, college-binge drinking, promiscuous sex, teenage pregnancy, and pornography.

15. Students learn how to cut corners and cheat to pass, survive, and graduate.

16. Failing students have seven options:
Option 1. Failing students go to summer school
Option 2. Failing students change schools
Option 3. Failing students choose homeschooling
Option 4. Failing students drop out and earn a G.E.D.
Option 5. Failing students drop out and get a job
Option 6. Failing students are misdiagnosed with learning deficits, learning disabilities, or A.D.H.D.
Option 7. Failing students drop out, commit a crime, and go to prison

17. Students who pass, survive, and graduate from the malfunctioning American education system suffer from the "Pain of Inadequacy" and graduate bearing the "Scars of Incompetence." Students earn a diploma, but not an education: No in-depth comprehension, no long-term retention, and no mastery of the academic material.

Appendix E
Academic Insanity

Appendix F: Academic Insanity

Q: Are educators running a school for academic success or an education asylum riddled with academic insanity?

Academic Insanity 1. *The Quantity Over Quality Curriculum*
Teaching and learning are sacrificed to push the curriculum forward at a frenetic pace to meet the education goals dictated by the "Higher Standards." Every day is a cutthroat competition for academic survival.

Academic Insanity 2. *Difficult Courses*
A difficult course is when the teachers won't have time to teach it and students won't have time to learn it, but teachers will have time to test students on it.

Academic Insanity 3. *How Does Learning Take Place?*
Educators do not know how to nurture and cultivate the awesome power of the human brain. You cannot stuff a whole sandwich into your mouth. Facts are brain food. You have to take small bites and chew, chew, chew, and digest. You have to take small amounts of information and chew (in-depth comprehension), chew (long-term retention), and chew (mastery of the academic material).

Academic Insanity 4. *No In-Depth Comprehension*
Teachers do not have time to teach for in-depth comprehension, but always find time to test students on significant and trivial details that they don't have time to teach.

Academic Insanity 5. *No Time to Teach the Craft of Writing*
Teachers do not have time to teach the craft of writing (ten to twenty rough drafts), but do expect students to be able to write well.

Academic Insanity 6. *No Time to Teach Critical Thinking Skills*
Teachers do not have time to teach "Critical Thinking Skills," but do expect students to analyze, synthesize, and evaluate academic material in an English essay or research paper.

Academic Insanity 7. No Time for Continuous Feedback of Strengths and Weaknesses
Teachers don't have time to correct writing errors. Students don't learn from their mistakes and make them over and over again.

Academic Insanity 8. Students Do Not Have Learning Tools
Students do not have "time to learn" or learning tools to "learn and process" voluminous academic material for instant recognition and recall on abusive (tricky) hotdog exams. Faulty regurgitation of academic facts destroys a student's self-esteem and American dream.

Academic Insanity 9. Abusive (Tricky) Hotdog Exams
Q: How many hotdogs do you have to stuff into your mouth in an hour to win the Coney Island Hotdog Contest in Brooklyn?

Q: How many academic facts do students have to cram into their mind with meager comprehension, no learning tools, and for short-term retention, to regurgitate under psychological duress and a stopwatch onto an abusive (tricky) hotdog test to earn a diploma? Two weeks after the test, academic facts disappear into a black hole.

Academic Insanity 10. The Mental Health Clinic
a. Take anxious, stressed, and depressed students off caffeine, recreational drugs, and alcohol and replace or supplement them with psychotropic drugs, a dangerous crutch with serious side effects.

b. Tell students to seek help for their depression, and after they admit that they have "suicidal thoughts," expel them from school.

Academic Insanity 11. Educators cut corners and cheat students out of an education, and in return, students also learn how to cut corners and cheat to pass, survive, and graduate to earn a diploma.

Academic Insanity 12. The Education System Has No Beneficiaries
Teachers don't benefit. Students don't benefit. Parents don't benefit. Teachers don't have time to teach. Students don't have learning tools. Parents are asked to fill in the gaps (gigantic potholes).

Academic Insanity 13. Graduate with Astronomical Financial Debt
Students graduate without any practical business skills to earn a living and they have to pay off school loans with 40-year repayment plans.

Dear Ms. Sugar,
My son was enrolled in one of the best schools in the country and he almost dropped out... but now he's back on top. We weaned him off the anti-depressant medication.

Tom's report card was TERRIFIC.

Thank you for helping Tom overcome his anxiety and fear of testing by teaching him to be organized and prepared.

 So...drumroll...here are the grades:
 Science B+... which considering he started the year with a D is amazing.
Math A-... can you believe it? Tom was amazed!
Latin A-
Social Studies A-
Art A-
English A
Theatre/Communications A

So that's about it... almost a straight A student... but close enough for me!

Have a good summer and thanks again.

William Robertson

P.S. SMARTGRADES is my favorite school supply company!

Appendix F
Thinkers in Education

Sharon Rose Sugar
The Paladin of Education for the 21st Century

Ms. Sugar Brought Us All Fifteen Steps Closer to World Peace

Sharon Rose Sugar
The Paladin of Education for the 21st Century

Mission: To place the new learning technology, **SMARTGRADES** Processing Tools, directly into the hands of all students and parenting tools into the hands of all parents.

The Monumental Contributions to Education

1. Pioneered **SMARTGRADES** 10 Step Processing Tools
2. Pioneered Education Paradigm: Learning-Processing Education System
3. Pioneered The Universal Gold Standard of Education
4. Pioneered How Does Learning Take Place?
5. Pioneered Eight Goalposts of Education

6. THE SILENT CRISIS DESTROYING AMERICA'S BRIGHTEST MINDS:
   a. The 15 Stumbling Blocks of Academic Failure
   b. The 15 Stepping Stones to Academic Success
   c. The Downward Spiral of Academic Failure
   d. Academic Insanity
   e. The Misdiagnosis of A. D. H. D., "The Incurable Brain Disorder"
   f. The 3 Stages of Child Abuse: Cripple, Parasite, and Predator

7. Integration Therapy for Intrapersonal Growth, Development, and Maturity, The 13 Steps to True and Everlasting Happiness

8. Feed the Whole Child: Mind, Body, and Spirit; The Spiritual Affirmations

9. Coined the word, "democrisy," a democracy laden with hypocrisy

10. **PHOTON SUPERHERO OF EDUCATION**

11. C.A.P.S. Children's Science Curriculum, Grades 1-4

12. In One Hour, Read Hebrew

You Can Do More Than Survive, You Can Succeed

Appendix F

Thinkers in Education

One Small Step Forward for Women and One Giant Leap Forward for Education and World Peace

Alain, Aristotle, Avicenna, Bello, Bettelheim, Binet, Blonsky, Al-Boustani, Buber, Cai Yuanpei, Claparede, Comenious, Condorcet, Confucius, Cousinet, Dawid, Decroly, Dewey, Diesterweg, Durkheim, Eotvos, Erasmus, Al-Farabi, Ferriere, Freinet, Freire, Freud, Frobel, Fukuzawa, Gandhi, Al-Ghazali, Giner de los Rios, Glinos, Goodman, Gramsci, Grundtvig, Grzegorzewska, Hegel, Herbart, Humbolt, Husen, Hussein, Illich, Jaspers, Jovellanos, Jullien de Paris, Kandel, Kant, Kerschensteiner, Key, Ibn Khaldun, Kold, Korczak, Krupskaya, Locke, Makarenko, Marti, Mencious, Miskawayh, Montaigne, Montessori, More, Naik, Neill, Noikov, Nyerere, Ortega y Gasset, Owen, Pestalozzi, Piaget, Plato, Priestley, Al-Qabbani, Read, Rogers, Rousseau, Rudenschold, Sadler, Salomon, Sarmiento, Sergio, Skinner, Spencer, Steiner, Suchodolski, **Sharon Rose Sugar (Sharon Esther Lampert)** Sun Yat-Sen, Tagore, Al-Tahtawi, Tolstoy, Trefort, Trstenjak, Ushinsky, Uznadze, Varela, Vasconcelos, Vico, Vives, Vygotsky, Wallon

Smart Power Is in Your Hands and at Your Fingertips

WORLD PEACE IS COMING TO PLANET EARTH

The Official Emblem of Photon
The Super Heroine of Education on Planet

Super Hero Refresher Course

Clark Kent is Superman

Bruce Wayne is Batman

Peter Parker is Spiderman

Diana Themyscira is Wonder Woman

Sharon Rose Sugar is Photon

WORLD PEACE IS COMING TO PLANET EARTH

My Superhero Pledge for World Peace

"I Pledge to Safeguard Your Mental Health,
Promote Mental Health in Your Family,
Create an Atmosphere of Peace Among Your Friends,
Inspire Good Will Among Your Neighbors, and
Build a Foundation of Stability in Your Community."

PHOTON
SUPERHERO OF EDUCATION
www.BooksNotBombs.com

CRAWL. WALK. FLY. SOAR...

WORLD PEACE IS COMING TO PLANET EARTH

Welcome All Earthlings
Feed the Whole Student: Mind, Body, and Spirit

PHOTON'S Spiritual Illuminations

- My Self-Esteem Affirmation

- My Empowerment Affirmation

- My Circle of Responsibility Affirmation

- The World Peace Equation

- My 5 Superpowers of Making Dreams Come True

- My 7 Superpowers of Stress-Relief

- My Special Gifts

- **SMARTGRADES** Tools for Academic Success

- The 22 Spiritual Illuminations

- The Moon Quote for World Peace

CRAWL. WALK. FLY. SOAR...

WORLD PEACE IS COMING TO PLANET EARTH

PHOTON'S Spiritual Illuminations

My Self-Esteem Affirmation

I love you (insert your name).
I will do everything in my power to help you achieve your dream.
My dream is to become a _____
Everything else that I say to myself is just NOISE.

"When you recite the self-love affirmation, please stand in front of the mirror and make eye contact with yourself."

PHOTON
SUPERHERO OF EDUCATION
www.booksnotbombs.com

CRAWL. WALK. FLY. SOAR...

WORLD PEACE IS COMING TO PLANET EARTH

PHOTON'S Spiritual Illuminations

My Empowerment Affirmation

I have only one life.
My life is a valuable gift.
I am responsible for my destiny.
I changed my life to ensure my happiness.
Each day is lived fully with
purpose, enthusiasm, and joy.

PHOTON
SUPERHERO OF EDUCATION
www.booksnotbombs.com

CRAWL. WALK. FLY. SOAR...

WORLD PEACE IS COMING TO PLANET EARTH

PHOTON'S Spiritual Illuminations

My Circle of Responsibility Affirmation

My Problems Have Solutions
When I Take
RESPONSIBILITY
for my problems have solutions
when I take responsibility for
my problems have solutions
when I take responsibility for
my problems have solutions
when I take responsibility for
my problems have solutions
when I take responsibility for
my problems have solutions
when I take responsibility for
my problems have solutions
when I take responsibility for
my problems have solutions
when I take responsibility for
my problems have solutions
when I take responsibility for
my problems have solutions
When I Take
RESPONSIBILITY.

PHOTON
SUPERHERO OF EDUCATION
www.BooksNotBombs.com

CRAWL. WALK. FLY. SOAR...

PHOTON'S Spiritual Illuminations

The World Peace Equation

$$VG + VL = VP$$

Virtue of the Good + Value of Life = Vision of Peace

The Mathematical and Philosophical Proof for World Peace

$$VG + VL = VP$$
$$VP = VG + VL$$
$$VP = V(G+L)$$
$$P = (G+L)$$

Peace = Good + Life

Peace = Goodlife

PHOTON
SUPERHERO OF EDUCATION
www.BooksNotBombs.com

CRAWL. WALK. FLY. SOAR...

WORLD PEACE IS COMING TO PLANET EARTH

PHOTON'S Spiritual Illuminations
5 Superpowers to Make Dreams Come True

1. TIME Is Nonrefundable
(Don't Waste Your Time)

2. ENERGY Is Rechargeable
(Get a Good Night's Sleep)

3. MONEY Goes Round and Round
(Money is Passed from One Person to Another)

4. SELF-WORTH Is Infinite Potential
(Know Your Strengths, Work on Your Weaknesses)

5. LOVE Everything You Touch
(Put Your Heart into Everything You Do)

PHOTON
SUPERHERO OF EDUCATION
www.BooksNotBombs.com

CRAWL. WALK. FLY. SOAR...

WORLD PEACE IS COMING TO PLANET EARTH

PHOTON'S Spiritual Illuminations

7 Superpowers of Stress-Relief

1. RECOGNIZE Your Star Qualities

2. LISTEN to Your Inner Voice

3. PROTECT Your Needs and Desires

4. Have COURAGE to Abandon Relationships with insensitive people

5. Attach Your HEART to Your HEAD and Make Decisions in Your Best Interest

6. EMPOWER Yourself to Make the Necessary Changes to Ensure Your Happiness

7. Have the VISION to See Beyond Present Difficulties and Create a Stress-Free Lifestyle

PHOTON
SUPERHERO OF EDUCATION
www.BooksNotBombs.com

CRAWL. WALK. FLY. SOAR...

WORLD PEACE IS COMING TO PLANET EARTH

PHOTON'S Spiritual Illuminations

My Special Gifts

Inside of Me Are

SPECIAL GIFTS

I am able to use my special gifts,
If I focus on my positive qualities.

I am ready to use my special gifts,
to enhance the quality of my life.

I will use my special gifts for myself,
my loved ones, and to benefit humanity.

PHOTON
SUPERHERO OF EDUCATION
www.BooksNotBombs.com

CRAWL. WALK. FLY. SOAR...

PHOTON'S SMARTGRADES
10 Step Processing Tools

Step 1. Estimation Tool
Step 2. Divide and Conquer Tool
Step 3. Active-Reading Tool
Step 4. Extraction Tool
Step 5. Condensation Tool
Step 6. Association Tool
Step 7. Test-Review Note Tool
Step 8. Conversion Tool
Step 9. Visualization Tool
Step 10. Self-Testing Tool

"I am on a mission to place **SMARTGRADES** Processing Tools into the hands of all Earthlings."

PHOTON
SUPERHERO OF EDUCATION
www.BooksNotBombs.com

CRAWL. WALK. FLY. SOAR...

WORLD PEACE IS COMING TO PLANET EARTH

PHOTON'S
22 Spiritual Illuminations

Life Over Death
Strength Over Weakness
Deed Over Sin
Love Over Hatred
Truth Over Lie
Wisdom Over Stupidity
Optimism Pessimism
Sharing Over Selfishness
Praise Over Criticism
Loyalty Over Abandonment
Responsibility Over Blame
Gratitude Over Envy
Reward Over Punishment
Generosity Over Stinginess
Creation Over Destruction
Education Over Ignorance
Cooperation Over Competition
Freedom Over Oppression
Compassion Over Indifference
Forgiveness Over Revenge
PEACE Over War
Joy Over Suffering
© www.stressstar.com

PHOTON
SUPERHERO OF EDUCATION
www.BooksNotBombs.com

CRAWL. WALK. FLY. SOAR...

PHOTON'S Spiritual Illuminations

Moon Quote

"If it is possible to send a person to the moon to search for signs of LIFE, then it is PULSEABLE to search for signs of LIFE within the HEARTS of all peoples on PLANET EARTH to find PEACE."

PHOTON
SUPERHERO OF EDUCATION
www.BooksNotBombs.com

CRAWL. WALK. FLY. SOAR...

#1 Poetry Website for School Projects

STUDENT FAN MAIL

Hi Sharon!

My name is Alexa & I'm a junior in high school!

I love your poems, especially about world affairs.

I will be doing a poetry analysis on three of your poems (I've chosen Sandstorm in Iraq, Tsunami, and There Is No Flower in Darfur) and also a presentation to inform the class of your works, accomplishments & biography.

If you can it would be greatly appreciated if you could tell me a little about your childhood, parents, education, religious beliefs, and maybe some experiences that have shaped your views or positions in regards to your poetry!

Thanks so much!

Have an amazing day!

Alexa Young

Almost Always, The Creative, Dedicated Minority Has Made the World Better.
Rev. Martin Luther King Jr.

How to Read a Poem by Sharon Esther Lampert

1. Sharon's Poetry Paintings
Similar to the poet William Blake, her poems are accompanied by elaborate visu
graphics that enrich and compliment the text. The poems are wall hangings, and
her poems are framed by ardent fans and hang in their living spaces, like painting

2. Sharon is a Master of Condensation
Sharon is a master of the art of condensation. She is able to condense a major
world event in world history into a one-page poem. Sharon can condense a
600-page book into a single page (p. 113). Her immortal liteary gems come
in a variety of lengths: A single sentence, a single page, and grand sweeping epics

3. Sharon is a Literary Photographer
Her poems are telescopic of the main event and microscopic of the infinite
details.

4. Sharon Can Pack a Single Verse to the Brim
Sharon's poems are known for her ability to weave poetry, philosophy, and
comedy into a single verse.

5. Documentary Poet: Poems are Cinematic Journey's Through History
Sharon's poems take you on a cinematic journey, and make you feel as if you
are reliving the event, as if it happened today.

6. Sharon's Poems Are Completed Literary Works
Sharon's poems are completed works of art. Every word is essential to the poem
You cannot remove or replace a word. There are no extra words. Every word ha
its rightful place and fits to perfection.

7. Sharon's Poems Are All Inspired Works of Art
All of her poems are inspired. There are no rough drafts. Like giving birth to a
baby, the poem incubates in her "creative apparatus" and is birthed in minutes.
Like a baby, the poems are delivered whole and complete.

8. Sharon's Signature Endings: The Epiphany (Spiritual Illumination)
The last verse of every poem delivers a message that educates, enlightens, and
empowers. Her searing signature endings find their way into your heart, open
your mind to a deeper understanding, and stay with you forever.

The Sole Intention of My Poetry is to Add Light to Your Soul.
Sharon Esther Lampert

www.PoetryJewels.com
Diamonds, Emeralds, Sapphires, Rubies, and Pearls

Please Handle My Poems Gently.
These Poems Are My Remains.
Sharon Esther Lampert

www.PoetryJewels.com
Diamonds, Emeralds, Sapphires, Rubies, and Pearls

The Greatest Poems Ever Written on Extraordinary Events
www.WorldFamousPoems.com
#1 Poetry Website for School Projects

Ten Poems on America

The World Trade Center Tragedy (America)
Spiraling Downward, Upward We Stand United

The California Wildfires (America) **Angry Red Embers**

Kansas Twister (America) **The Return of Dorothy Gale**

Katrina: **Drowning in the American Dream**

New York: Central Park Violence (America)
Water, Fight, Flight, and Tears
(most published poem on the web)

New York City Blackout (America)
The Return of the Cavewoman

N.Y.C. Its a Bird, Its a Plane, Its Super-Sullenberger

EDUCATE NOT

STOP CAMPUS RAPE

POETRY WORLD RECORD
120 WORDS OF RHYME FROM ONE FAMILY OF RHYME
"Through The Eyes of Eve"
"I gave Biblical Eve a voice and liberated her
from 5000 years of misogyny"
-- Sharon Esther Lampert

SEE THE WORLD THROUGH THE EYES OF A CREATIVE GENIUS

www.PoetryJewels.com
Diamonds, Emeralds, Sapphires, Rubies, and Pearls

BE BORN

Be Born
Become Educated
Love Your Work
Make a Meaningful Contribution
to Yourself, Your Family, and Humanity
Be a True Friend to Yourself First
Have Sex with Someone You Love
Make Love with Complete Abandon
Enjoy Unconditional Love from Your Devoted Pet.
Make Time to Read the Funnies and Laugh
Save Enough Money to Visit the Popular,
Pretty, and Peaceful Places of the World.
Read Great Literature, Listen to Great Music
See Great Art, Watch the Great Movies
Play the Fun Sports, Dance till Dawn
Taste the Great Culinary Delights of the World
Eat Slowly, Enjoy Every Bite, and Stay in Shape.
Plan One Great Adventure and Stick to the Plan
Grow Old and Wise. Leave Your Money to Someone
You Love - Who Loves You Back.
Die in Your Sleep.

Sharon Esther Lampert

SEE THE WORLD THROUGH THE EYES OF A CREATIVE GENIUS

www.PoetryJewels.com
Diamonds, Emeralds, Sapphires, Rubies, and Pearls

THE 22 COMMANDMENTS
ALL YOU WILL EVER NEED TO KNOW ABOUT GOD
A UNIVERSAL MORAL COMPASS FOR ALL PEOPLE,
FOR ALL RELIGIONS AND FOR ALL TIME

1. LIFE Over Death
2. STRENGTH Over Weakness
3. DEED Over Sin
4. LOVE Over Hatred
5. TRUTH Over Lie
6. COURAGE Over Fear
7. OPTIMISM Over Pessimism
8. SHARING Over Selfishness
9. PRAISE Over Criticism
10. LOYALTY Over Abandonment
11. RESPONSIBILITY Over Blame
12. GRATITUDE Over Envy
13. REWARD Over Punishment
14. ALLIES Over Enemies
15. CREATION Over Destruction
16. EDUCATION Over Ignorance
17. COOPERATION Over Competition
18. FREEDOM Over Oppression
19. COMPASSION Over Indifference
20. FORGIVENESS Over Revenge
21. PEACE Over War
22. JOY Over Suffering

Sharon Esther Lampert
8TH Prophetess of Israel

SEE THE WORLD THROUGH THE EYES OF A CREATIVE GENIUS

www.PoetryJewels.com
Diamonds, Emeralds, Sapphires, Rubies, and Pearls

APRIL 30
Poetry In Your Pocket Day

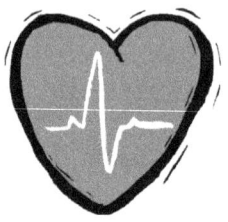

TRUE LOVE
True Love is Unconditional.
True Love is Found in the DEED.
True Love is Found in the WE.
True Love Unites the MIND,
BODY, and HEART as ONE.

Sharon Esther Lampert

Put this poem into your pocket and the positive vibrational energy will bring TRUE LOVE into your life.

SEE THE WORLD THROUGH THE EYES OF A CREATIVE GENIUS

www.PoetryJewels.com
Diamonds, Emeralds, Sapphires, Rubies, and Pearls

APRIL 30
Poetry In Your Pocket Day

POE T REE

Ink needs a pen
Pen needs paper
Paper needs a poem
Poem needs a poet
Poet needs a muse
Muse needs a poet
Poet needs divine inspiration
Divine inspiration needs divine intervention
Divine intervention needs divine grace
Divine grace needs immortality
Immortality needs eternity
Eternity needs readers of poetry

Sharon Esther Lampert
Poet, Philosopher, Peacemaker, Prophet, and Prodigy

SEE THE WORLD THROUGH THE EYES OF A CREATIVE GENIUS

Sharon Esther Lampert

The Gift of Automatic Writing: No Drafts

PRODIGY
10 Esoteric Laws of Genius and Creativity

PROPHET
WHO KNEW GOD WAS SUCH A CHATTERBOX
GOD TALKS TO ME: A WORKING DEFINITION OF GOD

THE 22 COMMANDMENTS
All You Will Ever Need To Know About God
A UNIVERSAL MORAL COMPASS
For All People, For All Religions, and For All Time
www.GodIsGoDo.com

POET
POETRY WORLD RECORD: 120 WORDS OF RHYME
The Greatest Poems Ever Written on Extraordinary World Events
www.WorldFamousPoems.com

PHILOSOPHER
10 Esoteric Laws of Inextricability
The Sperm Manifesto: 10 Rules for the Road
www.PhilosopherQueen.com

Women Have All The Power But Have Never Learned How to Use It
www.WomenHaveAllThePower.com

PALADIN OF EDUCATION
SMARTGRADES BRAIN POWER REVOLUTION

PHOTON SUPERHERO OF EDUCATION
www.smartgrades.com

PEACEMAKER
WORLD PEACE EQUATION
SILLY LITTLE BOYS: 40 RULES OF MANHOOD

PRINCESS
8TH PROPHETESS OF ISRAEL: THE 22 COMMANDMENTS

PIN-UP
SEXIEST CREATIVE GENIUS IN HUMAN HISTORY

www.ingramcontent.com/pod-product-compliance
Lightning Source LLC
Chambersburg PA
CBHW060041230426
43661CB00004B/614